BATH HISTORY

VOLUME XIII

edited by Graham Davis

Published by Bath Spa University

Supported by Bath Preservation Trust and
Bath and North East Somerset Council

2013

The production of this volume has been made possible thanks to the generous support of the following organisation:

Bath Spa University
Bath Preservation Trust
Bath and North East Somerset Council

First published in 2013 by Bath Spa University, Newton Park, Bath

Typeset in Palatino

Printed in Great Britain by WHP, Newbury, Berkshire

Design by Steve Hayes www.stevehayescreative.com

ISBN 978-0-9926338-0-6

British Library Cataloguing-in-Publication Data:

A catalogue record for this book is available from the British Library

MIX
Paper from
responsible sources
FSC® C100190

Contents

Editorial

We are delighted to announce that Bath Spa University has agreed to support the publication and development of *Bath History*. Dr Roberta Anderson, who is the university representative on the Editorial Board has helped to create a new website wwwbathhistory.org.uk through which the first ten volumes of the journal (1985-2006) are now accessible online for the benefit of all those interested in the city's history. The involvement of the university owes much to the vision and drive of the new Vice Chancellor, Professor Christina Slade. This development is part of a range of partnerships between BSU and various organizations in Bath.

Volume XIII, in addition to locally-based authors, has an unusually international cast of contributors: Iftikhar Malik, of Pakistani origin and based at BSU, Martin West, Colleen Denney, and Stephen Waddell of the United States, and Cynthia Hammond from Canada. This reflects Bath's international appeal and significance, not only as a World Heritage Site but because so many people of renown had an important connection with the city, so adding to the richness of its history.

Peter Adelard, an eminent medieval scholar, was born in Bath and travelled widely throughout Europe and the Middle East. Professor Malik's essay draws on extensive research to hail Adelard as a pivotal figure in bringing ideas from the Muslim world via the legacy of classical antiquity into the mainstream of Western thought in early medieval Christendom.

Barbara White's entertaining piece on 18th century highwaymen questions the validity of the romantic myths surrounding the 'gentlemen of the road', and shows how unwary travellers passing in the vicinity of the city could be subjected to brutal treatment.

Martin West is a descendant of the celebrated American artist, Benjamin West, renowned for his major historical canvases and as a member of the Royal Academy and court painter. He also spent time working in Bath where he painted local subjects such as Bladud and local pastoral scenes.

While celebrities flocked to Bath as part of the fashionable company, life could be perilous for children in the city. Jan Chivers has combed the records of the Coroners' Inquests to report eyewitness accounts of tragic accidents and deaths. Continuing with the theme of the lives of the unfortunate, Graham Davis recounts the story of the Rev. Thomas Spencer and the Reform of the Poor Law in 1834. Spencer was the first chairman of the Bath Board of Guardians and a champion of the reformed poor law system. The language of the 'deserving' and 'undeserving' poor was employed to target the able-bodied pauper on 'parish poor' as the cause of rising poor law expenditure. However, the diagnosis of the 1834 commission was mistaken. The great majority of those on poor relief inside and outside the workhouses proved to be children and old people.

The Age of Reform, 1830-50, was also marked by evangelical fervour, not least in Bath where the relentless pursuit of pleasure was challenged by the new mood of moral earnestness. Stephen Waddell identifies William Jay, the star preacher at the Argyle Chapel, as the key figure in the transformation of Bath away from its Georgian decadence, to become one of the most religious cities in Britain. The legacy of Bath's many Victorian churches and chapels bears witness to the religious spirit of the age.

Green Park was one of the places in Bath inhabited by Jane Austen. Alan Thwaite has trawled through the Victorian censuses to find out who else lived there during the nineteenth century. In the process, he identifies the social changes that occurred in one particular street as a reflection of a wider social transformation in the city. Occupations of inhabitants as well as the number of servants per household emerge as key factors marking a process of social descent.

The year 2012 was the bicentenary of the birth of Charles Dickens. In a short piece, the events are recalled that marked the celebrations in Bath. Dickens's association with Bath and the setting for scenes and characters in his novels is remembered with affection despite the satirical barbs he directed at the city, most famously in his first novel, *Pickwick Papers*, featuring the Master of Ceremonies, Angelo Cyrus Bantam Esq.

Among many labels attached to Bath, the city proclaimed itself the 'Queen of the West', and appropriately the next three articles have women in leading roles.

In a powerful essay, Suffragette City, Cynthia Hammond maps the incidence of suffrage activity in and around the city. Readers may be familiar with the recuperation at Batheaston of suffragettes who had been imprisoned and force-fed, but this formidable mapping of places in Bath demonstrates the strong presence of the women's suffrage movement in the city itself. It is a riveting and well-researched account, which may well add another tourist attraction with suffragette tours in future.

Colleen Denney offers a feminist take on the remarkable character, Madame Sarah Grand, who was part of the 'new woman' movement in the later Victorian period, a popular novelist, and later to become lady 'Mayoress' of Bath alongside Cedric Chivers in the early twentieth century.

Much attention is paid to Sarah Grand's public image, featuring the Praga portrait of her in the Victoria Art Gallery, amidst a discussion of changing ideas of women's role in society. Maud Forrester-Brown (1885-1970) was a different kind of pioneer; Britain's first female orthopaedic surgeon. John Kirkup writes an affectionate tribute of her from a personal acquaintance and a deep knowledge of the history and practice of orthopaedic surgery. Following the First World War, Forrester-Brown spent an important part of her outstanding career in the Royal United Hospital in Bath from where she set up clinics around the West Country.

The final piece of this volume continues the tradition of interviews with distinguished historians of Bath. William Hanna interviews Professor Angus Buchanan, a leading international authority on Industrial Archaeology, who spent virtually his whole career at one seat of learning. He started at the Bristol College of Science and Technology which, after its move to Claverton Down in Bath, ultimately became the University of Bath. His many important national and local publications, including his biography of I.K. Brunel, and academic honours may be well known, but equally fascinating is the early involvement with the Sheffield Industrial Mission, a shared involvement with Brenda, his wife and fellow historian and a former editor of *Bath History*.

Finally, the images that illuminate the articles for volume XIII have once more been carefully selected and beautifully presented by our picture editor Dan Brown of Bath in Time who has given generously of his time for this publication.

Graham Davis,
editor.

Newton Park Mansion House, Bath Spa University

Foreword

"As an Australian who has travelled and worked in many parts of the world, I am delighted to live in the beautiful city of Bath, as the Vice-Chancellor of Bath Spa University. Since taking up the post, I have learned the importance of the links between the city and the university. It has been impressed upon me that the public profile of Bath Spa University owes a great deal to the City of Bath and its World Heritage status. Over many years, and under different titles, we have been fortunate to recruit many very able students to our courses. We have excellent staff; people like living in Bath."

Professor Christina Slade, Vice-Chancellor, Bath Spa University

Bath receives some 4 million visitors a year. The city forms the backdrop for numerous period and modern films, and is recognised by UNESCO, not only for its Roman remains and Georgian architecture, but also for its history and literary heritage. Its re-invention as a 'festival city' builds on its historical tradition in the arts, music and literature and this fits well with the academic strengths of departments at BSU. The relationship between the city and the university is a two-way street, of mutual interest and benefit. Students benefit from access to the resources and institutions of the city. The Roman Baths, Bath Central Library, Bath Record Office, the Victoria Art Gallery, the Holburne Museum, Museum of Bath at Work and the Building of Bath Museum have between them an amazing collection of sources and expertise that can enrich the student experience. Student work-experience in these institutions provides valuable support and a genuine engagement with activity in the city.

The university's involvement with *Bath History* is part of a closer collaboration with organisations and events taking place within the city. Having met members of the editorial board, which now has university representatives on it, I am happy to give my personal endorsement to a beautifully presented volume XIII. Fittingly, it will be launched in Bath in September at the BSU conference entitled *Georgian Pleasures* to be held at the Bath Royal Literary Society and Scientific Institution and the Holburne Museum.

Professor Christina Slade
Vice-Chancellor, Bath Spa University.

Notes on Contributors

Jan Chivers - After a career in Primary Education, Jan obtained a Combined Honours BA from Bath Spa University, followed by an MA in Local and Regional History. She graduated from the University of the West of England with a PhD in July 2007. Her doctoral thesis was based on Poor Law records, charity records and Coroners' records for the city of Bath for the period 1775 to 1835. Her publications include 'Bath Penitentiary and Lock Hospital, 1816-1824' in *Women's History Magazine*, Issue 51, Autumn 2005, and 'Infanticide in Bath, 1776-1835' in *Bath Exposed! Essays on the Social History of Bath*, 1775-1945, edited by Graham Davis, (2007), 'James and George Norman and the rise of the Casualty Hospital, 1783-1861' in *Bath History* vol. XI, (2009), and 'John Curry, Overseer for the Poor for the parish of Walcot, Bath' in *Bath History* vol. XII, (2011).

Graham Davis - retired as Professor of History at Bath Spa University in 2008 and continues to give talks to local and family history societies, as well as acting as editor of *Bath History*. His Bath publications include *Memoirs of a Street Urchin* (1985), *Bath beyond the Guide Book* (1988), co-author with Penny Bonsall of *Bath: A New History* (1996), and *A History of Bath: Image and Reality* (2006), editor of *Bath Exposed: Essays on the Social History of Bath, 1775-1945* (2007), and author of *Bath as Spa and Bath as Slum: The Social History of a Victorian City* (2010). He has also written extensively on Irish and British migration: *The Irish in Britain, 1815-1914* (1991), *Land! Irish Pioneers in Mexican and Revolutionary Texas* (2002) and editor of *In Search of a Better Life: British and Irish Migration* (2011). He has lived in and around Bath since 1968.

Colleen Denney - is an art historian who currently holds the titles of Director and Professor of the Gender and Women's Studies Programme at the University of Wyoming in Laramie, USA. Sarah Grand, as a feminist and avid cyclist, holds a special place in her heart. Dr Denney has just received her college's Seibold Professorship for 2013-14 which will allow her to travel to England, France and New Zealand for several new projects on the visual culture of women's suffrage, including a book in progress entitled *Raise Your Banner High! The Visual Culture of Women's Activism from London to Paris, 1860 to the Present*, and a novel entitled *Desire*, whose female protagonist is based in part on the character of Sarah Grand.

Cynthia Hammond - is Associate Professor in the Department of Art History, Concordia University, Montreal, Canada, where she teaches courses in art and architectural history and feminist cultural landscape theory. In addition to publishing on women, architecture, public space and landscapes, she is also a practicing artist. Dr. Hammond has a longstanding interest in and deep affection for Bath, visiting in 1993, and studying and painting the city ever since. Her doctorate and several articles focus on the intersection of public memory, women's history and architectural heritage in Bath. Her book, *Architects, Angels, Activists and the City of Bath, 1765-1965: Engaging with Women's Spatial Interventions in Buildings and Landscape* was published by Ashgate in 2012.

William Hanna - was educated at the City of Bath Boys School and read History and Political Institutions at the University of Keele. After National Service with the Somerset Light Infantry in Germany and Malaya, he served for twenty years in the Territorial Army. He worked in personnel in a number of public and private sector organizations, his last appointment being Director, Staff Relations in the Civil Aviation Authority. Retirement allowed him to develop his interests in military and local history. He is a Field worker for the National Inventory of War Memorials, a Regional Volunteer for the War Memorials Trust, a member of the Society for Army Historical Research and programme secretary for the History of Bath Research Group.

John R. Kirkup - Educated at Kettering Grammar School, Emmanuel College, Cambridge and St. Mary's Hospital, Paddington, he first visited the city (1950-2) to play rugby against Bath on beautiful September afternoons. Recalling the latter prompted his successful bid to work in the city's hospitals in 1959 and to gain a permanent post as consultant orthopaedic surgeon in 1964. Later he introduced ankle joint replacement to the U.K. His interest in the history of medicine stimulated books on 17th to 21st century surgery, including an edited version of *The Surgions Mate* by John Woodall (1617), *A Historical Guide to British Orthopaedic Surgery* (1992), *The Evolution of Surgical Instruments from Ancient Times to the 20th century* (2006), and *A History of Limb Amputation* (2007); *A History of Hip Surgery* is in press. He has been President of the British Society for Medical History, Archivist to the British Orthopaedic Association, Curator of the Historical Instrument Collection at the Royal College of Surgeons and Lecturer in the History of Surgery to the Society of Apothecaries. Awarded the Sir Arthur Keith medal of the College of Surgeons, he has advised widely on museum collections especially in the UK, Portugal and Australia.

Iftikhar Malik - Professor Malik teaches History at Bath Spa University and has authored a considerable number of books and papers on the recent history and politics of South Asia, Muslim communities in the West and U.S. policies towards the Muslim world. He is a fellow of the Royal Historical Society and a member of the Common Room at Wolfson College, Oxford. His special interests and expertise have made him very much in demand for interviews in the British media.

Alan Thwaite - On retirement in 1992 he was Deputy Director of Education in Newcastle upon Tyne. Since then he has followed a number of interests, in particular industrial archaeology and wider aspects of 18th and 19th history. He has written articles for the Jane Austen Society, of which he is a member. Initially provoked by Jane Austen's comments about 'dampness in the offices' (basements) of Green Park Buildings in Bath, he has spent a considerable time over the last few years investigating the history of these houses and developments there, and the residents past and present.

S. Blair Waddell - is currently a PhD candidate at the University of Stirling. His thesis is on William Jay of Bath. He has a general interest in the history of Evangelicalism in South West England. He resides in the United States with his wife and four daughters.

Martin West - holds an M.A. in public history and was director of Fort Ligonier in Pennsylvania, 1981-2011. He has been adjunct lecturer at the University of Pittsburgh, Saint Vincent College and Clark State Community College, concentrating on the eighteenth century. Serving on the Council of George Washington Scholars, Mount Vernon, Virginia, West edited and annotated the general's autobiography in *George Washington Remembers*. He is a collateral descendant of artist Benjamin West.

Barbara White - has retired as Director of an American study abroad programme based in Bath, after twenty years service. She was awarded a PhD in 1980 for her study of early modern assize sermons. She has since published widely on sermon literature, censorship and criminal biography and has contributed articles to the *Dictionary of National Biography,* and to encyclopaedias of censorship, the Victorian era, and erotic literature. She has also co-edited a collection of essays entitled *Writing and Fantasy* (Longmans, 1999), and is a regular contributor to *The Bath Magazine.*

REGULE ABACI

dragma
deunx
triens

Adelardus philosophorum assecla ultimus H. suo salute. Cum inter nonnulla fercula philosophie mense apposita nobis dextrorsum solitarius discumbentibus. proximum commune de parte secunda tripliciter sumerent: et me de quadrifida lance pauca ori tuo instillante omnia fastidires: quippe que ab aliis seposita et hactenus intemptata, tibi videres pituitorum antidotum ante plibasti

Pytagorici vero hoc opus composuerunt. ut ea que magistro suo pytagora docente audierant. oculis subiecta retinerent: et firmius custodirent. Et ipsi quidem mensam pithagoream ob magistri sui reverentiam. sed posteri tamen abacum dixerunt. Decuplacione enim totum opus texitur, quod ex nominis interpretatione signatur. Abacus enim vel abax decuplex interpretatur. vocatur etiam radius geometricus quia cum ad multa pertineat maxime per hunc geometrice subtilitates nos illuminantur. Dicitur etiam abacus a tribus primis litteris grecorum vel latinorum a quibus singule sillabe huius nominis incipiunt. Materia in hoc opere est numerus. secundum contrarias passiones augmenti et detrimenti consideratus. Intencio philosophorum in hoc opere de hac materia tractare ad divisiones et multiplicaciones numerorum Lectorem instruere. Fiunt tribus modis hic scilicet simpliciter. id est sine differentiis quod nos aureum dicimus et composite i. cum differenciis quod nos ferreum vocamus. Permixtum quod nos aureum et ferreum nuncupamus. Sciendum est quod omnes numeros ab uno usque ad x. digitos omnes vero limites. i. x. et xx et supra articulos antiqui vocaverunt hec improprie esse dicta et quedam alia in hoc opere invenimus sicut dominus Gybertus testis est. qui hoc opus nostris ytallis restituit et regulis succintim compositis illustravit. Digitus enim articulum esse videtur: cum plures articuli in digito contineantur: Sed quoniam articulus in digito finem facit. Vero limes numerorum dicitur.

Quinque sunt species divisionis. Due in simplicibus divisoribus. tres in compositis que et accidentibus et differenciis informamus: preter quas nullam inveniet poterius.

Prima est que fit in simplici dividendo per simplicem divisorem et in una eademque linea invicem sedere sortitur. Denominaciones a neutro fiunt nec a partibus nec a toto. Singularis singularem dividens. Simplex simplicem: minime requirit differenciam. Ita quidem decenus ad decenum. centenus ad centenum se habet et deinceps. Sed denominaciones a singulari non promovebunt. Collocentur quatuor divisor et novenarius dividendus sede limites

Peter Adelard and Islam:
Bridging the Medieval Worlds

Iftikhar H. Malik

Bath's Peter Adelard (c.1080-c.1151) **[fig. 1]**, Adelardus Bathoniensis, or Adelardus Bata (Latin), was surely one of the earliest and most far reaching intermediaries and bridgeheads between 'East' and the 'West,' at a time when both these distant civilisational regions, despite their pluralities, either lay indifferent to each other, or were at daggers drawn. His exposure to education on the Continent steered him towards a sustained foray in Asia Minor, Syria, Palestine and possibly Iraq, at a time when Spain and Sicily had already become the western focal points of a growing Islamic civilisation, itself a hybrid trajectory of several preceding intellectual traditions. Ironically, not enough has been written about this West Country philosopher, traveller, scientist, translator and ornithologist, though people seem to know more about Pierre Abélard since the former often gets confused with the latter.[1] His personal life, travels and scholarly works reveal a dynamic, tolerant and inquisitive seeker of scholarship, who went beyond the contemporary *othering* of the 'Orient; and took upon himself to introduce Eastern knowledge into the religious and mundane citadels of his own native England and beyond.[2] A man of several disciplinary interests, this Medieval scholar, like many of his contemporaries, began his profession as a budding ecclesiast, before venturing into astrology, astronomy, algebra and philosophy, which duly benefited from an enduring immersion in Arabic and Arabo-Islamic heritage. Despite our limited knowledge about his times and works, Adelard is not only the intellectual face of Medieval Bath and the West Country, he is also one of the fountainheads in re-introducing Classical Greek and Near Eastern intellectual heritage into Europe, where religious conformity had been resisting critical or contrarian thinking. According to Bertrand Russell, he was the pioneer translator of *Elements,* authored by Euclid, the Greek classicist. The work had been previously unavailable in Europe for a long time and it was only from its Arabic translations and commentaries that Adelard was able to render it into Latin, and thus provided the earliest version of this major treatise. **[fig. 2]**[3] By introducing classical Greek philosophy, Arabian natural sciences and Indian research on similar subjects besides numerology, Adelard left a lasting

fig 1: **Adelard of Bath teaching - Adelardi Bathensis Reguli abaci, c.1400**
Leiden University Library, ms. SCA 1, fol. 1v

Facing: Adelard of Bath teaching - Adelardi Bathensis Reguli abaci, c.1400
Leiden University Library, ms. SCA 1, fol. 1v

imprint at a time, when either that 'East' was an unknown, obscure landmass of non-white, 'uncouth' people of a competing faith, or was simply a place of exotic rivals.

Adelard's journey across the Muslim world, exposure to Eastern scholarship, and then its transference to Western Europe, put him in his own league, long before the travellers, explorers, colonials, fortune seekers and other curious individuals from these shores began visiting Africa, the Americas and Asia. Despite his religious upbringing and further disciplinary training in theology in France, Adelard did not carry any of the anti-Muslim rancour that characterised some sizeable sections of contemporary West European societies. Situating himself well beyond fanaticism and Crusading, demonisation, or pejoratively seeing Muslims as bogeymen, especially following Pope Urban II's declaration of Crusades in 1096, he, instead, opted to build upon mutualities with the Muslims and steered clear of those tormenting channels which wrought havoc on all the three Abrahamic communities for a major part of the Medieval era. Other than the Crusades as a backdrop of Adelardian quest, the contemporary Muslim+Christian+Jewish interface through Muslim Spain and Sicily, not only operated as a major incentive, it equally prepared him to undertake his extended journey to and stay in the Levant. Thus, while investigating Adelard and his scholastic and theological pursuits on the Continent and in the Near East, it is imperative to undertake academic inquiry into the Crusades, Arabo-Norman Sicily and, certainly Muslim Spain, as the mainsprings of this cross-cultural interface.

fig 2: Euclidis - Elementorum libri XV Paris, Hieronymum de Marnef & Guillaume Cavelat, 1573 (second edition after the 1557 ed.)
Private collection Hector Zenil /
http://commons.wikimedia.org

In other words, a study of Adelard of Bath affords us an opportunity to go beyond the parameters of biographical history by allowing us to contextualise him within some of the most significant historical crosscurrents of his times. Not only Muslim Spain and Sicily continue to reverberate in Muslim consciousness as the major losses and traumatic mishaps, but the Crusades themselves have refused to wither away from the memory on all sides.

Life and Times.

As mentioned earlier, general knowledge about Adelard has been quite limited though the philosophical writings and some more recent works have begun to show significant interest in his pursuits. A follower of Adelard, like several others in Bath, has thus lamented a lack of general information about this greatest Medieval scholar, who pioneered studies on the Islamic East long before anyone else. Thus begins the brief biographical note by Michael Davis: 'It could be a valid opinion that Adelard is our greatest Bathonian, by a long way. He was world-famous in his day and, for several centuries, Bath was known primarily as the birthplace of Adelard. But today, in his native city, he is entirely forgotten in a strange case of civic amnesia. The few people who think they have heard of him get him mixed up with the Frenchman Peter Abelard of the ill-fated love affair with Heloise (they were contemporary and almost certainly met).'[4]

Even an otherwise modern classic on the relationship between Islam and the *Christian West* mentions him only once and that too in an endnote though, one may state that Norman Daniel was more focused on theological issues in this interchange and less on other realms such as philosophy and natural sciences.[5] Various biographical entries do not have a consensual year of birth for Adelard, and often oscillate between 1079 and 1080 AD, though 1151 AD is generally accepted as the year of his demise. This was the time when 10,000 Normans venturing in from across the Channel had captured England, then inhabited by about two million people of predominantly Anglo-Saxon extraction. Interestingly, this was also the last time that England had ever been conquered by the invaders from the Continent, controlling its landmass and resources besides relegating the natives to a lower hierarchical order. Adelard was just eight when Bath's Anglo-Saxon church, where Edgar had been enthroned in 973, was destroyed. Following the Conqueror's death there had been a dispute over the royal succession and despite Robert, Duke of Normandy, being a major contender he did not turn up and instead opted to go on the Crusades to fight the Muslims. As a consequence, the revolt did not succeed and King William Rufus sold a bruised, war-torn Bath to John de Villula of Tours, who had been the Conqueror's physician. John became the Bishop of Bath and Wells and subsequently moved the Diocese to Bath from the latter and built a new Cathedral. This new structure preceded the present Abbey and was one of the grandest of its type in the whole of Europe. [fig. 3]

fig 3: 1st Seal of the Chapter of St Peter's Cathedral, Bath in use from the middle of the 12th to close of 13th century. Drawn by J.T. Irvine c.1870s
Bath in Time - Bath Central Library Collection

The Norman supremacy was extended with the recent conquest of Sicily, and several other Mediterranean islands from Muslims. Some of those Norman Kings in Sicily, such as Roger II, were totally Arabised though without diminishing their own Christian ethos and, like their Spanish successors on the Iberian Peninsula and in southern Italy, they ensured the assimilation as well as expulsions of Muslims from Bari, Sicily and Malta. On the one hand, they benefitted from Muslim craftsmen in developing the Arabo-Norman architecture besides diversifying irrigation systems and crops; simultaneously they taxed Muslims and Jews specifically to build new cathedrals. The appropriation of Muslim and Jewish lands, resources, skills and institutions, besides their gradual assimilation into Catholicism, preceded what was to become a *fait accompli* in Spain following the fall of Granada in 1492. Inquisition, conversions and finally the expulsions ensured a grievous form of ethnic cleansing in Spain which, in the case of Spanish Muslims, continued until the early seventeenth century and certainly retarded the socio-economic progress in that erstwhile cross-cultural society. While the Ottomans benefitted by bringing in Jewish and some Muslim Spaniards, Spain itself was reduced to a marginalised status from a trans-continental power. Despite dislocation of these two significant communities and imposition of a cultural straightjacket, their legacies in various realms continued to permeate for some time until Muslims and Jews disappeared even from the historical accounts except for a few rudimentary or derogatory references to some past invasions. All the way from 1492 until 1988, not a single mosque was built in a country which once was home to three Abrahamic faiths.[6]

At a time when colleges in Oxford and Cambridge were still non-existent, young Englishmen, like their Muslim contemporaries, would attend seminaries and special schools run by ecclesiasts. Here, the emphasis would be on biblical knowledge, imparted in Latin through faith-dominated teaching, and the knowledge of other creeds, as well as languages, remained almost non-existent. Given the understandable logistical and other technical restraints, clergy meticulously controlled and even monopolised academic domains and disciplinary realms with very limited receptivity shown for Greek, Roman or other pre- or non-Christian pedagogies. An element of self-sufficiency certainly was in common currency, though in reality it was the fear of secular and 'alien' influences that deterred these monks and priests from encouraging a more 'secular' scholarship. Philosophy, sciences, philology and certainly the study of other Abrahamic traditions, or curiosity about 'distant' lands, were not prioritised causing a serious disconnect with those vital strands.

Adelard's parentage is not that well-known, though one comes across a certain Fastred, possibly his father, who was a tenant of the Bishop of Wells, John de Villula. Adelard is certainly an Angle-Saxon name, which could have meant a rather subordinate position for his family under the Norman suzerainty. Bishop John had moved from Wells to Bath in 1090 and, following his early education in Bath's Cathedral school, we find Adelard, like the Bishop, on his way to Tours in France to gain higher instruction in theology. There he studied Trivium and Quadrivium though remained in the lower echelons of the Benedictines. A few years later he returned to Bath and took a group of younger people including his nephew to study in France. While in France, both as a student and then in his capacity as a teacher, Adelard was inspired by a 'wise man of Tours' to study astronomy, which became his lifelong pursuit. He had moved to Laon in 1109 along with his tutees and, after a teaching sojourn of seven years, decided to move further east by embarking on a visit to Norman Sicily in 1116.

Even before reaching Sicily, he must have been exposed to Islamic scholarship, which certainly was at its zenith, by combining Greek, Persian, Indian, Jewish and African traditions through a critical inquiry and comments, along with their own innovative disciplinary works. The rise of Muslim civilisation during the early Medieval period was not merely flagged by military conquests, and building up caliphates in the Middle East, Persia, Northern India,

Central Asia, Asia Minor, North Africa, Sicily and the Iberian Peninsula, as it equally assimilated plural intellectual and scientific influences. Certainly, the conquests endowed Muslims with more confidence and greater resources along with affording access to traditional centres of learning and philosophical thoughts, yet their own statecraft was deeply influenced by non-Arab strands. Here the Greek and Persian influences proved to be of enduring nature, where both secular and sacred flourished allowing greater space for scientific and philosophical pursuits. Arabic being the language of Islam and of the early Rashidun, Ummayyid and Abbasid caliphates (636 to 1258), most of the translations and newer scholarly treatises were written in Arabic, followed by Persian and other contemporary languages. Central Asian and Turkic scholars, along with the Jewish academes in Spain and Sicily, often used Arabic for their intellectual and theological works, though for literary and poetic purposes languages such as Persian, Hebrew and Turkish flourished without the former displacing them. As a consequence, the geographic location of the caliphate and Muslim kingdoms, and receptivity towards older and newer learning, energised Muslim scholarly discourses, something that was not lost on a perceptive Adelard. Sicily proved to be his springboard in orientating himself to Arabo-Muslim

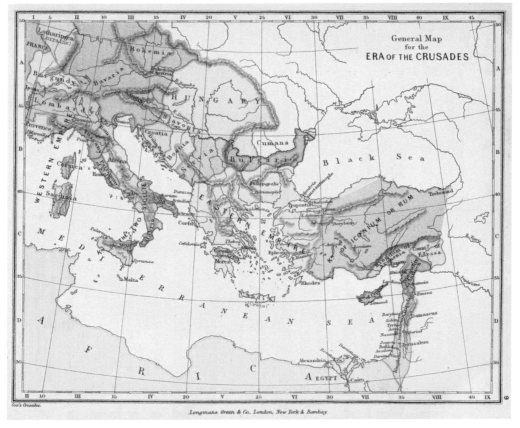

fig 4: General Map for the Era of the Crusades, 1095-1272
University of Texas at Austin. From The Public Schools Historical Atlas edited by C. Colbeck, 1905

scholarship and, unlike many contemporary Crusading European counterparts, his journey took him to Syria through Anatolia. In the wake of a crusading frenzy and heightened emotionalism this must have been a tense period, but Adelard's venture for learning Arabic, and initiation into classical and contemporary philosophical and scientific disciplines, overrode other considerations for his health and safety. Consequently, he proved to be the first Englishman to undertake this journey. The major transformation in the East-West equation, often away from the Mediterranean shores, happened in more recent times whereas the early Arabo-Muslim civilisation or the Islamicate continued with its tradition of inquiry and acceptance of plural scholarly conventions. This had persisted until the early modern era despite the debilitating developments such as the Crusades, Reconquista and the Mongol invasions, which crucially weakened Muslim political power at various places though it failed to weaken their literary and intellectual pursuits.

Though there is greater need to reconstruct Adelard's seven years of intellectual engagements in Syria and Palestine [fig. 4], yet the fact remains that on his return to England he busied himself in transferring a whole domain of his findings into Latin. Adelard must have faced numerous challenges in reintroducing his fellow ecclesiasts to Greek scholarship, besides some totally new disciplines such as algebra and geometry, and possibly Arab numerals, including the concept of zero imported into the Middle East from India. His contemporary doyens of Christian learning, both in England and elsewhere in Western Europe, entertained serious reservations against inducting Greek scholarship including the language, which emanated from the clergy's self-limiting attitude. This introversion certainly hindered a more forward-looking acceptance of classical and subsequent research in vital areas, with superstitions and defensiveness characterising priestly groups though the Bible itself had been written in Greek, and Jesus, more like future apostles, used Greek as a powerful medium of exchange. This reticence towards mundane philosophy, rationalism and natural sciences was not just reserved for Greek classics; it was equally symptomatic of a wider malaise where clergy could sit in judgment on everybody else by proscribing some more daring realms.

As mentioned earlier, amidst Adelard's several translations, Euclid's *Elements* and Al-Khwarzimi's *Zij* are the most prominent ones. Both helped develop interest in algebra besides strengthening astronomy. Based on his research at Tours, his earliest philosophical work was *De Eodem et Diverso,* which affirms Adelard's stature as an original teacher steeped in deeper pedagogical issues. One of his monumental works was titled as *Quaestiones Naturales* that he completed on his return and which remained a standard treatise for the next several centuries. In this book, Adelard himself mentions that seven years have passed since his lecturing in schools at Laon, which may mean that his stay in Antioch, and beyond in the Arab Middle East, happened during those seven years. However, one cannot be sure about his visit to Spain, which is still largely conjectural due to a lack of documentary evidence. He styled this work as a compendium on Arabic learning, based on research and interaction in Antioch, and raised 76 questions in the form of a classical dialogue about meteorology and natural sciences. The book, despite its incarnation several centuries before the printing press and with the contemporary literacy rates being dismally low, soon turned into a prized text both in England and France until the Renaissance ushered in more openness towards Plato and Aristotle. Here, Adelard has built up the case for the primacy of reason in understanding philosophy and natural phenomena, over and above faith, besides vouchsafing for Arab literary style of reasoning complex mundane and theological issues. Both these new strands must have posed a challenge to orthodox thinking and conformity, yet Adelard's care as well as personal status obviated the possibility of any vetoing clerical backlash. In addition, his close interface with the contemporary English royalty ensured his personal safety and integrity.

Adelard's scholarly pre-eminence was consolidated by his translation of Euclid's 13 *Elements of Geometry* [**fig. 5**], which dated from 300 BC, and had been lost in the West due to lack of general interest in such early classics. The Arabs had earlier translated *Elements* into Arabic and Muslim architecture, among other areas, had been a beneficiary of this seminal work. Adelard's other and no less significant contribution was his translation of Al-Khwarizimi's *Zij*, or the Star Tables, which played a significant role in changing the attitudes towards heavens, the place of humanity in this universe and the overall location of the earth in a rather complex system of stars and planets with varying sizes, locations and circular movements. Future researches by Galileo and Copernicus, among many more, were destined to benefit from this landmark work in Astronomy that was translated into Latin along with all the accompanying diagrams. Moreover, Adelard pioneered the introduction of the abacus and the astrolabe,

fig 5: The frontispiece of an Adelard of Bath's Latin translation of Euclid's Elements, c. 1309–16, portraying a woman with set-square and dividers teaching a group of students.
The British Library Board - Burney 275, f.293

two major, multi-purpose Muslim inventions that greatly systemised cartography as well as time-keeping in Europe. He wrote operational manuals for these astrological tools and dedicated them to the young Prince, soon to be crowned as Henry II, a scholarly and enlightened monarch in his own right.

During this period of anarchy while the young prince resided in Bristol with his mother, Empress Matilda, Adelard's native Bath was under King Stephen's control, though the philosopher maintained amiable relations with both the rival camps. It is possible that Adelard might have been a tutor to the future king, as in his dedication he exhorts him to acknowledge Muslim scientific grandeurs and contributions, instead of simply confining himself to the contemporary clerical discourses.[7] There is a strong possibility that it was Adelard, who translated Al-Khwarzimi's major work, *Kitab al-Jabar* (The Book of Completion/Algebra), commonly known as Algorismi, which inducted the Arab numerals and zero into English usage by gradually replacing Roman numerals. This was not a minor achievement given the fact that both the ancient Greeks and Romans were not familiar with zero and had their own formulas of arithmetical measurements.

Other than his scholarly work as a teacher, translator and an influential medium for Arabo-Islamic sciences, knowledge and inventions in England, Adelard held various public offices under King Henry and thus lived a busy life, possibly excluding the possibility of a marriage. In his teaching methodology, he followed the Aristotelian and Platonic precepts of dialogue, where students participated in the discourse by raising issues or attempting their own responses to various scholarly questions. He was a man of various personalities and devotion, proving himself to be a genius for all seasons. In *A Little Key to Drawing* there are several recipes attributed to Adelard, including the preparation of sweets by using sugar cane, which for a long time was only known to the Arabs. Originally, they had imported it from West Africa; the earliest sugar cane plantation took place on the Iberian Peninsula until with the introduction of coffee and tea, the demand for sugar caught up subsequently allowing the development of sugar plantations under British tutelage. In line with his role as a chemist, he is reported to have introduced new methods in brewing alcohol, itself an Arabic word. Though he was not a physician, but like other contemporary medieval men of learning, he carried some basic know-how on minor surgeries that he had picked up during his sojourn in the Middle East. In addition, Adelard authored a shorter book, *de Cura Accipitrum,* a manual on the upkeep of birds of prey such as hawks, which has been a lifelong pastime of many Arab people, and was equally popular among English monarchs and aristocrats.[8] His immersion in Arabo-Islamic culture at testing times, such as the Crusades and Reconquista, is certainly not a minor achievement, which affirms his stature beyond and above the contemporary proclivities and biases. In the post-9/11 atmosphere of mutual suspicions, it is all the more important to relocate his contributions as a pioneering intellectual intermediary, who set up a higher standard of objective learning without falling into the trap of what Edward Said defined as Orientalism.[9]

Medieval Views of Islam: A Contrarian Discourse.

Adelard's pioneering work must have been a bit out of sync with the contemporary cynical view of Islam within the Latin world, spread around due to two Medieval texts-*Risalah* and *Contrarietas*-polemical Latin works authored by some pseudo converts from Islam. They influenced the early Christian thinking in Europe including the works by Peter the Venerable, St. Thomas Aquinas, Matthew Paris and Sir John Mandeville. Peter the Venerable had, in fact, commissioned the Cluniac translation of the Quran by Robert of Ketton, and like Mark of Toledo's translation of the Muslim holy book, it too suffered from its own lacunae. The Quranic respect for Biblical prophets as divine messengers of Islam, and shared resemblance with the other two Abrahamic creeds, certainly astonished early theologians, especially in Spain which was now witnessing the Muslim suzerainty since its conquest by the Ummayyids in 712. The suspicion and hostility towards Muslims, due to their conquests and a high rate of conversions, began to be met by the martyrdom movement in Cordova, soon to be followed by the papal decree for the holy war. Spanish San Pedro, while impressed by Quranic teachings and beliefs, still could not bring himself to accept its divine origins viewing Islam as a revealed message. Early Christians, like him and their disciples elsewhere, were baffled by Muslim belief in the Quran being a revealed and not a created text. To San Pedro, despite all its merits, the Quran had been written down twenty years after Muhammad began to preach and thus merited questions about its authenticity. However, these theologians, with a lasting imprint on future generations across the Christian world could not see what Daniel summed up several centuries later, when he commented: 'The Quran in Islam is very nearly what Christ is in Christianity: the word of God, the whole expression of revelation. For the most Bible-loving, Protestant or Catholic, the Bible derives its significance from Christ; but Muhammad derives his from the Quran. In their failure to realise this, Latins persistently contrasted Christ and Muhammad, and nothing marks more clearly the distance between Islamic and European thought.'[10] Here, in this dominant Latin discourse on theology, other than the Quran and its relationship with the Prophet, Muhammad's own integrity, came under serious review with personages like William of Tyre openly calling him a liar and imposter, something which reverberated in Dante's *The Divine Comedy.* Sensationalised stories about his wives, especially Zaynab and Ayesha, were exaggerated to deny him even a normal humanity, with San Pedro being astonished for the earth not having devoured Muhammad for simulating epileptic fits to obtain other men's spouses.[11] Within a common context of a fervent Christianity over every other creed, the latter two writers and the future succession of British scholars on Islam held a slightly different and balanced views on Islam, revelations, the Quran and the Prophet. This slight change, possibly due to Adelard's contributions, had begun to occur in the twelfth century though cannot be viewed as a radical departure from the erstwhile serious reservations about the youngest Abrahamic tradition.

Through a distorted view during the Medieval period, Islam, like today, was believed to have justified violence through conquests and conversions; whereas the same was legitimated against it through the Crusades and here leading theologians such as Thomas Aquinas, Hubert of Romans, St. Bernard, and Pope Urban II ended up often being apologists for the holy wars. Strong social reservations against Muslims and Jews featured in some of the contemporary polemics suggesting a type of ordained ostracisation. For instance, soon after Adelard's death, an edict emanating during the thirteenth century from San Ramon de Peniaforte to the Friars Preachers and Friars Minors in Morocco, prohibited even a friendly social intercourse with the Muslims. Earlier, under a canon law, Muslims and Jews living under the Christian Kings were to be 'tolerated' as neighbours in an evangelical sense. In 1179, the Christians were forbidden from rendering any services in the Jewish and Muslim households under any circumstance and were destined for excommunication for living among the latter. In 1215, Jews and Muslims in the conquered territories were ordered to wear distinctive clothings to differentiate them from Christians, and a century later, the Clementine of 1312 forbade Muslim calls for daily prayers or undertaking pilgrimage to the Hejaz from within the territories of Christian princes. Following Reconquista and other serious exclusionary policies as seen in Spain and Sicily, the Medieval Muslim communities initially turned into smaller isolated islands and a few generations down the line were assimilated or were simply expelled.[12]

While highlighting such historic prejudices and partisan policies, Norman Daniel's summation does not seem to be out of place, as he noted: 'The Muslim communities of mediaeval Europe ceased to exist, converted under pressure, if not by force, or expelled, all of which now is contrary to Western practice.'[13] This early 'clash of faiths' assumed annihilative proportions during the Crusades and left bitter memories on all sides and despite initiating a multiple interaction between Europe and the Middle East in various innovative areas; they seem to reverberate even in today's conflictive lexicons.[14]

The Arabo-Islamic Culture: A High Point!

While the Latin views of Islam, the Quran, the Prophet and Muslims in general were selective and, as noted above, often hostile largely out of theological and political considerations of the clerical and political elite during the Medieval era, there was still a strong sense of Muslim achievements in areas other than statecraft. In 1112 locust attacks had laid a waste in Antioch whereas two years later, on November 13th, an earthquake struck the town that housed a sizeable community of Crusaders, and was now the home to Adelard. While Walter the Chancellor, a long-time cleric and 'Frankish' administrator of Antioch attributed it to Divine retribution for the moral extremities committed by fellow Christians, Adelard kept himself busy learning Arabic and gathering Eastern knowledge. A few years earlier, the combined Norman and Genoese forces had captured the nearby city of Tripoli laying waste to its vast library. Thousands of those works were given to merchants in Antioch, which due to its strategic location and cross-cultural influences was a natural choice for Adelard to pursue his intellectual ambitions. Saint Peter had once served in the city and now locusts and a devastating earthquake still did not deter the Bathonian to make it his home for the next several years. He was certainly aware of the atrocities being committed against the Jews and Muslims by some of his co-religionists, 'who had seen only evil in the Muslim infidel, [whereas] Adelard sought the light of the Arab wisdom.'[15] Even before reaching the Holy Land or adjoining Muslim regions in the Near East, Crusaders had been eliminating Jewish communities from across the Continent and occasionally did not spare their fellow Christians belonging to non-Catholic denominations.[16] However, their main hostility was reserved for Muslims and given the frenzy created by senior Church leaders such as Peter the Hermit, Gregory, Urban II and their successors who never relented in their anti-Muslim animus, the destruction and bloodshed in the Arab lands by *Frankish* forces knew no bounds. The Arabs were themselves shocked with this degree of violence, which did not spare even the holy places in the Old City, where the Dome of the Rock and Al-Aqsa Mosque were full of human and equine corpses since the population had been ordered to gather there. Other than their cruelty, the Crusaders shocked local people by their cannibalism during the food shortages in 1098 especially in the Syrian town of Mara. Radulph of Caen, a contemporary witness, while defining Muslims as infidels, recorded: "Our troops boiled pagan adults whole in cooking pots; they impaled children on spits and devoured them grilled." Another witness, Albert of Aix, wrote unabashedly: "Not only did our troops not shrink from eating dead Turks and Saracens, they also ate dogs."[17]

The characterisation of Muslims as heathens, idol worshippers and lesser humans, had facilitated the papal propaganda to justify these invasions which went on for centuries and proved to be the most far reaching historical development during the Medieval times. The Norman conquest of Sicily in the mid-eleventh century coinciding with the Reconquista had certainly unleashed this 'problematique' of relations with Muslims. Curiously, on the one hand, Muslims were viewed as outsiders and barbarians while concurrently their statecraft, monotheistic devotion and receptivity towards plural mundane disciplines and arts were deeply envied. Thus, even though by default, the Crusades proved to be a formidable channel between the Muslim intellectual and scientific achievements and their diffusion in Europe. This interchange also resulted in the transfer of knowledge and specialised skills in natural sciences, architecture, nutrition and vital inventions such as the astrolabe and abacus. Adelard's earlier visits to Salerno, Palermo and Syracuse had enthused him to visit the Islamic heartland where cities like Damascus, Aleppo [fig. 6], Antioch and certainly Baghdad had become the focal points of scholarly and scientific pursuits. The Abbasids, following their victory over the Ummayyids in 750, had decided to build their capital, Baghdad, in central Mesopotamia as a planned metropolis of knowledge and inquiry, and caliphs like Al-Mansur, Haroon al-Rashid and Abu Jaafar Mammun had ensured its global stature as the centre of wisdom and knowledge. The libraries, observatories, seminaries and private intellectual platforms had turned Baghdad into a global *Baitul Hikmah* or the House of Wisdom, until the Mongols destroyed it in 1258. Baghdad's completion happened in 762, just fourteen years before Caliph Abu Jaafar Mammun al-Rashid's birth. and given the attention and patronage from Caliphs Mansur and Rashid, the city assumed a pre-eminent status as a world leader in intellectual, cultural, artistic and religious pursuits. Some of the ablest men of letters were brought to Baghdad by these early Abbasid caliphs and its library became the largest of its type, exactly like Alexandria's a millennium earlier.

Caliph Mammun, a great scholar in his own right, encouraged scholarly investigations of secular and sacred subjects besides sponsoring a very ambitious translation programme. For instance, Hunayn bin Ishaq, the Christian Arab scholar, was commissioned to translate works of Greek classicists, including Galen whereas Banu Musa Brothers specialised in translating works in Physics and Astronomy. However the greatest philosopher of the time was an Iraqi named Al-Kindi or Al-Kundus (801-73) who tried to bridge Philosophy with Theology. In the

fig 6: The Citadel of Aleppo, Syria, 2010
Simon Jenkins of Mumbles

same vein, the most reputable geographer and mathematician in the contemporary Abbasid caliphate was Muhammad Ibn Musa al-Khawarizimi (780-850), who along with Al-Kindi tried to introduce the Hindu decimal system in their works. Another known contemporary philosopher was Al-Farabi (870-950), the thinker, who was of Turkish origin whereas Abu Rehan Al-Beruni (978-1048) could be safely called a noted geographer and perhaps the first anthropologist. Born in eastern Afghanistan, Al-Beruni completed his research in northwestern India-present-day Pakistan-and came out with his tome, *Kitabul Hind* (*Indica*), in 1000. It is an impressive record and research on geography, contemporary religions and cultural sociology of India. Like these and some other creative geniuses, the Abbasid period in the Middle East and its contemporary Ummayyid caliphate in Spain came to form the golden age of Islamic arts and letters. Other than Spaniard scholars such as Mohy-ud-Din al-Arabi (1165-1240), commonly known as Ibn-e-Arabi, the most familiar name in philosophy and medicines remained that of Ibn-e-Sina, or Avicenna (980-1037), who could be called the Erasmus of Islam during this golden age. Other than philosophical commentaries on ancient works, his Canon of Medicine (*Al-Kimiya*) became a universal text on medicines and surgeries across Europe. By virtue of his philosophical contributions, Avicenna proved one of the most notable links between Greek philosophy and Muslim theology, whereas in the realm of rationalism, Ibn-e-Rushd or Averroes (1126-98), a native Cordovan, has been acknowledged as the greatest philosopher in northern Mediterranean.

Baghdad attracted Muslim, Zoroastrian, Jewish, Hindu and Christian thinkers and scientists from across the world including some from Spain and Sicily. Inter-denominational tolerance and the diversification of Sufi orders equally owed to a more tolerant attitudes across the caliphate and thus philosophers, poets, architects, Sufis and publicists moved from one end to the other. In the same vein, Cordova, Toledo, Zaragoza, Seville and Granada flourished as centres of intellectual and artistic achievements under the Ummayyid caliphate that had come into existence in Spain, commonly known as Al-Andalus, and which rivalled the Abbasids further east. Between Muslim Spain and the Abbasid Middle East, the Fatimids had established their political centre in North Africa and had founded Al-Azhar University in their newly established capital of Cairo. Basically a Shia dynasty-as denoted by their dynastic name attributed to the daughter of the Prophet-the Fatimids patronised knowledge and inquiry and for a time ruled Sicily, but avoided converting their subjects to Islam. Following the destruction of the Abbasid caliphate and the prized city of Baghdad in 1258, cities such as Shiraz, Nishapur, Cairo, Granada, Lahore, Ghazni, Delhi, Qum, Samarkand, Balkh and Konya emerged as the focal points of philosophical and literary activities. The induction of erstwhile nomadic Central Asian Turkic tribes into Islam had brought fresh blood and energies into the erstwhile Perso-Arab civilisation of Islam and despite the acute adversities suffered during the Crusades and Mongol invasions along with the loss of Sicily and northern Spain, Muslim civilisation escaped a feared eclipse.

Thus, on the eve of the Crusades, the Muslim world featured several parallel centres of power and learning though numerous regional kingdoms also dotted various regions and their interaction with the Crusaders and other non-Muslim clusters is still to be documented. In this intra-Muslim pluralism during the medieval times, individuals such as Adelard and Stephens of Pisa, much like other seekers of knowledge, both Muslim and non-Muslim, became the fellow travellers. In a powerful way, this period, despite the hurt and tribulation of the Crusades

fig 7: Historical Map of the Mediterranean Lands after 1204
University of Texas at Austin. Historical Atlas by William Shepherd (1923-6)

and Reconquista, saw the evolution of medieval Jewish renaissance in Spain and North Africa. It is not surprising to see Maimonides (1135-1204), the pre-eminent Spanish Jewish philosopher, writing most of his works in Arabic and then moving from his native Cordova to Cairo to serve as a personal physician to Sultan Salah-ud-Din (1137-93).[18]

The presence of many Muslims in Southern Italy, especially in Sicily, and the Italian interaction with North Africa and larger Middle East **[fig. 7]**, afforded greater opportunity for Adelard to gain orientation into Eastern learning. In addition, Sicily's Christianity itself had a strong Greek persona, which allowed a diverse perspective that a growingly dominant Catholic factor deeply resented. The Norman monarchy under Roger II was attempting a delicate balancing act amongst these testing and often polarized trajectories until Greek, Muslim and Jewish influences were rigorously purged. It was soon after Adelard's return to his native Bath that King Roger II, in 1138, invited Al-Sharif al-Idrisi to move to Sicily to supervise research on geography and head the royal project of cartography. A well travelled poet, botanist, scientist and scholar of Latin, Arabic, Persian, Greek, Byber and Sanskrit, the Muslim academic decided to work under the patronage of the Norman King, who himself reflected contrasting attitudes towards Muslims varying from suspicion to adulation. Roger had refused to join the Popes on Crusades yet had made every effort to assimilate Muslims into a re-energised Christian Sicily. According to some contemporary reports several 'rumours swirled among the people that their king was really a secret Muslim, a reputation no doubt enhanced by Roger's frequent clashes with the Popes…'.[19] In addition, there was a pronounced Muslim interaction between Sicily and Spain and several Muslim families, in fact, migrated to Spain following the Norman conquest and a few centuries down, their descendants like other Spanish Muslims were confronted with the powerful forces of Inquisition and Expulsion with history repeating itself in Northern Mediterranean regions.

Adelard certainly augured serious scholarly and scientific interest in Eastern intellectual heritage, after gaining first-hand experience and despite the volatility as exhibited during the Crusades, visible interest in Islam continued at monasteries across Britain. Adelard's defiance of clerical indifference towards other intellectual and scientific traditions might have not transformed the contemporary mindset towards Muslims, but it certainly opened up new vistas, which eventually helped spawn the Renaissance, and comparative and even critical thinking in successive centuries. The emergence of the Ottoman, Safawid and Mughal empires, long after the caliphal era and dissolution of Muslim societies in Spain and Italy, continued to elicit interest across Britain, and individuals like Thomas Dallam (1570-1614),[20] Robert Sherley (1581-1628)[21] and Thomas Coryate (1577-1617), considerably added to those cross-cultural contacts in those early centuries.[22] Their efforts to reach out to the Muslim regions soon followed the destruction of the Armada with the crucial Ottoman assistance in 1588 and, with the formation of the East India Company in 1600, a new paradigm in relationship began to take shape, which certainly anchored itself on a different set of imbalances.[23]

Notes

1. Other than some of his own works and a few biographies, Adelard remains largely unknown if not totally confused with Abelard. In addition to sharing his name with some modern-day IT experts and financial wizards, Adelard has a few shorter biographical insertions on the Internet. Along with a Wikipedia entry, which surely acknowledges some useful references, there are a few shorter entries on Adelard, which fall short of academic rigour. Adelard's style of answering philosophical questions through active conversations with his nephew – inclusive of three separate words – have definitely elicited some recent translations and comments. For instance: Charles Burnett, *Adelard of Bath, Conversations with his Nephew,* (Cambridge: Cambridge University Press, 1998), and Jill Kaye and W.F.Ryan, (eds), *Adelard of Bath,* (London: Warburg Institute, 1987).

2. The biographical essay by Michael Davis of Bath Royal Literary and Scientific Institution (BRLSI) is a brief outline of Adelard's life and works. Davis happens to be the convener of the Adelard Society aimed at creating greater awareness on this prominent Medieval philosopher and runs the 'Adelard returns to Bath' programme. Michael Davis, 'Adelard of Bath: A Synopsis', BRLSI, October 2009. This short sketch was sent to the present author in reference to a possible lecture on Adelard and Islamic Scholarship, which was eventually held in Bath in 2010.

3. Bertrand Russell, *A History of Western Philosophy,* (London, Routledge, 2004), p.212.

4. Davis, 'Adelard of Bath', p.1.

5. Norman Daniel, *Islam and the West. The Making of an Image,* London, 1992), p.401. (Chapter X, endnote 4).

6. Michael Portillo, a Conservative politician, has occasionally used television programmes on cross-cultural themes, and in July-August 2012 he led a series on Muslim Spain on Radio 4, highlighting the legacy as well as on-going tensions between Muslims and Christians in today's Spain. 'Stepping Stones of Islamic Spain', July 29th 2012, BBC Radio Four, video: www.bbc.co.uk/iplayer/episode/b01l5pls/Stepping_Stones_of_Islamic_Spain_Episode_1/

7. Davis, p.3.

8. 'He was also a musician, having studied Music in the Quadrivium at Tours, and played the Cithara. On his return from the Middle East he played it for Queen Matilda (Henry 1's wife) at Easter 1116 (at Bath?).' Davis, p.4.

9. Edward Said's seminal work and postulation has caused an entire flurry of academic and ideological debate that has been claimed and challenged by a wide variety of opinion groups varying from critical academics to neo-conservative cheerleaders and Islamist radicals. See, Edward Said, *Orientalism,* (London, 1978). His future works on the Empire, Media and the Middle Eastern politics further elaborated imbalances within Islam-West interface though Niall Ferguson and several other historians would find those very features rather 'civilising'. For critics such as Talal Asad and Hamid Dabashi, the reawakening of biases and serious fissures within an exclusive cultural prism could themselves be a form of 'Neo-Orientalism', often appropriated by the post-colonial elite, both from the Western and non-Western regions. See, Talal Asad, (ed.), *Anthropology & the Colonial Encounters*, (Amherst: Humanity Books, 1998); and Hamid Dabashi, *Dark Skins: White Masks*, (London: Pluto, 2011).

10. Daniel, p.53.

11. Quoted in Daniel, pp.51-2.

12. Amidst a growing historiography, one finds more works on Islam in Sicily and Spain underlining an enduring though no less tragic tradition that once existed in Medieval Europe. On Spain, one finds several new books, papers and visual documentaries though more and more primary sources are also being unearthed. For instance: Francisco Nune Muley, *A Memorandum for the President of the Royal Audiencia and Chancery Court of the City and Kingdom of Granada,* edited and translated by Vincent Barletta, (Chicago: The University of Chicago Press, 2007); Iftikhar H. Malik, *Islam and Modernity: Muslims in Europe and the United States,* (London: Pluto, 2004); and, Matthew Carr, *Blood and Faith: The Purging of Muslim Spain.* (London: Hurst & Company, 2009): also, Alex Metcalfe, *The Muslims of Medieval Italy,* (Edinburgh: Edinburgh University Press, 2009).

13. Daniel, p.316. However, he did acknowledge a visible tradition of awareness of Islam during that period, which transmitted its lasting impact all the way until recent times: 'Summing up the Western view of Islam, we can say that it was based in the crucial period on a good deal of sound knowledge, but it is also accepted a great deal that is now seen, and was seen by many then too, to be nonsense. Nonsense was accepted, and sound sense was distorted, because whatever seemed useful to faith was thought likely to be true, a failure of logic, and indeed of faith as well, which is not peculiar to this subject or these people.' p.302.

14. Soon after 9/11, George W. Bush and several other Western leaders and policy makers fell back upon the typologies associated with the Crusades and holy warfare, which in the same vein, were responded by the Islamist radicals such as Osama bin Laden. The Afghan Taliban, essentially a Pushtun-based movement fighting the NATO troops since 2001, have often labeled these countries and troops as 'Saleebi'-cross-carrying Crusaders. In a recent interview, Western journalists were again informed of the Taliban resistance to persist with the resistance against what they termed as 'the Crusaders'. It is interesting to note that groups like the Taliban or even Al-Qaeda consciously avoid labeling Western forces as 'infidels' rather invoke the Medieval imagery of enduring confrontations. Commenting on a Taliban video documenting a suicide attack on NATO's Camp Salerno in eastern Afghanistan on June 1st 2012, a Western report noted: 'Grinning for the camera, the suicide bomber fondly patted his truckload of explosives. "We will defeat these crusader pigs as they have invaded our land," he declared as he revved the engine.' Declan Walsh and Eric

Schmitt, 'New Boldness From Militants Poses Risk to U.S.-Pakistan Ties', *The International Herald Tribune,* July 30ᵗʰ 2012. Often-quoted autobiography of one of the founders of the Taliban and a former Guantanamo internee has also tried to differentiate between the erstwhile pre-1989 Soviet troops and the post-2001 NATO forces in Afghanistan. See, Abdus Salam Zaeef, *My Life with the Taliban,* (London: Hurst & Co., 2010).

15. Jonathan Lyons, *The House of Wisdom. How the Arabs Transformed Western Civilisation,* (London: Bloomsbury, 2010), p.2.

16. The most serious pogroms were carried out on the French and German territories though places like London and York had their own less savoury records in anti-Jewish campaigns. At Worms in 1096, forces led by Count Emicho, the German aristocrat, killed five hundred Jews though they had sought the protection from the local Catholic leadership. More than one thousand Jews were killed in Mainz while others began to commit mass suicides and mothers were reportedly slaughtering their own children before killing themselves. Anonymous of Mainz in Shlomo Eidelberg, (ed. and trans.) *The Jews and the Crusaders. The Hebrew Chronicles of the First and Second Crusades,* (Madison: University Press), p. 110, quoted in Lyons, pp.13-4.

17. Quoted in Lyons, p.20.

18. It is quite curious to note that several Jewish scholars opted for Arabic to express their literary and philosophical ideas and some of their students and followers elsewhere complained about Hebrew being sidelined by its own speakers. Yet, given the stature of Arabic as a lingua franca, the Jewish luminaries did not shirk from using Arabic as their preferred medium. For a very interesting perspective on leading Jewish voices from Spain and their works, see Esperanza Alfonso, *Islamic Culture Through Jewish Eyes: Al-Andalus from the Tenth to Twelfth Century,* (London: Routledge, 2008).

19. Lyons, p.93.

20. Thomas Dallam (1570-1614) was the doyen of a well-known family of blacksmiths from Lancashire who specialised in making organs. The Ottoman Caliph, Sultan Mehmet III, to build and deliver a special organ for the royal court in Constantinople, commissioned Thomas Dallam.

21. Sir Robert Shirley/Sherley(1581-1628), like his brother, Anthony Shirley, served the Safvid King, Shah Abbas and lived in Isfahan. He, along with his Circassian wife, led a Persian Embassy to the court of King James I, seeking alliance for the Shia regime against the Sunni Ottomans.

22. Thomas Coryate (1577-1617) was a West Country historian, traveller and courtier who was born in Somerset and walked all the way to India to meet the Mughal Emperor, Jahangir. His arrival in India coincided with the presence of Sir Thomas Roe, who had been deputed by East India Company's directors in Threadneedle Street to open up trade relations with the Sub-continent. Coryate was born in Crewkerne near Ham Hill and after studying at Oxford, decided to see the world on foot. In 1608, Coryate undertook a tour of Europe, followed by his publication of memoirs entitled *Coryat's Crudities* (1611). In 1612, Coryate began his journey towards South Asia to meet up with the Mughal Emperor, visiting Greece, the Asia Minor, Palestine and Persia on the way, and eventually reached the Sub-continent. From Agra, the Mughal capital, he sent letters describing his experiences, published in 1616 as *Greetings from the Court of the Great Mogul.* A similar volume of his letters appeared in 1618, a year after he died of stomach illness in Surat, the main port in Western India. After Adelard, Coryate is viewed by many to have been the first known Briton to accomplish a grand tour

of Europe and Asia, which eventually proved a favourite trend among English upper classes seeking knowledge and recreation on the Continent. See, R. E. Pritchard, *Odd Tom Coryate: The English Marco Polo,* (Stroud: Sutton, 2004); Michael Strachan, *The Life and Adventures of Thomas Coryate*, (London: Oxford University Press, 1962); and Dom Moraes and Sarayu Srivatsa, *The Long Strider: How Thomas Coryate Walked from England to India in the Year 1613*, (Delhi: Penguin, 2003).

23. For those early intellectual and literary contacts, see Nabil Matar, *Islam in Britain, 1558-1685*, (Cambridge: University Press, 1999); and, Humayun Ansari, *The Infidel Within: The History of Muslims in Britain, 1800 to the Present*, (London: Hurst, 2004).

'Stand and Deliver':
Bath and the Eighteenth-Century Highwayman

Barbara White

Why is a Highwayman the most godly man? Because he lives by preying!
(Ben Johnson's Jests, 1755)[1]

D r. Archibald Maclaine (1722-1804) **[fig. 1]** who, from 1796 until his death in 1804, lived in 'dignified retirement' at 18, Belvedere in Bath would not have appreciated jokes like this which appeared in highly popular jest books throughout the eighteenth century.[2] Before his retirement, and between 1747 and 1796, Maclaine had been a highly respected Presbyterian minister at the English Church in The Hague and was 'admired and beloved by all who courted and enjoyed his society' in his adopted home of Bath.[3] This particular 'godly man' had more reason than most to disapprove of jokes that irreverently likened clerics to highwaymen for he was possibly the only resident in Bath to be related to a notorious 'Knight of the Road'. Maclaine was the elder brother of 'Gentleman James Maclean', one of the most infamous highwaymen in England. **[fig. 2]**

Maclean (1724-50), whose exploits famously included holding up Horace Walpole's (1717-97) coach at Hyde Park, was executed at Tyburn on October 3rd 1750. He was a frequent visitor to Bath and it was alleged that he had a dalliance with Fanny Murray (1729-1778), Richard 'Beau' Nash's (1674-1761) cast-off mistress when she was a successful courtesan in London.[4] She may even have been the mystery woman who was found in Maclean's bedroom in St. James's on the fateful day of his arrest.[5] Maclean's dashing bravado captured the public imagination and over three thousand people saw him in Newgate Prison as he awaited execution. Numerous prints, pamphlets and ballads were published during Maclean's lifetime, and after his death, which not only made him a household name but also mythologised him into the romantic figure of 'The Gentleman Highwayman'.[6] One of the most popular prints of the day showed the dissolute Lady Caroline

fig 1: **Archibald Maclaine D.D. by Henry Bone R.A. Miniature**
Private Collection, sold at Bonhams 21 July 2005

Petersham (1722-84) and her friend Miss Elizabeth Ashe (c1731-?) weeping for Maclean in his cell shortly before his death. **[fig. 3]** Walpole was quick to recognise the parallel between Captain Macheath, the leader of a gang of highwaymen in John Gay's *The Beggar's Opera* (1728),

Facing: Detail of An exact Representation of Maclaine the Highwayman Robbing Lord Eglington on Hounslow Heath on the 26th June 1750)
Courtesy of The Lewis Walpole Library, Yale University

and the grief of his two wives, Polly Peachum and Lucy Lockit, as Macheath was led to the scaffold, and the affected grief of Maclean's aristocratic doxies:

> "the chief personages who have been to comfort and weep over this fallen hero are Lady Caroline Petersham and Miss Ashe: I call them Polly and Lucy, and asked them if he did not sing "Thus I stand like the Turk with his doxies around".[7]

Maclaine, who had braved the Newgate crowds to visit his brother and urge his repentance, was undoubtedly shocked by his brother's lack of contrition in his preparations for death and the crowd's celebration of him as a chivalrous hero. Shamed by his brother's life of criminality and the celebrity that grew up around him, the venerable cleric publicly renounced his brother during his final incarceration in Newgate and changed his name from Maclean to Maclaine in an attempt to conceal his filial relationship. It was to no avail, for the public at large was too entranced by the myth of the highwayman hero to let such connections go unnoticed. Well into the nineteenth century, published accounts of Maclaine's exemplary life, and indeed his 1804 obituary notice, could not resist referencing this revered Bath resident's connection to a famous highway robber. 'It will be no reproach to this worthy man's memory' noted *The Annual Register* in 1805, 'that he was brother to the highwayman who went by the name of "The Gentleman Highwayman"'.[8]

fig 2: The Ladies Hero or the Unfortunate James
McLeane Esq. (sic)
National Portrait Gallery, London

Maclaine was not alone in having to reconcile personal shame with a public fascination, and indeed glorification, of the highwayman as popular hero. When Eliza Wheeler (d. 1794) made her debut on the Bath stage on Saturday October 24th 1789, there would have been an undoubted frisson in the theatre had members of the audience known that her husband, Francis Malloy, whom she had married on September 28th 1787, was a highwayman.[9] When he was arrested for a highway robbery at Maidstone in Kent in March 1791 newspapers concentrated on the light irony, rather than the seriousness of his crime, remarking that 'in her performance of Polly, in *The Beggar's Opera*, little did she expect she would so soon meet with - a real Macheath'.[10] Mrs. Malloy was not so amused and changed her stage name to Mrs. Murray and after 1792 became Mrs. Cotter 'either by marriage or whim'.[11]

fig 3: Newgate's Lamentation or the Ladys Last farewell of Maclean

Trustees of the British Museum

The Beggar's Opera, **[fig. 4]** which had its own connections to Bath, was first performed on January 29th 1728 at the playhouse in Lincoln's Inn Fields. Likening the leading politicians of the day to a gang of highwaymen, to the highwaymen's benefit, the play was an overnight sensation and ran for an unprecedented sixty-two consecutive performances in its first season. During its second season when *The Beggar's Opera* toured the provinces, it was performed a staggering fifty times in Bath and Bristol, more so than anywhere else in the country: the play 'spread to all the great towns of England, was played in many places to the 30th and 40th time; at Bath and Bristol 50'.[12] Even some twenty years after its first performance in the city, Bath audiences greeted the play enthusiastically. *The Bath Journal* reported that

> THE BEGGAR'S OPERA was perform'd last Saturday Night at the Theatre in Orchard-Street, to a very polite Audience, with great Applause; and by Particular Desire, will be perform'd again this Night.[13]

The play's success led Dr. Thomas Herring (1693-1757), King's Chaplain and afterward Archbishop of York and Canterbury, to denounce *The Beggar's Opera* for its moral laxity in encouraging criminal activity, glamourizing highwaymen and, in its finale, for allowing Macheath to triumph unpunished.[14] John Gay (1688-1732) **[fig. 5]** was tickled by Herring's denunciation and wrote to Jonathan Swift (1667-1745) in May 1728, at the height of Macheath fever, when he was beginning a six-month stay in Bath to take the waters:

> I suppose you must have heard that I have had the honour to have had a sermon preached against my works by a court chaplain, which I look upon as no small addition to my fame.[15]

The popularity of *The Beggar's Opera* in Bath confirmed that, in the morality debate that followed Herring's condemnation, Bath society, ever addicted to scandal and pleasure, was firmly on Gay's side, and that of his highwaymen. Bath took Gay to its heart and he enjoyed all the amusements the city had to offer: Swift feared that 'Mr Gay will return from the Bath with twenty pounds more flesh, and two hundred less in money'.[16] Rather than taking to the gambling tables, however, Gay devoted some of his time to coaching a company of actors who played Bath in July 1728, in the performance of his play. This had 'so good an effect that they

fig 4: A Scene from The Beggar's Opera, 1728/9 by William Hogarth. Oil on canvas.
National Gallery of Art, Washington, Paul Mellon Collection

have not only gained a great deal of money by it, but universal applause, insomuch that they played it all last season at Bath'.[17] Gay also found Bath conducive to playwriting and it was in the supportive atmosphere accorded by the city that he completed *Polly*, his less successful sequel to *The Beggar's Opera*. The preface to *Polly* explained that 'the very Copy I delivered to Mr. <u>Rich</u> [theatre manager] was written in my own Hand, some Months before, at the <u>Bath</u> from my own first foul blotted Papers'.[18]

The concern that *The Beggar's Opera* actively encouraged young men to take to the road was legitimate. In 1773, the magistrate Sir John Fielding (1721-80) warned David Garrick (1717-79), actor manager of the Drury Lane Theatre, against performing the play, arguing that it was never 'represented on the stage, without creating an additional number of real thieves'.[19] Similarly, Herring's sermon was held by some to be prophetic for:

> Experience afterwards confirmed the Truth of his [Herring's] Observations, since several Thieves and Street robbers confess in <u>Newgate,</u> that they raised their Courage at the Playhouse, by the Songs of their Hero <u>Macheath,</u> before they sallied forth on their desperate nocturnal Exploits.[20]

The twenty-one year old Isaac Darkin (c.1740-61) was a case in point. With Macheath an undoubted role-model Darkin, the son of a cork-cutter from Eastcheap, fashioned himself into a well-mannered and courteous gentleman with an eye for the ladies and a strong sense of his own style.[21] He even had a mistress called Polly although her surname was Cannon rather than Peachum. In his short, three-year career as a highwayman, it was estimated he earned some £600 which financed his affected gentlemanly life-style.[22] 'He frequently visited places of public

fig 5: John Gay, author of the Beggar's Opera, mezzotint, c.1730
V&A Image/Victoria and Albert Museum

Scene from Claverton Down near Bath

fig 6: **Scene from Claverton (Clarken) Down, near Bath, 1824 by Benjamin Barker. Lithograph**
Bath in Time - Bath Central Library Collection

diversion, drove his phaeton, and constantly appeared upon the turf'.[23] In Bath, where he was a regular visitor, he supplemented his income by robbing 'invalids going to, or returning from, the waters' but he also took to highway robbery on the surrounding roads.[24] On June 22nd 1760, Darkin was taken at an inn at Upavon and sent to Salisbury for trial after an unsuccessful attempt to rob Lord Percival of about 14 guineas as he travelled by post-chaise over Clarken (Claverton) Down. **[fig. 6]** Darkin was acquitted when neither Percival nor his driver could give a positive identification but accounts of his dashing, gentlemanly ways had already transformed Darkin from a common criminal into a heart-throb as the women of Salisbury flocked to see him in prison and pinned their romantic dreams on him.

> To Bath in safety let my lord
> His loaded Pockets carry;
> Thou ne'er again shall tempt the Road,
> Sweet youth! If thou wilt marry.[25]

Within two months of his acquittal, Darkin was awaiting trial in Oxford for the robbery on the Oxford Road of a Mr. Gammon on August 26th 1760. Found guilty, Darkin was executed on March 23rd 1761, yet during his incarceration it was *The Beggar's Opera* that sustained him.

> He diverted himself one Evening before his Trial, by reading the Beggar's Opera, when he appeared to enter thoroughly into the Spirit of Mackheath's Part, and seemed greatly to enjoy the Character. He dressed even then very neat, particularly in his Linnen; and had his Hair dressed in the most fashionable Manner every Morning; his polished Fetters were supported round his waist by a Sword-Belt, and tied up at his Knees with Ribbon.[26']

Thus, by associating the criminal Darkin with the fictional hero Macheath, his biographers disarmed him and made him safe, a process which was completed by effeminising and dandifying him in descriptions of his dress. This contrivance can also be seen at work in the representation of another highwayman with Bath connections, namely Jack Rann (c.1750-74) also known as 'Sixteen String Jack' because of the sixteen strings of brightly coloured silk ribbons he stylishly attached to the knees of his breeches. [**fig. 7**] Rann was born near Bath in about 1750 and worked as a pedlar around the city's streets until the age of twelve when he left for London. During his four-year career in the capital and on Hounslow Heath, he menaced numerous travellers including Dr. William Bell, chaplain to the Princess Amelia (1711-86), whom he robbed on the Uxbridge Road. Yet his danger to the travelling public was eclipsed in the popular imagination by his extrovert dandyism and his fashionable lifestyle. Thus, accounts of his final condemnation concentrated as much on what he wore - 'a new suit of pea-green clothes, his hat was bound round with silver strings, he wore a ruffled shirt' - as the crime for which he suffered.[27] Indeed, in one account of a hold-up at pistol-point, Rann's dandyism turned what was, in reality, a terrifying ordeal into an amusing anecdote with the joke dependent on a popular knowledge of Rann's fastidiousness about his appearance. The story goes that when Rann told Mr. Shuter to stand and deliver, (probably the actor Ned Shuter), Shuter replied, '*you see, <u>honest friend</u>, that I cannot*

"SIXTEEN-STRING JACK" AND ELLEN ROCHE IN THE DOCK.

fig 7: Sixteen String Jack - Highwayman Jack Rann
Half Hours with the Highwaymen by Charles G Harper, 1908

An Exact Reprefentation of MACLAINE the Highwayman Robbing LORD EGLINGTON on Hounflow Heath on the 26.th of June 1750.

MACLAINE is said to be born in the North of Ireland, of Scotch Parents, is a tall genteel young Fellow, and commonly very gay in his Drefs. On the 27.th of July laft, he was Apprehended for a Robbery on the Highway, and committed to the Gatehouse Westminster by Juftice Lediard; Among others whom he robbed, was Lord Eglington. The Stratagem he made use of was very extraordinary, being as follows. On the 26.th of June, as his Lordfhip was going over Hounslow Heath early. Maclaine and his Companion Knowing they should have a good Booty refolv'd to rob him. But as he was well arm'd with a Blunderbufs; some Contrivance was necefsary, they therefore agreed, that one should go before the Poft-Chaise & the other behind it; he before the Chaise stopt the Poftillion, and screen'd himself in such a manner that his Lordfhip could not discharge his Blunderbufs at him without killing his own Servant; at the same time, Maclaine who was behind swore if his Lordfhip did not throw the Blunderbufs out of the Chaise, he would blow his Brains thro' his Face. His Lordfhip finding himself thus beset, was forced to Comply, and was robbed of his Portmanteau and 50 Guineas. His Lordfhip had two Servants about half a Mile behind.

Publifhed according to Act of Parliament Augft 13.th 1750 & Sold by P. Angier Engraver and Printseller at the Plume of Feathers in Windmill Street St. James's London.

Pr. 6.d Plain & 1.s Colour'd.

fig 8: An exact Representation of Maclaine the Highwayman Robbing Lord Eglington on Hounslow Heath on the 26th June 1750
Trustees of the British Museum

stand, but I can <u>deliver</u>, and immediately spewed all over him, and escaped from being robbed'.[28] Anecdotes which emasculated highwaymen by downplaying their brutality or turning them into figures of fun were always popular. One such account centred on Mr. Gill, who was 'an eminent pastry cook at Bath' in Wade's Passage where, according to Lydia Melford in *Humphry Clinker* (1771), one could 'take a jelly, a tart, or a small bason of vermicelli'.[29] Travelling alone in a post-chaise between London and Bath, Gill noticed a highwayman closing in on him. Believing discretion the better part of valour, he decided just to give the highwayman his money without putting up a fight. As the highwayman drew level with the post-chaise, Gill thrust his head out of the window but forgetting the glass was up, his head went straight through the window and smashed the glass to smithereens. Misreading the accident as 'invincible intrepidity' on Gill's part, the highwayman galloped away rather than confront such a 'lion hearted fellow'.[30]

The unmanning of the highwayman was never more obvious than in novel reports of transvestism on the highway, for it was always difficult to take seriously highwaymen in petticoats. *The Bath Chronicle* for 1761 reported how a criminal lay down in the road between Tetbury and Cirencester dressed in women's clothes and then robbed at pistol point the gentleman who came to 'her' assistance and rode off on the victim's horse.[31] One of the more

35

amusing set-pieces of cross-dressing, which was clearly designed to titillate, referred to Thomas Sympson, known as Old Mobb (d. 1690) who, at the end of the seventeenth-century, frequently robbed on the Bath roads. On one occasion, having spent some time in Bath, he had reconnoitred a lord who was leaving the city and devised a plan to separate him from the large retinue which was accompanying him in order the more easily to rob him. Having 'a tolerable good face', Old Mobb disguised himself in women's clothes and caught up with the lord on the road. The lord propositioned the 'maiden', the 'maiden' demurred but eventually yielded and suggested they went into the woods together for greater privacy.

> Taking up the petticoats, [the lord] found under them a pair of breeches. Quoth he, What a plague's the meaning of your wearing breeches, madam? Nothing, replied Old Mobb, but to put your money in. So putting a pistol to his lordship's breast, he said, If you make but the least resistance you're a dead man'. [32]

This sense of farce on the highway is compounded by reports of passengers themselves engaging in transvestism. *The Public Advertiser* for May 1766 described how two tradesmen who were carrying large sums of cash and bills hoped to escape the close attention of any potential highwayman by disguising themselves in women's clothes. Their men's shoes and stockings gave them away to their alarmed fellow passengers who feared a conspiracy to rob them.[33]

It is not surprising therefore, that although the hundreds of highwaymen who infested all the Bath roads could be both brutal and terrifying, eighteenth-century Bath remained captivated by the idea of the highwayman. The city revelled in its connection with John Gay who had created the most dashing highwayman of the eighteenth-century literary imagination and took a sneaking pride in its link to real-life highwaymen like James Maclean or Francis Malloy. It was a love-affair compounded by the numerous criminal biographies, prints, ballads and broadsides which did much to transform cold-hearted robbers into romantic, chivalrous heroes via a process of reinvention that created mythic, sexual creatures of legend for safe armchair consumption. This distanced the public from the real-life brutality of the highwayman by sanitising and dandifying him, turning him into a comic set-piece and unmanning him in women's clothing.[34] The lowly footpad played no part in the legend of the highwayman.

There were, however, enough residents and visitors to Bath to know that these inventions were a far cry from the reality of travelling on any of Bath's roads.[35] The 107 mile journey to and from London appeared especially perilous if only because of the large ratio of robberies to the volume of traffic on the road. John Wood the elder (1704-54) claimed that by the late 1740s Bath could accommodate a staggering 12,000 visitors, a figure that may have grown to 40,000 by 1800, and each visitor offered highwaymen the prospect of rich pickings as they made the two or three day journey from London to Bath for the season.[36] Between 1740 and 1777, there were up to forty-six coaches or 'Flying Machines' a week for highwaymen to choose from, a number that increased to 147 by 1800.[37] The more enterprising amongst the highwaymen fraternity infiltrated the various coach companies and had at least one employee on their payroll. Thus, the 39 year old Thomas Talbot, who was born at Wapping, began his criminal career by riding postilion on the Bath and Bristol coaches and passing intelligence about his passengers to an unnamed Irish highwayman who paid Talbot for 'a previous Account of the People, and their Circumstances'.[38]

Numerous highwaymen regularly lay in wait along the length of this often wild and desolate road with the vast 6,000 acre expanse of Hounslow Heath [fig. 8], as well as Colnbrook, Maiden Thicket, the wild Marlborough Downs and Cherhill in Wiltshire, the home of the notorious Cherhill gang, amongst their favourite haunts. One particularly unlucky passenger was robbed on Hounslow Heath in the summer of 1749 by two highwaymen, the 26 year old Michael Keys and the 24 year old James Poole, on her journey to Bath, and was robbed again by the self-same men as she returned to London some three weeks later.[39] It is little wonder that passengers often made their wills before setting out on a journey, even of only 50 miles, or that coaches were known as 'god permits' with arrival at one's destination dependent on 'god willing'[40]. When Joseph Clavey advertised his London schedules for the 'Froom Waggon' in *The Bath Journal*, he made clear that all journeys were only to be 'perform'd (if GOD permit).'[41]

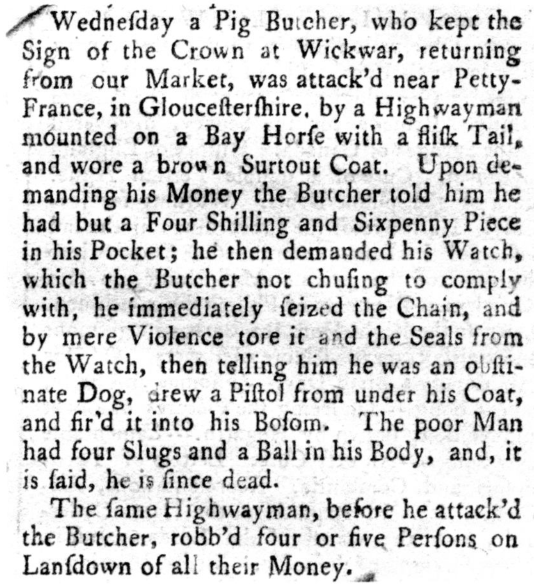

Wednesday a Pig Butcher, who kept the Sign of the Crown at Wickwar, returning from our Market, was attack'd near Petty-France, in Gloucestershire, by a Highwayman mounted on a Bay Horse with a flisk Tail, and wore a brown Surtout Coat. Upon demanding his Money the Butcher told him he had but a Four Shilling and Sixpenny Piece in his Pocket; he then demanded his Watch, which the Butcher not chusing to comply with, he immediately seized the Chain, and by mere Violence tore it and the Seals from the Watch, then telling him he was an obstinate Dog, drew a Pistol from under his Coat, and fir'd it into his Bosom. The poor Man had four Slugs and a Ball in his Body, and, it is said, he is since dead.

The same Highwayman, before he attack'd the Butcher, robb'd four or five Persons on Lansdown of all their Money.

fig 9: An account of a raid by a highwayman on a pig butcher near Petty-France, Bath Chronicle July 4 1763
Bath in Time - Bath Central Library Collection

In reality, any journey beyond the city boundaries, no matter how short, was fraught with danger for the roads to Bristol in the west via Twerton, Newton St. Loe and Keynsham, to Marshfield and Cold Ashton in the North, to Box and Batheaston in the East and especially Claverton Down and Kingsdown were all patrolled by highway robbers. The nature of robbery on these roads was different in that journeys tended to be made on foot, horseback or by post-chaise rather than by the speedier 'Flying Machines' and instead of fashionable visitors, travellers were often lone farmers, servants or local businessmen returning home from farmers' markets or Bath fairs. As a result, there was a proliferation of footpads who were skilled at pulling riders from their horses, as well as highwaymen, working these routes and accounts of their thievery, taken mainly from the brief reports that appeared in *The Bath Chronicle* and *The Bath Journal*, confirm that these men, for there were almost no women working the Bath roads, were anything but chivalrous or romantic figures.[42] For example, in 1763, a highwayman who robbed four or five persons of all their money on Lansdown shortly afterward killed a butcher who kept 'The Crown' at Wickwar in a robbery near Petty France in Gloucestershire. The butcher had been slow to hand over his valuables and so the highwayman, 'mounted on a Bay Horse with a flisk Tail' shot him in the chest as an 'obstinate Dog'. [fig. 9] [43] In 1756, as Mr Biggs, a maltster from Inglescombe (Englishcombe) was returning home from Twerton, he was attacked by highwaymen who robbed him of over four pounds and 'used him very ill'.[44] When the highwayman, George Wilkinson, was taken for his robbery of William Cox which took place half a mile on the Bath side of Keynsham, he had a brace of fully loaded pistols and nineteen bullets on him.[45] Footpads had a worse reputation for barbarity and regularly carried blunderbusses, pistols, cutlasses and bludgeons with which to threaten and intimidate.[46] When a terrified maidservant was pulled from her horse at the direction-post between Twerton and Newton St. Loe, the footpad threatened to blow her brains out if she made any resistance.[47] Sarah Doderage who was travelling to Bath from Bristol received a worse fate for she was also pulled from her horse, but was then violently beaten with a stick, robbed and raped with the footpad threatening to murder her if she cried out.[48] James Eames, a servant to Mr. Abraham of Bathwick, was also treated brutally when he was travelling on foot to Freshford. He was overtaken at Brassknocker Hill [fig. 10] by a stout footpad who stole his bag and 'beat him most unmercifully with a stick, leaving him almost dead, with six large wounds in his head'.[49]

Reports in the local newspapers provided very little detailed information on the hundreds of highway robberies that took place on Bath's roads throughout the eighteenth century. A brief account of the incident was customary, including where and when it had happened and what had been stolen. Details of the victim usually extended to no more than giving his/her name, place of abode and occupation:

> Last Tuesday Evening, about Six o'Clock, Mr Pedding , a Carpenter, of Weston, was robb'd of about twenty-six Shillings in Silver, a Mile from this City, in the Road to Wells. The Robber seem'd to be a tall Fellow; and had on a light-colour'd Coat.[50]

Where possible, physical descriptions of the highwayman were also provided but these were often vague when attacks took place at night or the victim was traumatised. The rape victim Sarah Doderage was unusual in being able to provide a reasonably detailed description:

> He is a well-set Man, not very tall; wore a blue Surtout-Coat, a small round-brimmed Hat, and had a brownish Silk Handkerchief on his Neck, a brown Wig, and was marked with the small pox.[51]

It was probably easier for a victim to stare into the face of a horse than a highwayman so that descriptions of horses were often very detailed and a horse with distinctive markings could prove fatal to its rider. The butcher, John Weston, who was robbed near Newton St. Loe on his way to Bristol described a 'dark-brown Gelding, with a Mane and Tail of a Blackish colour, and a whiteSnip on his Nose'.[52] As a result, highwaymen often rode stolen horses or, like Wilkinson, dismissed from the employ of a Bristol gentleman because of 'his bad Course of Life', they 'hir'd Horses at divers Places in this City, to carry on [their] illegal Courses'.[53] Concealing one's identity was of the essence and highwaymen made good use of wigs, hats and masks to disguise themselves. John Weston's assailant 'was a lusty Man, and wore a black Wig, a brown Great Coat, with his Hat uncock'd and his Face covered with something of a lightish Colour'.[54] Similarly the 'thick-set' footpad who attacked the servant of a Mr. Wood between Bath and Bitton, wore 'a long light-coloured Great Coat, a Grizzle Bob Wig; His hat

fig 10: Road to Bradford (Brassknocker Hill), 1804 by J.C. Nattes. Aquatint
Bath in Time - Bath Central Library Collection

slapped before' whilst another footpad who terrified the maidservant at the direction-post between Twerton and Newton 'had a Crape over his Face'.[55] The fear of being recognised also explains why highwaymen were constantly on the move and, as we shall see in the case of the Poulter gang, could range up and down the country. Michael Keys and James Poole, who held up the same female passenger twice, were finally apprehended in Swindon where they admitted to working the Bath road between Hungerford and Sandy Lane but also to a robbery at Petty France in Gloucestershire.[56] Similarly Joseph Somner, William Cole and Paul Coleman who robbed a gentleman in a post-chaise on Kingsdown Hill also admitted to robberies at Holt-Forehead near Staverton, Bradford-on-Avon, Appleshaw, Wayhill and on the Wilton Road near Salisbury.[57]

    As a result, highwaymen and footpads could suddenly move in and terrorise an area for a week or a month and as quickly disappear again. Newspapers did their best to protect the travelling public and when *The Bath Journal* warned that there had been several attacks by a particular footpad near the direction-post between Twerton and Newton 'Farmers and others who frequent Bath Market, and are necessarily obliged to travel that Road by Night, accompany each other for Fear of being robbed by him'.[58] Of greater concern was intelligence suggesting that organised gangs were in operation: for example, the two footpads who stopped a post-chaise on Totterdown Hill near Bristol were believed to be members of a larger London gang that had recently begun to work the environs of Bristol. Similarly, when Somner and Cole were arrested for a robbery near Staverton, it soon became apparent that they were part of a much larger outfit when they informed against some, but certainly not all, of their fellow gang members including Paul Coleman, Sam Lane and Peter Floyd, regarded as 'three desperate and leading villains', as well as Christopher Still and William Cromwell.[59]

Execution, transportation, imprisonment: the consequences of informing were devastating to fellow gang members which was why so many highwaymen preferred to work alone rather than risk treachery from confederates eager to save their own skins or make money. Victims tried to capitalise on this by offering generous rewards to tempt partners into betrayal. Thus, when William Tavennor, the servant of a Chippenham farmer named Salway was robbed, Salway offered a ten-guinea reward to any of the three robbers who would impeach his colleagues. Similarly, when Mr. Murray was attacked by six ruffians as he was riding from Bath toward Hemington, he also offered ten-guineas for information as well as a free pardon to the accomplice who would give evidence against the others.[60]

The outcome of one particularly spectacular betrayal was the publication of a pamphlet which exposed, in vivid detail, the secret world of a gang of highwaymen and the part played by Bath in its operation. In an attempt to save his life, John Poulter, alias Baxter turned King's evidence after he had been apprehended at Exeter in February 1753 for the robbery, committed with an Irishman named Thomas Lynch alias Burk, of Dr. Hancock, a physician at Bath, and his daughter as they travelled by post-chaise across Claverton Down.[61] Poulter signed a damning affidavit against his former confederates which was printed in two issues of *The Bath Journal* in April 1753 and which then formed the basis of his forty-page *The Discoveries of John Poulter, alias Baxter.* **[fig. 11]** [62] This described, in startling detail, Poulter's criminal career since 1749 and helpfully provided readers

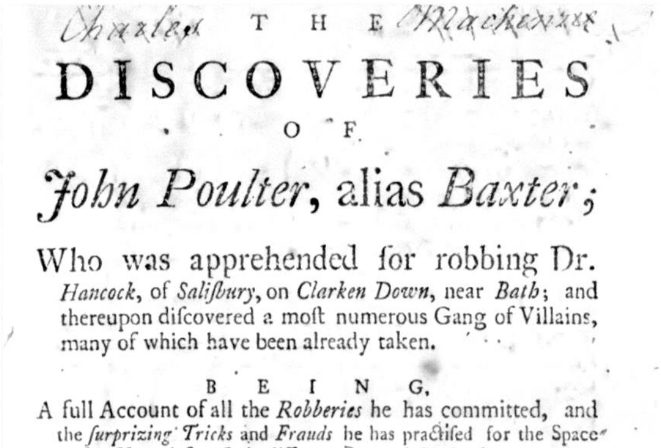

Charles   T H E   Mackenzie

DISCOVERIES
O F
John Poulter, alias *Baxter;*

Who was apprehended for robbing Dr.
Hancock, of *Salisbury,* on *Clarken Down,* near *Bath;* and thereupon difcovered a moſt numerous Gang of Villains, many of which have been already taken.

B E I N G,
A full Account of all the *Robberies* he has committed, and the *furprizing Tricks* and *Frauds* he has practiſed for the Space of five Years laſt paſt, in different Parts of *England.*

Written wholly by H I M S E L F.

To which he has added for the Service of the Publick, to make all the Amends in his Power for his paſt Offences,
DIRECTIONS to SECURE Houſes from being BROKE open. How to PREVENT HORSES from being STOLEN out of Grounds, Commons, or elſewhere. USEFUL CAUTIONS to Tradeſmen and Others who travel the Roads, to PREVENT their being robbed. And to prevent any unwary Perſons from being impoſed upon and defrauded, an exact Account of the Manner in which GAMBLERS and other SHARPERS impoſe upon People at Fairs, &c. The ARTS the HORSE DEALERS make Uſe of there to draw in People to buy or exchange their Horſes; and the various other CHEATS practiſed at Fairs, as giving Notes for Goods, Pricking at the Belt, exchanging Saddles and Great Coats at Inns, &c. In what Manner SHOP-KEEPERS are cheated by SHOPLIFTERS: With every other TRICK and SPECIES of VILLAINY made uſe of by ROGUES and SHARPERS, laid open in ſo plain a Manner, and their Behaviour and Language ſo fully deſcribed, that every one who reads the Book, may certainly know them at any Time, and ſo be upon their Guard againſt being cheated by them.

The TENTH EDITION, With ADDITIONS.

Printed for R. Goadby in Sherborne; and ſold by W. Owen, Book-ſeller, at Temple-Bar, London, MDCCLIV.

fig 11: The discoveries of John Poulter, alias Baxter; who was apprehended for robbing Dr. Hancock of Salisbury, on Clarken Down, near Bath… 1754
University of California Libraries / Internet Archive

with advice on how to avoid those tricks regularly used by gamblers, thieves and pickpockets. The pamphlet proved so popular that it had reached seventeen editions by 1779.

From the moment Poulter's affidavits were published, they must have sent a shudder through every gang member and associate involved in the intricate network of fences (those that received stolen goods) and safe-house inn-keepers, who had harboured and protected the gang along the length and breadth of England for the authorities moved quickly to arrest them all on the strength of Poulter's revelations. Edward and Margaret Lines, who were the landlords of the 'The Rock Tavern' near Stourbridge in Staffordshire, which Poulter described as the 'greatest Place of Rendezvous in England for Thieves', had regularly harboured the gang and received their stolen goods.[63] They were taken up as were Stephen and Mary Gea (or Gee) of Chapel Plaister near Box who had assisted Poulter and Burk after the robbery of Dr. Hancock.[64] Mary Brown, the wife of John Brown, Frances Allen, the wife of John Allen who had rooms in Bath and had often concealed Poulter's goods for him, were also arrested as was John Roberts and the silversmith John Ford for receiving. Roberts would die in prison shortly after his arrest.[65]

In the end, Poulter's fulsome exposé did not save his neck. Nash, along with other dignitaries, tried to intercede for him and he wrote to the Duke of Newcastle, on behalf of the Bath Corporation, to press that 'everyone here wishes he may not be executed'.[66] On October 22nd, the Duke of Newcastle won Poulter a reprieve but after a failed attempt to escape from Ilchester jail on February 16th, Poulter was finally hanged there on February 25th 1754. He died 'very peniently [sic], but with a decent Resolution' and it was noted that 'he never struggled once after he was turned off, but hung quite motionless from the first Moment'.[67] According to Goldsmith, Nash had good reason to look favourably on Poulter as it was through *The Discoveries*, that Nash had 'received a list of all those houses of ill fame which harboured or assisted rogues, and took care to furnish travellers with proper precautions to avoid them'.[68] Goldsmith added that Poulter's original intention had been for his work to be dedicated to Nash and he had arranged for a copy of the manuscript to be sent to Nash along with a covering letter which was reproduced in Goldsmith's 1762 biography of Nash.[69]

The Discoveries is a work of exceptional recall with details of the dates, names, conversations and crimes of Poulter's five-year career on the road minutely noted. Either Poulter kept careful records against the day he might need to save himself or *The Discoveries* was produced under duress as Poulter tried to save himself. Allowing for the caution that revelations written under such circumstances demand, Poulter's confession, if accurate, is particularly valuable in demonstrating the local part played by Bath within the gang's national network of highly organised criminal activity which ranged all over the counties of England from Durham to Devon and included Staffordshire, Oxfordshire and Worcestershire.

The centre of their Bath operations was 'The Pack Horse Inn' where Roberts was the landlord. The eponymous hero of Edward Bulwer-Lytton's nineteenth-century novel of highway adventure, Paul Clifford, alias Captain Lovett, took rooms above a hairdresser's in fashionable Milsom Street but used 'a mean-looking alehouse in a remote suburb' for the serious business of planning robberies with his confederates. By contrast, 'The Pack Horse Inn' was right in the centre of Bath for it was either the inn on Claverton Street or the one near St Michael's Church.[70] Being in the centre of town presented certain dangers to gang members and like any highwaymen visitors to Bath, it was essential to merge unobtrusively into the city without drawing attention to themselves. Not all highwaymen succeeded: the 27 year old Thomas Pollard and the 26 year old James Kirton who had both returned early and illegally from a sentence of transportation, had been recognised in the environs of the city, disguised as gypsies, and their sighting reported in *The Bath Chronicle*. Recapture would almost certainly cost them their lives.[71] The fictional Paul Clifford passed seamlessly for a dandy and was seen, and accepted, at all the fashionable assemblies as well as at the gaming tables. Darkin was more enterprising and early in his career gave himself a solid alibi by enlisting in the navy, joining 'The Royal George' at Portsmouth and becoming a midshipman, thus proving he had a respectable occupation if ever he were taken up for robbery. Michael Keys had kept a wine cellar in Bath before taking to the road and this may well have been a cover for his criminal activities. Poulter and his associates, however, chose the surprising personae of smugglers presumably working on the assumption that everyone, other than Revenue officers, liked a smuggler and goods at knock-down prices. To authenticate their roles, gang members 'used to give seven Shillings a Pound for Tea and sell it again for four Shillings and Six-pence, on purpose to make people believe we were Smugglers'.[72] This was clearly a popular persona for

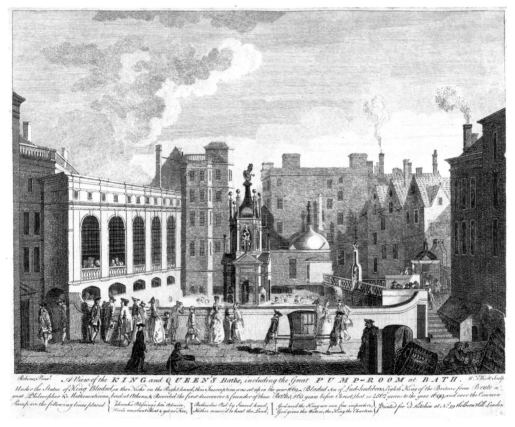

fig 12: A View of the King and Queen's Baths, including the Great Pump-Room at Bath, 1764, after Thomas Robins. Copper engraving.
Bath in Time - Bath Central Library Collection

when Somner and Cole 'skulked' around Melksham as the centre of their operations, they did so similarly 'under the Character of Smugglers'.[73]

Despite the dangers of being recognised, the diversions of Bath acted magnetically on highwaymen who often accumulated as many 'contributions' from the road as they could, specifically to enjoy themselves, as Darkin and Rann had done, at the fashionable spa. Poulter financed a six-week stay in Bath by robbing enough in the preceding weeks 'to bear our Expences to Bath for the Benefit of the Waters'. **[fig. 12]** [74] It was a similar story with other highwaymen: after the 29 year old Charles Cleaver, from Whitechapel who was executed at Tyburn near Marble Arch on June 8th 1744, had robbed an old farmer at Holt, he and his two confederates Matthew Mooney and one Tool, 'went immediately to Bath, where they repaired to the Gaming-Tables, and had not been there a Week, before they were stripped of their Money at play' and presumably were forced back on the road.[75] Around 1776, Thomas Boulter (c. 1748-78), the scourge of Salisbury Plain, visited Bath and Bristol 'where he got into company with some sharpers, who eased him of a good deal of his cash' which he made up by robbing around the city environs during the following months.[76] The light irony of a highwayman himself being robbed becomes much darker with the realisation that Bath's very reputation for gaming and pleasure ensured the city itself, as well as the highways beyond, were rife with highwaymen.

> As there are so many Nurseries for Vice, 'tis no great Wonder that so many
> Robberies, etc, are daily committed: Neither is it any Wonder how many
> Fellows live, who skulk about, and have no visible Employ'.[77]

The gang to which Poulter belonged planned their robberies from 'The Pack Horse Inn' and, for example, at the end of April 1752, when twelve members of the gang 'all Gamblers and Pickpockets' were at the inn, they organised themselves into 'three setts' and took off to Sampford Peverell in Devon to carry out a variety of crimes including, robbery, burglary and horse stealing. Closer to home, Roberts kept surveillance on all the guests at his inn, and briefed gang members on their routines and their wealth. In November 1751, he aided Poulter and Richard Branning in planning the robbery of a gentleman clothier who habitually travelled from Trowbridge to Bath in order to collect money to pay his workers. Roberts was not averse to participating in actual robberies himself and was involved in the Bell Warehouse robbery in Bristol but he was much better suited to co-ordinating the operation. He concealed stolen items for gang members until it was safe for them to collect and was instrumental in receiving and selling on stolen goods (including horses) as he had developed an extensive network of criminal contacts within Bath for passing on, or laundering, (sometimes literally!) stolen items. Thus, an unnamed dyer in Bath regularly dyed stolen fabrics to make them untraceable and it was probably through Roberts that Poulter met the silversmith Ford who was actually in the crowd on the day Poulter was hanged, loudly denying Poulter's accusations from the scaffold that he was implicated in the gang. After a robbery at 'The Crown Inn' at Blandford, Poulter alleged he sold his share including 'Bells, seal, Shoe Buckles, and Girdle Buckles, all of Gold', to Ford who 'melted them down before my Face, into an Ingot of Gold, not quite an Ounce'. Ford also melted down a silver tankard that Poulter had stolen from an inn at Corsham and the silver thread from an embroidered waistcoat but, complained Poulter, 'I never got above one Shilling of F[or]d for my Silver to this Day'.[78]

Poulter's confederates were not only highwaymen but could turn their hands to anything from opportunist thieving and burglary to horse-stealing. This was true of most highwaymen although it flies in the face of the romantic image of the highwayman as a 'Knight of the Road'. Darkin rather ignominiously robbed invalids going to and from the Baths whilst Still and Cromwell, who were impeached by Somner, were also involved 'in several Burglaries, and receiving, lodging, and dividing many stolen Goods'.[79] Thus, Poulter's confederates, William Elger, John Brown and John Allen made unsuccessful attempts in November 1753 to burgle a house in Wade's Passage that they had been watching, as well as a toy-shop and a watch-maker's in the Church Yard.[80] Brown was more successful on November 28th when he went 'on the sneak by himself' and robbed a Mr. Bartlet of North Parade of a portmanteau trunk from his home which was then quickly spirited away to 'The White Lion Inn' at Devizes.[81] Poulter's confederates were also consummate card-sharpers and they worked one particularly lucrative scam up and down the country. Known as 'Pricking in the Belt, or the Old Nob', the trick usually worked best with four gang members involved. Goldsmith described it as follows:

> A leathern strop, folded up double, and then laid upon a table; if the person who plays with a bodkin pricks into the loop of the belt he wins; if otherwise, he loses. However, by slipping one end of the strop, the sharper can win at pleasure.[82]

In attracting the 'fashionable company', Bath also drew in a host of undesirables: pickpockets, beggars, prostitutes as well as highwaymen and footpads. Thus, Bath visitors and residents were as much at risk from highwaymen within the city walls as they were without. Sometimes this was obvious as when a nursery-man named Philip Brown was attacked at pistol-point 'near the End of Terrass-Walk, in King's Mead' by two footpads.[83] Quite often, however, it was impossible to know when a highwayman was in the vicinity. Like Macheath, the finest gentleman upon the road, who could keep company with lords and gentleman at the gaming tables of Marylebone in London as easily as he could drink in taverns with his gang members, the adept highwayman could blend seamlessly into society at Bath.[84] Poulter's *Discoveries* demonstrated, to the deep unease of Bath's visitors and residents alike, that the highwayman who had robbed them at pistol-point the night before, could pass unobserved in their company the following day as Bath society took the waters at the Pump Room, attended the assemblies, played the gaming tables or bought their bargain packets of tea.

My thanks to Elaine Chalus and Ceri Sullivan for reading earlier versions of this article. I would also like to thank the staff of Bath Central Library for their kind assistance and Dan Brown of 'Bath in Time' for his generous help in sourcing the images that have appeared in this article. I also wish to express my thanks to Graham Davis for his helpful suggestions and careful editing.

Notes

1. Anon: *Ben Johnson's Jests: or the Wit's Pocket Companion. Being a new Collection of the most ingenious Jests, diverting Stories, pleasant Jokes, smart Repartees, excellent Puns, wise Sayings, witty Quibbles, and ridiculous Bulls. To Which is Added, a Choice Collection of the newest* <u>Conundrums</u>, *best Riddles, entertaining* <u>Rebusses</u>, *satirical* <u>Epigrams</u>, *humourous* [sic] <u>Epitaphs</u>, *facetious* <u>Dialogues,</u> *merry* <u>Tales</u>, *jovial* <u>Songs</u>, <u>Fables</u>, *etc. etc. etc.* 3rd ed., *With great Additions and Improvements,* (1755), pp.89 and 112.

2. 'A Gentleman of great Genius and Learning' would throw jest books 'promiscuously into a large Bag in one Corner of his Library to obviate Melancholy, or relax his severer Studies'. See *The Jests of Beau Nash, Late Master of the Ceremonies at Bath, consisting of a Variety of Humorous Sallies of Wit, Smart Repartees, and Bon Mots; which Passed Between Him and Personages of the First Distinction, and the Most Celebrated for True Wit and Humour. Dedicated to the Right Honourable the Earl of Chesterfield,* (1763), preface, p.i.

3. Dr. Maclaine was born in Monaghan in Ireland in 1722 of Scottish parentage and is best known for his translation of Johann Lorenz von Mosheim's *Ecclesiastical History* (1765). He is buried in Bath Abbey where a monument was erected to his memory. See, *The Monthly Magazine; or, British Register,* (1805), vol. xix, p.94; John Britton, *The History and Antiquities of Bath Abbey Church: including Biographical Anecdotes of the Most Distinguished Persons interred in that Edifice: with an Essay on Epitaphs, in which its Principal Monumental Inscriptions are Recorded,* (1825), pp.107 and 109-110.

4. Anon, *Memoirs of the Celebrated Miss Fanny M[urray],* 2nd ed., 2 vols. (1759), vol. 2, pp. 80-83.

5. Peter Cuningham, (ed.), *The Letters of Horace Walpole, Earl of Orford,* 4 vols. (Circencester: Echo Library, 2005), vol. 2, (1749-1759), p.83. Letter from Horace Walpole to Sir Horace Mann dated August 2nd 1750.

6. There are numerous biographies of James Maclaine: see, for example, John Barrows, *Knights of the High Toby: Theory of the Highwaymen,* (Peter Davies, 1962), pp.159-178; Charles G. Harper, *Half-Hours with the Highwaymen, Picturesque Biographies and Traditions of the 'Knights of the Road',* 2 vols. (Chapman & Hall Ltd., 1908), vol. 2, pp.271-300; Reverend Dr. Allen, *An Account of the Behaviour of Mr. James Maclaine, from the Time of his Condemnation to the Day of this Execution, October 3. 1750. By the Reverend Dr. Allen who attended him all that time, to assist him in his Preparations for Eternity. Drawn up and published at the earnest Desire of Mr. Maclaine himself,* (1750).

7. Cuningham, (ed.), *The Letters of Horace Walpole,* p.83. Letter from Horace Walpole to Sir Horace Mann dated August 2nd 1750. *"Thus I stand like the Turk."* is the finale of *The Beggar's Opera.*

8. *The Annual Register, or a View of the History, Politics, and Literature for the Year 1804,* (1806), p.510. See also, Sylvanus Urban, (ed.), *The Gentleman's Magazine,* vol. 96, (1804), p.1173; W. Kenrick, et al., *The London Review of English and Foreign Literature,* (1767), vol. 5, p.343; *The Plain Englishman: Comprehending Original Compositions, and Selections from the Best Writers, under the Heads of The Christian Monitor; The British Patriot; The Fireside Companion,* (Hatchard & Son; Windsor, Knight & Dredge, 1821), vol. 2, p.174.

9. See Philip H. Highfill, Kalman A. Burnim, Edward A. Langhans, *A Biographical Dictionary of Actors, Actresses, Dancers, Managers and other Stage Personnel in London 1660-1800,* 16 vols. (Carbondale and Edwardsville: Southern Illinois University Press, 1993), vol. 16, p.28. Another source gives the date of her marriage as 1786. See John C. Greene, *Theatre in Belfast 1726-1800,* (New Jersey: Associated University Presses, 2000), p.238.

10. Arnold Hare, (ed.), *Theatre Royal Bath: A Calendar of Performances 1750-1805*, (Bath: Kingsmead Press, 1977), p.123.

11. Highfill, Burnim and Langhans, *A Biographical Dictionary of Actors*, p.29.

12. *The Magazine of Magazines, compiled from Original Pieces with Extracts from the Most Celebrated Books, and Periodical Compositions, Published in Europe, for the Year 1754, the Whole Forming a Compleat Literary and Historical Account of that Period,* (Limerick, 1754), vol. 8, p.579.

13. *The Bath Journal*, November 4th 1754.

14. The sermon, which is now lost was preached in March 1728 in Lincoln's Inn Chapel. See, J.V. Guerinot and Rodney D. Jilg, (eds.), *Contexts 1:The Beggar's Opera*, (Connecticut: Archon Books, 1976), pp.118-124.

15. Walter Scott, *The Works of Jonathan Swift, D.D. Dean of St. Patrick's, Dublin; Containing Additional Letters, Tracts, and Poems, Not Hitherto Published; with Notes, and A Life of the Author*, 2nd ed., (Edinburgh, 1824), vol. 17, p.194.

16. Quoted in, Calhoun Winton, *John Gay and the London Theatre*, (Kentucky: The University of Kentucky, 1993), p.129.

17. Quoted in, David Nokes, *John Gay: A Profession of Friendship*, (Oxford: Oxford University Press, 1995), p.448.

18. John Gay, *Polly: An Opera. Being the Second Part of The Beggar's Opera*, (1729), preface, p.iv.

19. James Plumptre, *Four Discourses on Subjects Relating to the Amusement of the Stage: Preached at Great St. Mary's Church, Cambridge on Sunday September 25, and Sunday October 2, 1808, with Copious Supplementary Notes*, (Cambridge, 1809), p.174.

20. Guerinot and Rodney, *Contexts 1: The Beggar's Opera*, pp. 119-120.

21. Harper, *Half-Hours with the Highwaymen*, vol. 2, p.269.

22. *The Bath Chronicle*, March 26th and April 2nd 1761.

23. *The London Chronicle*, March 26-28th 1761.

24. Harper, *Half-Hours with the Highwaymen*, p.266.

25. Harper, *Half-Hours with the Highwaymen*, p.268.

26. *The Bath Chronicle*, April 2nd 1761.

27. G.T.Crook, (ed.), *The Complete Newgate Calendar Being Captain Charles Johnson's General History of the Lives and Adventures of the Most Famous Highwaymen, Murderers, Street-Robbers and Account of the Voyages and Plunders of the Most Notorious Pyrates, 1734; Captain Alexander Smith's Compleat History of the Lives and Robberies of the Most Notorious Highwaymen Foot-Pads, Shop-Lifts and Cheats, 1719; The Tyburn Chronicle, 1768; The Malefactors' Register, 1796; George Borrow's Celebrated Trials, 1825; The Newgate Calendar, by Andrew Knapp and William Baldwin, 1826, Camden Pelham's Chronicles of Crime, 1841; etc,* 5 vols. (1926), vol. 4, p.101.

28. Anon: *The English Roscius. Garrick's Jests, or, Genius in High Glee. Containing all the Jokes of the Wits of the Present Age, viz. Mr.Garrick, Ld. Lyttleton, Mr. Fox, Ld. Mansf—, Mr. Burke, Mr. Foote, Mr. Selwyn, Dutchess of K., Lady H—, Lady T—, &c. Being Humorous, Lively, Comical, Queer, Satirical Droll, Smart Repartees, Facetious, Merry Bon Mots &c. To which are added, A New Selection of Epigrams, Poems, Conundrums, Toasts, Sentiments, Hob-Nobs &c now in Fashion* (c.1785), p.92.

29. Angus Ross (ed.), *Tobias Smollett, The Expedition of Humphry Clinker*, (Penguin Classics, 1985) p.70. See also, Gavin Turner, (Introduction and notes), *The New Bath Guide by Christopher Anstey*, (Bristol: Broadcast Books, n/d), pp.159-160.

30. James Northcote, *The Life of Sir Joshua Reynolds, LL.D. F.R.S. F.S.A. etc. Late President of the Royal Academy. Comprising Original Anecdotes of Many Distinguished Persons; His*

Contemporaries; and a Brief Analysis of his Discourses, 2nd ed., 2 vols, (1819), vol.1, note to pp.200-201.

31. *The Bath Chronicle*, April 30th 1761.

32. Arthur L. Hayward, (ed.), *A Complete History of the Lives and Robberies of the Most Notorious Highwaymen, Footpads, Shoplifts & Cheats of Both Sexes Wherein their most Secret and Barbarous Murders, Unparalleled Robberies, Notorious Thefts, and Unheard-of Cheats are set in a true Light and exposed to Public View, for the Common Benefit of Mankind, by Captain Alexander Smith*, (George Routledge & Sons, 1926), pp. 39-40.

33. Quoted in Daphne Phillips, *The Great Road To Bath*, (Newbury: Countryside Books, 1983), p.143.

34. For a full discussion of this argument see, for example, Lincoln B. Faller, *Turned to Account, The Forms and Functions of Criminal Biography in Late Seventeenth- and Early Eighteenth-Century England*, (Cambridge: Cambridge University Press, 1987).

35. For a comprehensive discussion of the Bath Road, see, Brenda J. Buchanan, 'The Great Bath Road, 1700-1830', in *Bath History*,(Bath: Millstream Books, 1992), vol. 4, pp.71-94.

36. R.S. Neale, *Bath: A Social History 1680-1850 or a Valley of Pleasure, Yet a Sink of Iniquity*, (Routledge & Kegan Paul, 1981), p.46.

37. Graham Davis and Penny Bonsall, *A History of Bath: Image and Reality*, (Lancaster: Carnegie Publishing, 2006), p.112.

38. *The Ordinary of Newgate's Account of the Behaviour, Confessions, and Dying Words, of the Eight Malefactors Who were Executed at Tyburn on Monday the 17th June 1751*, (1751).

39. *The Bath Journal*, August 28th 1749.

40. See for example, *The Miscellaneous Works of William Hazlitt. In five volumes. The Spirit of the Age: or Contemporary Portraits*, 5 vols, (New York, Derby and Jackson, 1857), vol. 5, p.92; William Tyte, *Bath in the Eighteenth Century: Its Progress and Life Described*, (Bath, 1902), p. 78.

41. *The Bath Journal*, October 1st 1744.

42. Mary Abraham alias Mary Sandall (born c. 1754) operated around Wilton and is discussed in James Waylen (probable author) *The Highwaymen of Wiltshire; or a Narrative of the Adventurous Career and Untimely End of Divers Freebooters and Smugglers in this and the Adjoining Counties,* (E.&W. Books, 1970), pp.64-67. The book was probably first published in 1845. Alice Osman commonly called Jenny was sentenced to death at Salisbury Assizes, although this was commuted to seven years transportation, for robbing on the highway on December 22nd 1736 [sic] with two accomplices who escaped. See *The Bath Journal* August 5th 1745 and March 17th 1746.

43. *The Bath Journal*, July 4th 1763.

44. *The Bath Journal*, October 25th 1756.

45. *The Bath Journal*, January 27th 1755.

46. See for example, *The Bath Chronicle*, January 29th 1784 and January 18th 1787.

47. *The Bath Journal,* February 20th 1758.

48. *The Bath Journal*, January 23rd 1764.

49. *The Bath Chronicle,* November 1st 1781.

50. *The Bath Journal*, October 26th 1747.

51. *The Bath Journal*, January 23rd 1764.

52. *The Bath Journal*, February 14th 1763.

53. *The Bath Journal*, January 27th 1755.

54. *The Bath Journal*, February 14th 1763.

55. *The Bath Journal*, February 20th 1758.

56. *The Bath Journal*, August 28th 1749.

57. *The Bath Journal*, December 7th 1747.

58. *The Bath Journal*, March 20th 1758. See also *The Bath Journal*, March 13th 1758.

59. *The Bath Journal*, December 7th 1747. See also *The Bath Chronicle*, May 3rd 1778.

60. *The Bath Chronicle*, May 4th 1786.

61. Burk was apprehended in London on suspicion of being involved in November 1754. See *The Bath Journal*, November 4th 1754.

62. *The Discoveries of John Poulter, alias Baxter; Who was apprehended for robbing Dr. Hancock, of Salisbury, on Clarken Down, near Bath; and thereupon discovered a most numerous Gang of Villains, many of which have been already taken. Being A full Account of all the Robberies he has committed, and the surprizing Tricks and Frauds, he has practised for the Space of five Years last past, in different Parts of England. Written wholly by Himself. To which is added, as a Caution to prevent any unwary Persons from being imposed on and defrauded, An exact Account of the Manner in which Gamblers and other Sharpers impose upon People at Fairs and other Places; where their whole Tricks, Behaviour and Language, is so laid open, that any one who reads it, may certainly know them at any Time, and so be upon their Guard against being cheated by them. With some Precautions to secure Houses from being broke open, very useful for all Families: And likewise some Cautions to Tradesmen, and others who travel, to prevent their being robbed. With Directions how to prevent Horses from being stolen out of Grounds and Commons, 9th ed.,* (Sherborne, 1754). This edition appears in Philip Rawlings, *Drunks, Whores and Idle Apprentices: Criminal Biographies of the Eighteenth Century*, (Routledge, 1992), pp.139-177, which also has a useful introduction. See also, Harper, *Half-Hours with the Highwaymen*, vol. 2, pp.301-315.

63. Rawlings, *Drunks, Whores and Idle Apprentices*, p.151.

64. Buchanan, 'The Great Bath Road', p.84.

65. *The Bath Journal*, April 16th 1753. *The Bath Journal* reflected the large amount of interest in the exploits of the gang. See entries for April 2nd 1753, April 9th 1753, April 23rd 1753, August 13th 1753, September 3rd 1753, October 22nd 1753, December 17th 1753, February 25th 1754, March 4th 1754, April 22nd 1754 and November 4th 1754.

66. Rawlings, *Drunks, Whores and Idle Apprentices*, p.124. For a discussion of Nash's dealings with Poulter, see Oliver Goldsmith, *The Life of Richard Nash, of Bath, Esq; Extracted principally from His Original Papers,* (1762), pp. 130-139.

67. *The Bath Journal*, March 4th 1754. See also, *The Bath Journal*, February 25th 1754.

68. Goldsmith, *The Life of Richard Nash*, p.139.

69. Ibid, pp.131-132.

70. Edward Bulwer-Lytton, *Paul Clifford*,(Penguin Books, 2010), p.220. *Paul Clifford* was first published in 1830.

71. *The Bath Chronicle*, October 4th 1770.

72. Rawlings, *Drunks, Whores and Idle Apprentices*, p.136.

73. *The Bath Journal*, December 7th 1747.

74. Rawlings, *Drunks, Whores and Idle Apprentices*, p.136.

75. *The Ordinary of Newgate, His Account of the Behaviour, Confession and Dying Words, of the Malefactor Who was Executed at Tyburn, on Friday the 8th of June, 1744,* (1744).

76. Waylen, *The Highwaymen of Wiltshire*, p.27.

77. *The Bath Journal*, March 7th 1748.

78. Rawlings, *Drunks, Whores and Idle Apprentices*, pp. 137 and 144.

79. *The Bath Journal* December 7th 1747.
80. Toy shops sold souvenirs and fancy goods. The most famous toy shop in Bath was owned by Mrs Bertrand and it is mentioned in Alexander Pope's poem, written in 1739, 'On Receiving From the Right Honourable the Lady Frances Shirley A Standish and Two Pens'.
81. *The Bath Journal*, April 2nd 1753.
82. Goldsmith, *The Life of Richard Nash*, p.133.
83. *The Bath Journal*, December 9th 1751.
84. *The Beggar's Opera*, Act I Sc. IV.

Benjamin West in Bath

Martin West

In 1807, Benjamin West, president of the Royal Academy of Arts in London, journeyed to Bath, England for the sake of his wife's health. He had visited Bath only on one other occasion, forty-four years earlier. Born near Philadelphia in 1738, young West gained recognition as a precocious painter who impressed several wealthy residents of that city, led by William Allen, Chief Justice of Pennsylvania. They helped support his studying in Italy, 1760-63, the first American known to have done so. West not only viewed works of art available from various periods and copied original pictures for his patrons, but also he was exposed to, and was influenced by, Neo-Classical painters.[1]

West's initial trip to Bath occurred not long after his reaching London on August 20th 1763 from Italy via Paris. By the first of September, he had encountered William Allen, who, with his two daughters, Margaret and Anne, was coincidentally present in the great metropolis. In order to further his elder son's education, Allen had contemplated for several years a voyage to Great Britain but was unable to sail until the end of April 1763. Moreover, to forestall potential conflict, the Chief Justice intended to use his influence to dissuade Parliament from levying a controversial Stamp Act tax on the thirteen colonies.[2]

After greeting West, the Allens seem to have proceeded directly to Bath, but the painter, expecting only a temporary stay in the homeland of his father and maternal grandparents, first examined the art holdings at Hampton Court, Windsor, Oxford, Blenheim Palace and Corsham Court, before arriving in the popular resort city. West remained there for about a month with his benefactor. **[fig. 1]** [3]

While in Bath, West painted portraits of William Allen and his youngest child, Anne, apparently his first works in the medium of oil on canvas to be undertaken in England. West must have been exposed to the pictures of the most fashionable Bath artist, Thomas Gainsborough, and possibly to those of William Hoare,

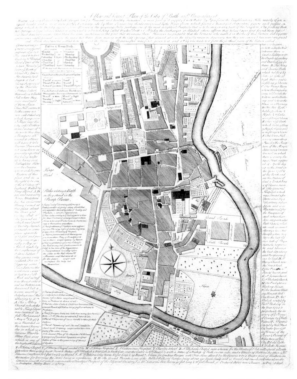

fig 1: **A New and Correct Plan of the City of Bath, Anon, c.1764**
Bath in Time - Bath Preservation Trust

Facing: Detail from Self-Portrait (Mr. West painting the portrait of Mrs. West in one picture half figures, large as life) by Benjamin West, 1806. Oil on canvas
The Pennsylvania Academy of the Fine Arts, Philadelphia. Gift of Mr. and Mrs. Henry R. Hallowell

fig 2: Abbey Street, the Abbey Green, Church Street and part of the Abbey, c.1785 by William James Blackamore. Pen on paper.

Victoria Art Gallery PD1918.453, Bath & North East Somerset Council

among other local painters. To further his career, Gainsborough, a native of Sudbury, Suffolk, had relocated from Ipswich to Bath in autumn 1759. From the following year to 1766, Gainsborough leased a new town house on Abbey Street **[fig. 2]**, where he maintained a large picture viewing room intended exclusively for exhibition.[4]

The young Pennsylvanian's likenesses of the Allens represent a change from his Italian style, because they resemble certain of Gainsborough's half-length portraits painted in Bath during the early 1760s, as determined by the authors of the authoritative Benjamin West *catalogue raisonné*, Helmut von Erffa and Allen Staley. That West scrutinised the Englishman's paintings is evidenced by his incorporating such Gainsborough touches as the averted gaze of the sitter and a complex landscape background. He may have been influenced by the works of Gainsborough, but whether or not West met in Bath with the artist eleven years his senior is questionable. According to Gainsborough biographer Susan Sloman, the painter was confined to bed for five weeks due to exhaustion and a presumed venereal disorder that almost took his life. Mistakenly reported dead by the *Bath Journal*, October 17th 1763, Gainsborough might have been too ill to see West, who probably arrived in Bath by the beginning of that month.[5]

Thus engaged with the Allens, West had little spare time to tour the surrounding area, but almost certainly he saw much of Bath, which could be accomplished easily by walking or by hiring one of the eighty or more sedan chairs then available. Upon departing the city, West continued his itinerary of inspecting various English collections on the return circuit to London, prior to his planned embarkation home to Philadelphia.[6]

These early months in England, 'the mother country, which we Americans are all so desirous to see', in West's words, presaged a rapid advancement as an artist so unprecedented and unexpected that his presence in London, intended as interim, soon became permanent. He realised that professional opportunities, especially his passion to paint history, were practically nil in provincial Philadelphia, where his fiancée, Elizabeth Shewell, was waiting patiently. West decided to send for her, and they were married in September 1764. Four years later, he was given his first commission from his exact contemporary, King George III, and became one of four principal founders of the Royal Academy. West exhibited his celebrated masterpiece derived from recent history, *The Death of General Wolfe* [fig. 3], at the Royal Academy in 1771. Based on events from history, literature and Scripture, history painting was the most dignified genre in the hierarchy of academic art; a 'grand manner' was attainable by incorporating the august and ennobling tenets of the classical era and Italian Renaissance. In less than a decade of his arrival, West had achieved spectacular success and international fame as the foremost history artist in the British Isles.[7]

*　　*　　*　　*　　*　　*　　*

Much of the information on Benjamin West's 1807 sojourn to Bath is found in the daily diary of Joseph Farington. A Lancashire native, Farington entered the Schools of the Royal

fig 3: **The Death of General James Wolfe (1727-59) by Benjamin West PRA, Ickworth. Oil on canvas**
National Trust Images

Academy in 1769, where he exhibited annually for over three decades, mainly as a topographical draughtsman and landscapist. He was elected to membership in 1785. Farington's sixteen volumes of diaries, kept from July 1793 until his death in December 1821, offer unique insights into the Royal Academy and London art scene for that period. Commencing about fifteen months after West's election to the presidency, the diaries indicate that although initially Farington was sceptical of the American-born painter, the two men would become close friends.[8]

Debilitated by a paralytic stroke in early 1805, Elizabeth West, the president's wife, contemplated travelling to Bath in order to take a course of the medicinal waters. In the opinion of their family doctor, Sir John McNamara Hayes MD, a reputable military physician, the preoccupied Benjamin West did 'not seem to be affected by what may happen. He feels only the present'. Hayes suspected that Elizabeth's condition was exacerbated by an aversion to the malodour of fresh white pigment redolent in the large painting room of her home. She had been weighing options since at least mid-November 1806 but complained to Farington that her husband could not afford a lengthy visit to Bath. The frugal alternative was nearby Windsor where the couple had rented a house for many years to facilitate the artist's numerous projects for the King. Eventually, sufficient funds were acquired, and Elizabeth West chose Bath **[fig. 4]**. Having diagnosed no possibility of her recovery, Hayes warned that a second major stroke would prove fatal. A now desperate West told Farington on July 8th 1807 that he would escort his spouse to Bath the following week, as 'It was Her only chance'. The painter engaged his Newman Street neighbour, Elizabeth Hooton Banks, widow of sculptor Thomas Banks, to accompany them as a carer.[9]

Familiar with London and Bath, Farington appreciated Elizabeth West's exigency to escape, if only temporarily, the vast urban centre for the salubrious spa community. The previous year he had entered in

fig 4: Self-Portrait (Mr. West painting the portrait of Mrs. West in one picture half figures, large as life) by Benjamin West, 1806. Oil on canvas

The Pennsylvania Academy of the Fine Arts, Philadelphia. Gift of Mr. and Mrs. Henry R. Hallowell

fig 5: George III Resuming Royal Power in 1789, c. 1789, by Benjamin West. Pen and brown ink with brown wash on laid paper
National Gallery of Art, Washington, John Davis Hatch Collection

his diary a provocative 'contest of opinion whether London or Bath should be preferred as a town residence' between a banker of South Mimms, Middlesex and a garrulous clergyman from St Albans, Hertfordshire. Farington explained that the former, in the long-standing debate of country versus city living:

> pleaded for Bath; said *there* something of the appearance of country was associated with the town,—that many articles of provision were a third cheaper,—and amusements might be had with the greatest convenience,— also friends and acquaintenance from all parts were occasionally met there, which was not the case in other places.— [The minister] contended for London; s[ai]d that as to situation those who looked over the *Parks* & in other parts had as great an advantage;—and London was free from that *gossiping* which prevailed as much at Bath as it could do in a country village. London also contained a variety which no other place can afford.[10]

West's party left in a hired carriage for 'the Great Bath Road', mid-July 1807. Historian Brenda Buchanan has demonstrated that no single road connecting London and Bath existed during this period, only 'a patchy, disorganized sequence'; even the exact route had not been fixed as of yet. The jarring trek necessitated at least two days of travel and one night for sleep at a nearby inn, but, by this time, with replacement drivers and frequent change of horses, the journey could be reduced to twelve hours, often made overnight. If he had the means, West may have selected the latter alternative to limit Elizabeth's suffering.[11]

Expecting to remain only a fortnight in Bath to complete his wife's arrangements, West, possibly detecting a growing rift between Elizabeth and her attending companion, decided to stay through the course of her treatments, which would extend to fifteen weeks. His reluctance to depart may have involved an added factor, however.[12]

At 68 years of age, Benjamin West could pause in Bath and reflect with satisfaction on his career, especially his unlikely relationship with King George III, involving over 60 commissions [fig. 5]. Starting in 1772, the sovereign's preferred artist had been made Historical Painter to the King, and, during the War for American Independence, West, ironically, served as portraitist to the immediate royal family. He was appointed to Surveyor of the King's Pictures in 1791, and, reaching the highest professional status, West, with the monarch's

fig 6: All Saints Chapel, Bath, July 29, 1807 by Benjamin West. Sketch
Victoria Art Gallery PD2007.7, Bath & North East Somerset Council

approval, was elected second president of the Royal Academy the following year, succeeding the late Sir Joshua Reynolds.[13]

These achievements notwithstanding, West faced an uncertain future because of his deteriorating association with George III. Having received reports of the artist's democratic tendencies and sympathy for the French Revolution, the recurrently ailing King, perhaps influenced by others, allowed suspension of West's royal projects in 1801, which were cancelled altogether one-half decade later, only a year before his second journey to Bath. His annual stipend of £1,000 from the crown was in jeopardy also (it would be terminated in December 1810). Furthermore, the Royal Academy had been the scene of chronic contention and unremitting turmoil that led to the harried West's resigning the presidency in December 1805. In July of the next year, Farington, speaking to a concurring Dr. Hayes, was shocked by the toll the office had taken on West, noticing 'that His personal appearance has much changed in the last 12 months; that he is become more *bony* & his flesh has fallen in.' Dissatisfied by his replacement, numerous Royal Academicians prevailed upon a reluctant West, who had been happily devoting his free time to painting, to stand for election the following year. Winning easily, he resumed his former position on New Year's Day 1807 and was never again seriously challenged for it. Almost eight months subsequently, West, over a hundred miles removed from court intrigue and Royal Academy politics, was enjoying the leisurely, pleasant Bath summer and must have concluded that taking an extended holiday could be remedial for him as well.[14]

At times afflicted by gout but apparently free of the malady while in Bath, West found ample opportunity to investigate the countryside during his wife's daily therapy. The artist retained the carriage that had conveyed his small party from London for 'all His excursions, hiring 2 or 4 Horses as the distance might require'. When not exploring, West spent his mornings preparing landscape sketches **[fig. 6]** and making 'a design of the discovery of the good qualities of the Bath waters.' He was extremely impressed by the local topography, and, Farington opined, his admiration and zeal for Bath were unequivocal. Following the return of the couple to London on November 7th, the diarist wrote on the tenth:

> [West] spoke of Bath & its vicinity with rapture as abounding with picturesque scenery. Take Bath & 20 miles round it He s[ai]d & there is not in the world anything superior to it. Rocks of the finest forms for a painter that He had ever seen, large, square forms. *Quarry's* worked out, now most picturesque & romantic. Wyck & Hampton rocks, Chedder Cliffs, most picturesque—distances the most beautiful—roads with occasional pools & streams of water falling from the Hills & Cattle & figures such as Berghem never saw. Take *Tivoli away* & Rome & its vicinity of 20 miles not to be compared with Bath & its neighbourhood.[15]

Local Bath artists, West ascertained, were 'much encouraged'. He met three of them: Thomas Barker 'of Bath', his younger brother, Benjamin, a landscapist and drawing master, and Joshua Shaw, a landscapist. In the president's view, the brothers were 'very ingenious'. Thomas Barker's name had been established by his work *The Woodman*, but West admired his 'admirably drawn. . .for truth of expression excellent, unrivalled' chalk drawings on tinted paper of peasants and landscapes, which he felt would be 'captivating' if portrayed in oil on

fig 7: Prince Bladud Contemplating the Medicinal Virtues of the Bath Waters by Benjamin West, 1807. Coloured chalk and wash
Royal Academy of Arts, London

canvas. The president assessed Benjamin Barker as a landscapist superior to his brother. West learned that while drawing masters were exceptionally well compensated, actual drawings sold poorly because oil paintings were the popular choice.[16]

The third artist, Joshua Shaw, boasted to West of his many commissions, which, placed as orders to be undertaken sequentially, were so numerous as to require eighteen months for execution. The Englishman further contended that he received about forty guineas for a kit-cat portrait. Should he have any idle hours, two dealers in Bristol wanted to purchase his pictures for resale, Shaw prated to his distinguished guest, and patrons throughout western England sought him to decorate their homes with chimney pieces and overdoors.[17]

West was also informed that a Bath art exhibition was scheduled for opening the following spring. Seeking his advice, the arrangers were counselled by the president to organize themselves on the Royal Academy model.[18]

During his stay in Bath, West completed four landscapes representative of the sights that had moved him. They featured subjects of the city and vicinity:

- *A View of the City of Bath, as seen from the high grounds eastward of Prior Park House*
- *A View within Prior Park, near the city of Bath*
- *A View on the river Avon above the city of Bath*
- *A View of the Rocks at Bristol Wells, with the ceremony of conducting down the river Avon the Man of War presented by the City of Bristol to Government* [19]

Additionally, West commenced a picture taken from a local myth entitled, *Prince Bladud Contemplating the Medicinal Virtues of the Bath Waters by Observing their Effect on Swine* [fig. 7], coloured chalk and wash, heightened with white, 28 by 41½ inches / 71.1 by 105.4 centimetres. Signed, *B. West Bath Sept 20 1807*, this work is pieced together from several sheets of brown tinted paper. Conceivably, as suggested by art historian Allen Staley, the terrain seen in the background of *Bladud* is derived from one of the landscapes listed above.[20]

Two of West's four landscapes feature Prior Park and might provide a clue to understanding his research for *Bladud*. Located about two miles south of the city, Prior Park House [fig. 8], a Palladian mansion, was under construction in 1735 by John Wood the elder, the prominent Bath architect and town planner, who wrote *An Essay Towards a Description of Bath*. West consequently was acquainted with the great house and the reputation of the late architect; he may have been aware also of the *Essay*, in which the author, basically accepting the prince as an actual figure of history and his story as established fact, recorded and embellished the Bladud fable.[21]

As with Wood, West was inspired by the enduring Bath legend. In brief, Bladud, the only son of Lud Hubibras, king of ancient Britain, was found to be a leper. Compelled to act, the king exiled the young man, who was obliged to labour as a swineherd. Having contracted

Prior Park in Somersetshire, the Seat of Mrs Smith.

fig 8: Prior Park in Somersetshire, the Seat of Mrs. Smith, 1785, after William Watts. Copper engraving
Bath in Time - Bath Central Library Collection

leprosy from the banished prince, his pigs, after wallowing several times in the mud of the thermal springs on the future site of Bath, became free of the disease. Astonished, the outcast immersed himself repeatedly into the warm ooze and found that he too was no longer leprous. Bladud, later reputed ninth king of Britain, was credited with founding Bath, place of his miraculous cure, circa 483 BC, according to Wood's singular calculation. West, who evidently classified his Bladud composition as a historical, rather than a mythological, subject, possibly accepted the rudiments of the traditional fable as fact. [22]

The biographers of Wood, Tim Mowl and Brian Earnshaw, have argued that he was obsessive and an incompetent historian, who adapted 'all information to suit previously fixed notions', in order to remake Bath within the architect's lifetime through his chimerical conception of a Druidic-Roman city. West's interpretation of *Bladud* may have been taken from the *Essay*, and his depiction of the Prince could have been informed by a print found in Wood's account **[fig. 9]**. The plate, engraved by Bernard Barton after an imaginative portrait by William Hoare, who resided and painted at No. 6 Edgar Buildings, Bath, is entitled, *BLADUD, To whom the GRECIANS gave the Name of ABARIS*. [23]

Hoare, through Barton, represents Bladud at middle age, his body thickened, and his head, almost in left profile, with short wavy hair and a whitening beard. Following his recovery, the Prince supposedly was educated in Greece, but he was described in the *Essay* as dressed in Athens like an inhabitant of Scythia, a vast Eurasian region to the northeast. His fanciful garb is reminiscent of both classical and anachronistic Ottoman Turkish styles. Depicted as a huntsman, the prerogative of Kings, Bladud is accoutred with a quiver of arrows, and his right hand grasps an unstrung reflex bow. Behind him, in agreement with Wood's text, is a Greek landscape. Bladud's dignified bearing embraces a sensitivity reflecting his bitter experiences as a young man.[24]

West's callow Bladud, turned slightly to his left, faces the viewer. Normally a careful researcher, the president evinced little or no knowledge of the raiment of ancient Britons and clothed the prince in classical Greek apparel. His eyes, nose and short wavy hair appear to resemble the older Bladud's corresponding features in the Barton-Hoare engraving. Slim and athletic, the youthful swineherd, otherwise weaponless, holds a long wooden staff in his right hand, similarly to the king gripping his bow. A frowning, but intensely curious Bladud, stares down in wonder at his recovering swine. In the background is West's romanticised rendering of the hills of Bath. [25]

*　　*　　*　　*　　*　　*　　*

The purpose of Benjamin West's second journey to Bath was a quest by his wife for relief from paralysis and discomfort. So the choice of the exile of Bladud theme, a topic they likely discussed together after arrival, was particularly appropriate. In September, Elizabeth West sent a letter to Dr Hayes and his wife, who showed it to Farington, indicating that her condition was 'very indifferent'. Painfully distressed by the therapeutic baths, Elizabeth's only improvement had come through a daily regimen of drinking Bath mineral water, offering hope of her surviving another winter. Encouraged, West had no intention of curtailing his Bath interlude, even by a day or two. In the past, he seldom, if ever, missed Royal Academy functions, but a missive by West posted from the resort city was read to the Royal Academy

General Meeting, November 2nd 1807, in which he apologised for his absence as a balloting was scheduled to elect an associate; all of his presidential business had to be postponed. The couple and the carer returned to London five days later, but Elizabeth West was no longer speaking to Elizabeth Banks, having had 'a certain difference' with her during their months together in Bath. More resilient than predicted earlier, Elizabeth West would live for another seven years in a failing state of health.[26]

Having conversed with West three days after his arrival, Farington, although still taken by the distinctive signs of ageing, thought his friend looked rested and well. The diarist dined with several other Royal Academicians, including artist John Hoppner, on November 11th. Once reportedly favoured by George III, Hoppner, without evidence, had held West responsible for his subsequent break with the King, but his antagonism might have waned since he had voted to return the ex-president to his former office the previous December. Hoppner expressed to Farington, 'West's admiration of Bath noticed'. Paraphrasing Samuel Johnson's opinion of poet James Thomson, Hoppner said of West, 'so poetical

BLADUD,
To whom the GRECIANS gave the Name of
ABARIS.

fig 9: Prince Bladud, frontispiece of John Wood's,
A Description of Bath Vol 1, after William Hoare, 1749.
Copper engraving
Bath in Time - Bath Central Library Collection

His mind. He could not see a farthing candle but with a poetical feeling'. Hoppner remarked that whatever belonged to the president, including his agreeable experiences in Bath, had to be 'always best'. [27]

Visiting the Wests' home at No.14 Newman Street on the snowy late afternoon of the nineteenth, Farington found the artist in his small painting room, with Elizabeth sitting nearby. He observed that West "was touching, with White Chalk, upon His design of 'the discovery of the virtues of the Bath waters by King Bladud' - a very able design". The work was initiated in

Bath, but Farington's entry proves that it was finished in London. Von Erffa and Staley have speculated that since *Bladud* consists of several sheets of paper, the president may have supplemented or revised the composition in his painting room. Perhaps West anticipated that the pieced-together image, afterward displayed at the Royal Academy, might encourage a wealthy patron, perchance one who esteemed the beauty of Bath and vicinity as much as he did, to commission an oil-on-canvas history picture of Prince Bladud in the grand manner.[28]

That night Farington wrote of West's four landscapes as well. He noted that the president 'shewed me also several studies He had made in & near Bath with Chalk & Crayon upon coloured paper, very good, His power seeming in no respect to have diminished'. [29]

In early December, Farington discussed West and his recent trip to Bath with two connoisseurs, Sir George Howland Beaumont, seventh baronet, and his wife, Lady Margaret Willes Beaumont, at their London home. They admired West's accomplishments. The diarist quoted Sir George's speaking 'in the highest manner of the excellent Landscape sketches' produced by West at the fashionable spa city, adding that "they were of as high a character as the designs of Nicolo Poussin, *the true Heroic Landscape*". Beaumont further commended the president for "His very able design of King Bladud discovering the virtues of the Bath Waters". Nevertheless, the elegant baronet criticized West's vanity, grammar and alleged overstatement of his welcome to Bath, by repeating a line of poetry Beaumont attributed erroneously to Alexander Pope but actually composed by Charles Churchill, 'A man so very high, so very low'. [30]

West disclosed to Farington in mid-December his deliberateness on considering a new composition, but once mentally committed he was 'a Child to everything else' until it was finished, and only then would the artist proceed to his next project. Hence, *Bladud* must have been done by that time, because the cold and darkness of the season, the president added, precluded most of his painting until the beginning of February. Placed on exhibition by West at the Royal Academy in spring 1808, *Bladud* and the four Bath landscapes were well received but quickly forgotten.[31]

Relieved by the improvement in Elizabeth's health and rejuvenated by almost four months in Bath, West, even without royal patronage, would experience resounding triumphs in ensuing years. Especially gratifying to the declining septuagenarian were several ambitious works, including two based on the life of Christ, which he painted on a genuinely grand scale. They brought to the venerable president some of the greatest popular acclaim and financial profits of his life.[32]

In March 1820, only six weeks after the death of King George III, West expired, and his collection was dispersed over the subsequent decade. *Bladud* was acquired from an unnamed seller on May 17th 1845 by the Royal Academy of Arts in London, where it can be viewed today. One of the landscapes, *A View of the City of Bath, as seen from the high grounds eastward of Prior Park House*, chalk and crayon on coloured paper, 24 by 38 inches/61 by 96.5 centimetres, was purchased for ten shillings by an unidentified buyer at Christie's, London, March 19th 1898. At some point before or after that date, the remaining pictures must have been sold or misplaced. Regrettably, the current locations of all four Bath landscapes by Benjamin West are unknown.[33]

Acknowledgements

Grateful appreciation is expressed to Brenda Buchanan, former editor of *Bath History*, for her advice, helpfulness and encouragement, Michael N. McConnell, historian of Colonial-Revolutionary America, and especially Allen Staley, the leading Benjamin West scholar today, for reading this article. As always, the West family of the twenty-first century, Penelope, Jane and Benjamin, provided assistance and support.

Notes

1. Helmut von Erffa and Allen Staley, *The Paintings of Benjamin West* (New Haven and London, 1986), pp. 21-25; Norman S. Cohen, 'Allen, William', John A. Garrety and Mark C. Carnes (eds.), *American National Biography* (New York and Oxford, 1999) 1: pp. 344-345; Allen Staley, email to writer, February 2nd 2012.

2. John Galt, *The Life and Works of Benjamin West, Esq. President of the Royal Academy of London, Subsequent to his Arrival in this Country; Composed From Materials Furnished By Himself* (London and Edinburgh, 1820) Part II:1, pp. 3-5; Robert C. Alberts, *Benjamin West: A Biography* (Boston, 1978), pp. 59-60; Cohen, 'Allen, William', *ANB* 1: pp. 344-345; 'William Allen to David Barclay, 20 October 1760', 'Benjamin West to Joseph Shippen, 1 September 1763', E.P. Richardson, 'West's Voyage to Italy, 1760, and William Allen', *The Pennsylvania Magazine of History and Biography* (January 1978) 102: pp. 14-15, pp. 23-24; Ann Uhry Abrams, *The Valiant Hero: Benjamin West and Grand-Style History Painting* (Washington, DC, 1985), pp. 90-91; Benjamin Franklin, *The Papers of Benjamin Franklin*, edited by Leonard W. Labaree (New Haven and London, 1966, 1967) 10: p. 415 n.l,11: pp. 34-35 n.9. The opposition of Allen to passage of a stamp act had been 'indefatigable', as reported by the *Pennsylvania Gazette,* May 10th and June 4th 1764. By utilising his access to officials in Britain, including members of the House of Commons, Allen helped prevent the proposed colonial tax legislation for that session.

3. Galt, *Life and Works of Benjamin West*, Part II: p. 5.

4. Von Effra and Staley, *Paintings of Benjamin West*, 23, pp. 486-487; Susan Legouix Sloman, 'Artists' Picture Rooms in Eighteenth-Century Bath', *Bath History* (1996) VI: pp. 132,134.

5. Von Erffa and Staley, *Paintings of Benjamin West*, pp. 486-487; Susan Sloman, *Gainsborough in Bath* (New Haven and London, 2002), p. 51, p. 193; Hugh Belsey, 'Gainsborough, Thomas', H.C.G. Matthew and Brian Harrison (eds.), *Oxford Dictionary of National Biography* (Oxford, 1999) 21: pp. 266-272. West and Gainsborough were founding members of the Royal Academy in 1768, and, following the Englishman's move from Bath to London six years later, their affiliation continued. In 1788, Benjamin West was a pallbearer at the funeral of Thomas Gainsborough.

6. Trevor Fawcett, 'Chair Transport in Bath: The Sedan Chair Era', *Bath History* (1988) II:124; Galt, *Life and Works of Benjamin West*, Part II: p. 5.

7. 'Benjamin West to Joseph Shippen, 1 September 1763', Richardson, 'West's Voyage to Italy 1760, and William Allen', *PMHB* pp. 102:23; Von Erffa and Staley, *Paintings of Benjamin West*, pp. 23, 50-51, 168, 211-213; Abrams, *The Valiant Hero*, pp. 97-98, 103, 146, 154, 170; David H. Solkin, *Painting for Money: The Visual Arts and the Public Sphere in Eighteenth-Century England* (New Haven and London, 1985), pp. 254-255, 269. In *The Death of General Wolfe* (National Gallery of Canada), 1770, West combined classical sculpture prototypes with contemporary military clothing and equipage to create a sensation. This immensely popular picture extolled the heroic death of Major General James Wolfe while commemorating his British victory in 1759 at Québec, Canada during the Seven Years' War (1756-63). He frequently had visited his parents in Bath, who resided at what is now No. 5 Trim Street. In 1758, his health impaired by two Atlantic Ocean crossings and the successful siege of Louisbourg in Nova Scotia, the general wrote to a friend, 'I am going to Bath to refit for another campaign'. During his stay, Wolfe was betrothed to Katherine Lowther, whom he seems to have met in Bath the previous year. Stephen Brumwell, *Paths of Glory: The Life and Death of General James Wolfe* (Montreal and Kingston, 2006), pp. 105, 185-186, 293; Brenda J. Buchanan, 'Sir John (later Lord) Ligonier (1680-1770), Military Commander and Member of Parliament for Bath', *Bath History* (2000) VIII: p. 96.

8. Von Errfa and Staley, *Paintings of Benjamin West*, 424; Evelyn Newby, 'Farington, Joseph', *ODNB* 19:45-47; Alberts, *Benjamin West*, p. 197.

9. Gordon Goodwin and Claire E.J. Herrick, 'Hayes, Sir John McNamara, first baronet', *ODNB* 26:35; Julius Bryant, 'Banks, Thomas', *Ibid.*, 3: pp. 698-700; Joseph Farington, *The Diary of Joseph Farington* (New Haven and London, 1982), 14 November 1806 8: p. 2906, 5 May 1807 8: p. 3038, 8 July 1807 8: p. 3083, 13 July 1807 8: p. 3087; Alberts, *Benjamin West*, pp. 124, 307 n.2, 336-337, 437 n.124.

10. Farington *Diary*, 18 July 1806 8: pp. 2816-2817.

11. *Ibid.*, 13 July 1807 8: p. 3087; Brenda J. Buchanan, 'The Great Bath Road, 1700-1830', *Bath History* (1992) IV: pp. 71-76. Measured from Hyde Park Corner, an original one-hundred-mile stone marker on a London-Bath road variant displays the remaining distance to Bath at precisely seven miles, for a total of 107 miles. An image of the marker is reproduced on page 76.

12. Farington, *Diary*, July 8th 1807 8: p. 3083.

13. Von Effra and Staley, *Paintings of Benjamin West*, pp. 51, 83, 97.

14. Alberts, *Benjamin West*, 190 n.8, pp. 319-320, 322, 332-335; Farington, *Diary*, July 9th 1806 8: p. 2807; Von Effra and Staley, *Paintings of Benjamin West*, pp. 90, 97-98.

15. Farington, *Diary*, November 10th 1807 8: pp. 3138-3139; Alberts, *Benjamin West*, pp. 336-337. The ageing West praised, perhaps wistfully, several places in the Bath area that can be identified as the 'Wyck rocks', lining both sides of a scenic glen by the village of that name in South Gloucestershire, the 'Hampton rocks', a notable outcrop of rock near the village of Bathampton, Somerset, and the dramatic 'Chedder [*sic*] Cliffs', rocks and ravine on the south side of the Mendip Hills, located close to the village of Cheddar, Somerset. To emphasise the loveliness of Bath and the surrounding area, West compared them favourably to the scenes painted by Nicholas Berghem, or Berchen, a Dutch landscapist of the seventeen century. When touring Italy as a young man, West had been inspired by Tivoli, site of the Aniene River waterfalls issuing from the Sabine Hills. Located about twenty miles east of Rome, Tivoli has splendid views of the *Campagna*, a landscape of traditional artistic importance. [No author,] *Gazetteer of the British Isles* (Edinburgh, 1963), pp. 51, 143, 725; Andrew Wilton and Ilaria Bignamini (eds.), *Grand Tour: The Lure of Italy in the Eighteenth Century* (London, 1996), p. 143; Abrams, *The Valiant Hero*, pp. 90-91.

16. Farington, *Diary*, November 10th 1807 8: pp. 3138-3139. At minimum, Thomas Barker executed five variations of *The Woodman*; a 1792 engraving of it by Francesco Bartolozzi (who also made prints after Benjamin West) was the most popular and recognised version. Ellen Wilson, 'A Shropshire Lady in Bath', *Bath History* (1996) IV: p. 121 n.7-122 n.7.

17. Farington, *Diary*, November 10th 1807 8: pp. 3138-3139. A kit-cat portrait is a standarised canvas, measuring about 36 by 48 inches/91.5 by 71 centimetres, usually including the head, shoulders and one hand. Edward Lucie-Smith, *The Thames and Hudson Dictionary of Art Terms* (London, 1984), 'Kit-cat', p. 109. West and Shaw had future contact. The Bath landscapist accompanied the president's gift of the massive religious painting, *Christ Healing the Sick in the Temple* (Pennsylvania Hospital of Philadelphia), 1815, to the United States in 1817, after which Shaw became an American citizen. Edward J. Nygren, 'Shaw, Joshua', Jane Turner (ed.), *The Dictionary of Art* (London and New York, 1996) 28: p. 560.

18. Farington, *Diary*, November 10th 1807 8: pp. 3138-3139.

19. Von Erffa and Staley, *Paintings of Benjamin West*, p. 424; John Dillenberger, *Benjamin West: The Context of His Life's Work with Particular Attention to Paintings with Religious Subject Matter* (San Antonio, Texas, 1977), pp. 196-197.

20. Von Erffa and Staley, *Paintings of Benjamin West*, pp. 186, 424; Staley, email to writer, 2 February 2012. West's work is also known as *Exile of Bladud*. Paul Hutton, 'A Little Known Cache of English Drawings', *Apollo*: *The Magazine of the Arts* (January 1969) 89: p. 54.

21. John Wood, *An Essay Towards a Description of Bath* (London, 1765) I: pp. 6-8, 72-77; Tim Mowl and Brian Earnshaw, *John Wood: Architect of Obsession* (Bath, 1988), pp. 101-118,185-187; Von Erffa and Staley, *Paintings of Benjamin West*, pp. 186, 424, 484. Interestingly, the West catalogue authors have listed *Bladud* under the category of 'Historical Subjects', instead of 'Mythological Subjects'.

    John Wood's *An Essay Towards a Description of the City of Bath* appeared in Bath, 1742-3. Revised, corrected and enlarged, it was published in London in 1749; a second edition of the latter was issued in London sixteen years later and reprinted, 1769.

22. Wood, *Essay* I: pp. 6-8, 72-77; Mowl and Earnshaw, *John Wood*, p. 184.

23. Andor Gomme, 'Wood, John', *ODNB* 60: pp. 112-114; Wood, *Essay* I: pp. 38-39, 72-77; Sam Smiles, *The Image of Antiquity: Ancient Britain and the Romantic Imagination* (New Haven and London, 1994), pp. 82-83; Mowl and Earnshaw, *John Wood*, pp. 184, 219; Gordon Goodwin, 'Hoare, William', *ODNB* 27: pp. 368-369; Von Erffa and Staley, *Paintings of Benjamin West*, pp. 186, 424. Prior Park House was commissioned by Ralph Allen, the entrepreneur and philanthropist who helped lead the rebirth of Bath. Brenda J. Buchanan, 'Allen, Ralph', *ODNB* 1: pp. 812-814.

24. Wood, *Essay*, Part I: p. 38. The physical appearance of Bladud, or Abaris (although lacking documentation, Wood insisted that they were one and the same 'historical' figure), was described in the *Essay*: 'Abaris came to *Athens* holding a Bow, having a Quiver hanging from his Shoulders, his Body wrapt up in a Chlamys [a Greek mantle fastened at the shoulder], girt about his Loins with a gilded Belt, and wearing Trowzers reaching from his Waste to the Soles of his Feet'.

25. Brenda J. Buchanan, email to writer, May 28th 2011.

26. Farington, *Diary*, September 4th 1807 8: p. 3117, November 2nd 1807 8: p. 3138, November 10th 180.7 8: p. 2138; Alberts, *Benjamin West*, p. 337.

27. Farington, *Diary*, November 10th 1807 8: p. 3138, November 11th 1807 8: p. 3139; Alberts, *Benjamin West*, pp. 175-6. Hoppner's probable source for the West reference was James Boswell's biography of the lexicographer and essayist, Samuel Johnson. On July 28th 1763, Johnson told Boswell that James 'Thomson, I think, had as much of the poet about him as most writers. Every thing appeared to him through the medium of his favourite pursuit. He could not have viewed those two candles burning but with a poetical eye'. Seventeen years later, Johnson, in his *The Lives of the Poets*, expanded this view of Thomson that Hoppner also may have read:

    He thinks in a peculiar train, and he thinks always as a man of genius; he looks round on nature and on life, with the eye which nature bestows only on a poet; the eye that distinguishes, in every thing presented to its view, whatever there is on which imagination can delight to be detained, and with a mind that at once comprehends the vast, and attends to the minute.

    James Boswell, *Boswell's Life of Johnson*, edited by George Birkbeck Hill, revised and enlarged edition by L.F. Powell (Oxford, 1934) I: p. 453; Samuel Johnson, *The Lives of the Poets*, edited by John H. Middendorf (New Haven and London, 2010) 3: pp. 1291-1292; James Sambrook, 'Thomson, James', *ODNB* 54: pp. 516-523.

28. Farington, *Diary*, November 19th 1807 8: p. 3144; Von Erffa and Staley, *Paintings of Benjamin West*, p. 186.

29. Farington, *Diary*, November 19th 1807 8: p. 3144.

30. Felicity Owen and David Blayney Brown, 'Beaumont, Sir George Howland, seventh baronet', *ODNB* 4: pp. 656-658; Farington, *Diary*, December 4th 1807 8: pp. 3156-3157. Nicolas Poussin, the intellectual French artist of the seventeenth century who painted in the classical style, was admired greatly in the 1700s, and sometimes West was compared to him.

    Two lines of Charles Churchill's satire, *The Rosciad* (1761), provide the context of the Beaumont-Farington quotation:

    Ludicrous nature! Which at once could show

    A man so very high, so very low.

    Charles Churchill, *The Rosciad, The Poetical Works of Charles Churchill* (Edinburgh, 1794) in *The Works of the British Poets with Prefaces, Biographical and Critical* (London, 1795) 10: p. 461; James Sambrook, 'Churchill, Charles', *ODNB* 11: pp. 592-595.

31. Farington, *Diary*, December 17th 1807 8: p. 3173; Von Erffa and Staley, *Paintings of Benjamin West*, p. 186.

32. Alberts, *Benjamin West*, pp. 348, 355, 364, 369.

33. Von Erffa and Staley, *Paintings of Benjamin West*, p. 23; Alberts, *Benjamin West*, pp. 186, 424. The Bladud work appeared in the exhibition under the title, *Prince Bladud, eldest son of Lud Hudibras, King of Britain; he first discovered the medicinal virtues of the Bath springs by observing the salutary effect those waters produced on swine.* Dillenberger, *Benjamin West: The Context of His Life's Work*, p. 197.

An Inquisition Indented taken at the Gu…
in and for the said City of Bath the first ——— day of May ———
in the Year of our Lord One Thousand Seven Hundred and Seventy Se…
Before Henry Wright ——— Esquire Mayor of the said City and a…
Coroner of our Sovereign Lord the King in and for the same City upon t…
of the Body of Elizabeth Read Spinster then and there lying dead near…
River Avon in the Parish of Saint Michael within the said City upon th…
of Elias Sumption John Reeves Thomas Rogers William Hill James Dogg…
Charles Jones Henry Mullins Thomas Lewis John Rose John Arnold Thom…
Jones Jonathan Whatley & Thomas Rodbone good and lawful men of the…
City who being sworn and charged to inquire on the part of our Lord the…
when where how and in what manner the said Elizabeth Read came to he…
Do say that the said Elizabeth Read on the thirtieth day of April in the yea…
aforesaid at the Parish and in the City aforesaid about the Hour of six o'Clo…
in the Evening of that day accidentally casually and by misfortune fell int…
River Avon in the parish and City aforesaid and was then and there suffoc…
and drowned of which said Suffocation and Drowning She the said Eliza…
Read then instantly died and so the Jurors aforesaid do say that the s…
Elizabeth Read in the manner and by the means aforesaid accidentally…
and by misfortune came to her Death and not otherwise In Witness where…
will the aforesaid Coroner as the Jurors aforesaid have to this Inquisi…
set their hands and Seals the day and year and at the place aforesai…

H. Wright Mayor
and Coroner

Henry Mullins

Thomas Lewis

Elias Sumsion

John Reeves

John Rose

Tho. Rogers

John Arnold

The mark
of Thomas Jones

William Hill

The Accidental Death of Children in Bath, 1777-1835.

Jan Chivers

It is not easy to access the daily lives of the children of 'ordinary' families in the eighteenth century. Through records of their deaths detailed in the Coroners' Records [fig. 1], however, it is possible to learn something of the lives of children in this period: where they played, how much freedom they had to roam the city, gender differences revealed in the nature of their deaths and the working practices of parents, particularly single mothers.[1] This study does not include the deaths of infants, many of whom were possibly victims of infanticide, as this has been dealt with elsewhere.[2]

From the 1750s, medical opinion argued that maternal breastfeeding rather than sending babies to a wet nurse not only had physical benefits but also led to what today we would call 'mother/child bonding'.[3] This suggests that attitudes to children were changing from the idea that children were essentially sinful and, therefore, in need of correction and punishment to a softer approach to child rearing.

G.J. Barker-Benfield has identified the growth in the eighteenth century of what he called 'the culture of sensibility', which, he has suggested, developed into a 'culture of reform' and encouraged humanitarianism.[4] Humanitarian reformers sought to address a number of issues in response to what was seen as commercial capitalism's exploitation of vulnerable sections of society including the mistreatment of children.[5] Notable among reformers involving themselves with children were Thomas Coram who founded the London Foundling Hospital in the 1740s and Jonas Hanway who founded the Marine Society in 1756. Both of these organisations aimed to raise children in benevolent conditions in order to produce a healthy workforce.[6]

In the late eighteenth and early nineteenth centuries, several acts of parliament were passed that indicate a concern for the working conditions of children. The Chimney Sweepers Act of 1788 prohibited the apprenticeship of boys before the age of eight and addressed the conditions in which they lived and worked. The Factories Act of 1802 concerned the age and condition of children working in textile mills as did the Cotton Mills and Factories Act of 1819. Reformers concerned themselves with the age at which children joined the labour force, usually set at the age of eight or nine, and the conditions and hours of child labour.

fig 1: City of Bath Coroners' Examinations and Inquisitions, 1776-1835
Photograph by Dan Brown

Labouring families often needed to put children to work at a young age in order to contribute to the family income. The fact that some of the children featured in the Bath Coroners' Records were at play might suggest that they did not come from the poorest families and that there was a growing understanding of the nature of childhood. On the other hand, it might mean that children were turned out of the house during the day to fend for themselves.

The Bath Coroners' Records rarely record the age of the deceased but cases involving the deaths of children were an exception. Childhood is a cultural designation that changes over time. Some of those classed as children by the writer of this article were around twelve years old and might not have been considered children by contemporaries. Two of these older children were working as apprentices and their deaths were the consequence of their working conditions.[7] They have been included in this study.

In eighteenth-century Bath, the Mayor was also the Coroner and it would appear that he held all inquests promptly and efficiently [**fig. 2**]. Inquests into the deaths of children were accorded the same weight as those concerning adults with juries varying in number between twelve and seventeen, the usual number being thirteen. In the years covered by the Coroners' Records, 1777-1835, the Coroner conducted 491 inquests of which forty-four (9%) involved the death of a child. Of these, thirty-two concerned boys and twelve concerned girls.

Although the number of children's deaths that resulted in an inquest remained steady over the period of the records at one or two a year, some years had no record of a child's death at all. As one would expect given the rise in the population of Bath, the total number of inquests increased over the period. Child deaths increased slightly in the 1820's but not as much as one might have expected. Table 1 shows an increase for 1821. We do not know why child inquests did not increase in line with adult inquests. It may be that there is an issue of the under-reporting of child deaths, or that there were particular, unknown, reasons why some deaths resulted in the involvement of the Coroner.

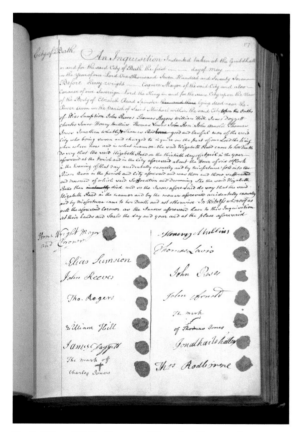

fig 2: City of Bath Coroners' Examinations and Inquisitions, 1776-1835
Bath Record Office - Bath & North East Somerset Council

Table 1: Adult and child inquests

Date	Adult inquests	Child inquests
1790	9	1
1801	6	1
1811	4	0
1821	16	3
1831	17	1

Source: Bath Coroners' Records

Children were not only the subjects of inquests but also appeared as witnesses. The ages of witnesses varied between four years and nine years. Several were five years old. When in August 1808, an inquest was held following the death of Hannah Weeks, aged five years, the only witness called by the Coroner was her younger sister, aged four years. Hannah had been left in charge of her three younger siblings while their mother went down to the courtyard to fill her kettle. The mother spent some time chatting to her neighbour and when she returned, she found that Hannah, in attempting to revive the fire with a pair of bellow, had caught alight her muslin gown. Hannah's mother took her to the Casualty Hospital but the child died later of her burns. Hannah's sister was the youngest witness recorded. It is easy to imagine that attendance at the Coroner's Court to give evidence must have been a frightening event for a young child, especially as he or she had just witnessed a fatal accident often involving a family member. One can imagine court officials attempting to prise information from a scared and tearful child overawed by its surroundings and by the trappings of officialdom.

Water has always fascinated children and eighteenth century children were no different. The river, while providing a playground, was also the site of a number of drownings. Little girls picked flowers on the banks, washed their hands or peered into the water with fatal consequences. The first recorded inquest involving a child tells how Elizabeth Read, in May 1777, was on the riverbank with her seven year old sister [**fig. 2**]. When the younger girl fell in the water, Elizabeth jumped into the river in an attempt to save her little sister. Samuel Broad and Thomas Pearse, fishermen, tried to save both girls. They managed to save the younger girl but Elizabeth drowned.

Boys were more adventurous but with equally tragic results: they fished in the river, they fell off trees into the water, they played at building rafts and attempted to fish dead cats out of the water. Henry Selway, in September 1815, drowned after falling in the river while retrieving his hoop [**fig. 3**]. Two other boys died by drowning but not in the river. In May 1807, John Horwell who was nine months old fell from a box in which he was sleeping into a pan containing two quarts of water, and in January 1808, two year old John Smith fell into what was described as 'a fourteen inch garden well'.

The other major cause of childhood accidental death was fire, something that also fascinates most children. The death of Hannah Weeks, mentioned above, was not unusual. Harriet Carnell was only three and a half when, in February 1820, she was left alone for a while. She found some matches and caught her clothes alight. Despite being taken to hospital,

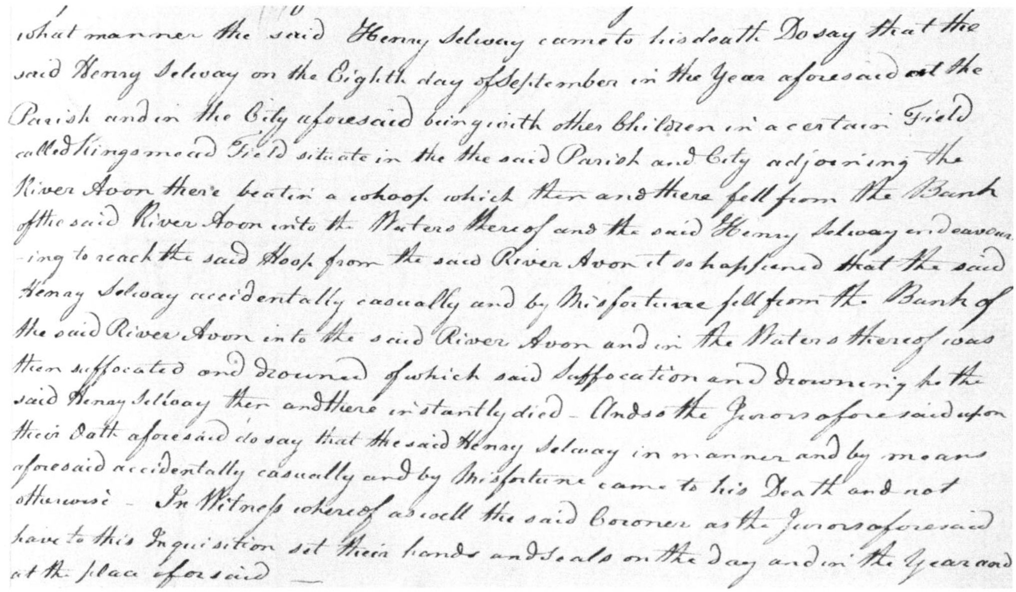

...that manner the said Henry Selway came to his death. Do say that the said Henry Selway on the Eighth day of September in the Year aforesaid at the Parish and in the City aforesaid being with other Children in a certain Field called Kingsmead Field situate in the the said Parish and City adjoining the River Avon there beating a whoop which then and there fell from the Bank of the said River Avon into the Waters thereof and the said Henry Selway endeavouring to reach the said Hoop from the said River Avon it so happened that the said Henry Selway accidentally casually and by Misfortune fell from the Bank of the said River Avon into the said River Avon and in the Waters thereof was then suffocated and drowned of which said Suffocation and drowning he the said Henry Selway then and there instantly died – And so the Jurors aforesaid upon their Oath aforesaid do say that the said Henry Selway in manner and by means aforesaid accidentally casually and by Misfortune came to his Death and not otherwise – In Witness whereof as well the said Coroner as the Jurors aforesaid have to this Inquisition set their hands and Seals on the day and in the Year and at the place aforesaid –

fig 3: Extract from City of Bath Coroners' Examinations and Inquisitions, 1776-1835
Bath Record Office - Bath & North East Somerset Council

she died of her injuries [**fig. 4**]. Girls at the time wore long dresses, petticoats and bibbed aprons tied with ribbons. The combination of long skirts and open fires was potentially lethal to small girls.

Lewis Doble, at four years old, was not much older than Harriet when his pinafore caught fire in the kitchen in June 1827. He was also taken to the Casualty Hospital but later died. It was usual for little boys to be dressed in pinafores, not unlike girl's clothing, until they were breeched at around four years. It was Henry Cole's shirt, however, that caught fire when he was in a dining room with an unguarded fire a few months later. His mother rushed him to the hospital but later his father took him home where he died. He was six years old.

These narratives and the other records of accidental deaths of children lead to some understanding of differences in the treatment of boys and girls. Table 2 shows that more boys had fatal accidents outside the home than inside whereas the reverse is true for girls. This suggests that boys were more at liberty to roam the city while girls were more likely to be confined to the home. Of the boys that died indoors, two were less than one year old, and two were still in pinafores. Sixteen of the boys who died outdoors drowned in the river. Anne Laurence in *Women in England* wrote 'Little boys, allowed to stray away from home, often drowned. … … The number of girls drowned was smaller … suggesting that they stayed closer to home.'[8] The fact that boys were able to play at large in the city and gravitated towards water explains the fact that more boys than girls became the subject of inquests, although the home was far from safe for girls or boys.

Table 2: Place of death, 1777-1835.

Outdoors	Girls	5
	Boys	23
Indoors	Girls	7
	Boys	9

Source: Bath Coroners' Records.

What is, perhaps, surprising to the modern reader is the fact that there is no written record of any concern shown by the Coroner or his jury about the causes of these deaths. We are used to Coroners calling for whatever safety measure they may think desirable to stop children dying preventable deaths. As can be seen from the numerous adult deaths resulting from building work in the city at this time, this was an age long before health and safety issues came to be of any interest.

It is risky to extrapolate from the small number of children appearing in the Coroners' Records to assumptions about parenting and parental attitudes. Some historians have suggested that, because of the high mortality rate of children, parents were unwilling to invest emotionally in their off-spring, but that attitudes changed throughout the eighteenth century with parents becoming more affectionate towards their children.[9] Both Paul Langford and Roy Porter were writing about children of 'middling' and wealthy parents, citing the growth in portraiture of children and the growth in the market for books and playthings for children as evidence. It is probably safe to assume that the children who appeared in Bath Coroners' Records did not come from the wealthier section of Bath society.

The number of children apparently left unsupervised points to the necessity for both parents to work to provide enough money for the family to survive. A study of the Poor Law Records in Bath suggests that the arrival of children meant that the mother was unable to work

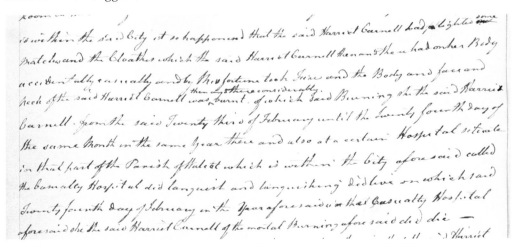

fig 4: Extract from City of Bath Coroners' Examinations and Inquisitions, 1776-1835
Bath Record Office - Bath & North East Somerset Council

fig 5: A Crying Boy at Bath by John Nixon, 1801. Watercolour sketch

Victoria Art Gallery 1994.23, Bath & North East Somerset Council

and that the family fell into poverty at least until any children were old enough to add to the family income.[10] If there were no father, the situation became even more acute. Two of the most poignant inquests illustrate the problems faced by single mothers and the economic necessity that drove them to leave their children unattended.

On the evening of Christmas Eve 1830, the mother of William and Joseph Jones prepared to go to work leaving the two young boys on their own. There is no record of the nature of her work but, as a night worker, it is possible that she was a prostitute. The family lived in 'a hovel' at the back of the Westgate Inn. It was an exceptionally cold night and the boys attempted to block up the gaps in the walls with rags. They then begged a chafing dish of coals from a neighbour. The boys' mother had asked another neighbour to look in on them while she was out but when the neighbour checked at six in the morning she found both boys dead in bed. An inquest was held on Christmas Day when the jury concluded that because of insufficient ventilation they had suffocated due to smoke and sulphurous fumes from the coals in the chafing dish.

When Ann Davis went to work on the morning of November 17th 1835, she locked her eight-year-old daughter, also Ann, in their attic room with instructions not to play with the fire. At about five o'clock in the afternoon, a neighbour alerted Ann Davis's landlady, Mary Hallett, to the room where a child was 'crying murder'. It took some time to break down the door but when Mrs Hallett found her, Ann's clothes were alight. They undressed the child and rushed her to hospital and when her mother was found, she went straight to her bedside. It is worth quoting her evidence in full.

'I gain my livelihood by selling meat about the town which keeps me from home the grater part of the day. On the 17th November between the hours of 10 and 11 in the morning I left my daughter, the deceased, in my room which is in the attick story and locked the door of my room. There was a little fire in the grate and I cautioned the deceased who was about 8 years of age not to play with the fire. About 6 in the evening I heard that the deceased was in the united hospital dreadfully burnt. I remained with her till she died which was about 11 o'clock at night on the 24th instant. The deceased was perfectly sensible till her death and told me that she was playing with her playthings near the fender and that her frock caught fire.'

Mary Hallett's evidence ends with 'The deceased's mother was always very kind to her.' There is some slight evidence here that ideas about affectionate parenting had spread to the labouring poor.

Poor parents, single mothers in particular, without the support of family, many of them having come into the city from the surrounding hinterland, must frequently have found themselves having to leave their children unsupervised while they earned an adequate wage to keep the family from the Poor Law authorities. Application for poor relief was likely to end up with removal and the possible splitting up of the family. **[fig. 5]**

The Coroners' Records give us a unique insight into the world of children and families in the late eighteenth century. Bath was struggling at this time to attract visitors to the city and to sustain a large resident labour force. Inquests were public, important affairs held in the Guildhall and frequently reported in the press. The authorities in the city may not have wanted to draw attention to the accidental death of children at a time of national concern for the welfare of the young.

The death of a child is always a tragic event. Children were vulnerable to death from disease from birth but the preventable accidental death of a child seems particularly tragic.

Notes

1. City of Bath Coroners' Examinations and Inquisitions, 1776-1835, Bath Record Office, hereafter Coroners' Records.

2. Jan Chivers, 'Infanticide in Bath, 1776-1835, The Coroners' Records' in *Bath Exposed! Essays on the Social History of Bath, 1775-1945*, Ed. Graham Davis, Bath, 2007.

3. Lawrence Stone, *The Family, Sex and Marriage in England, 1500-1800*, London, 1977, chap.4.

4. G.H. Barker-Benfield, *The Culture of Sensibility: Sex and Society in Eighteenth-Century Britain*, Chicago and London, 1992, chap.6.

5. Barker-Benfield, *The Culture of Sensibility*, pp. 224/5.

6. The letterhead for the Foundling Hospital, designed by William Hogarth, shows children holding variously a sickle, a rake, a trowel, a plumb line, a sweeping brush, a spinning wheel and a card for carding wool. Jenny Uglow, *Hogarth*, London, 1997, p.331.

7. Ann Allen was a pauper apprentice domestic servant. (March 26th1782). James Head, 'a young boy' was working in Racey's Yard, Walcot Street, when a load of hay smothered him. (April 17th 1820).

8. Anne Laurence, *Women in England 1500 -1760 A Social History*, London, 1994, p.85.

9. Paul Langford, *A Polite and Commercial People England 1727-1783*, Oxford, 1989, pp.501-3; Roy Porter, *English Society in the Eighteenth Century*, London, 1990, pp.266-8; Boyd Hilton, *A Mad, Bed, & Dangerous People? England 1783-1846*, Oxford, 2006, pp.179/180.

10. Jan Chivers, '"A Resonating Void": Strategies and Responses to Poverty, Bath, 1770-1835', unpublished PhD Thesis, University of the West of England, 2006.

REASONS

FOR A POOR LAW

CONSIDERED.

PART I.

BY

THE REV. THOMAS SPENCER, M.A.

PERPETUAL CURATE OF HINTON CHARTERHOUSE, NEAR BATH;
FORMERLY FELLOW OF ST. JOHN'S COLLEGE, CAMBRIDGE;
AND DURING SIX YEARS A GUARDIAN
OF THE BATH UNION.

FOURTH THOUSAND.

LONDON:

JOHN GREEN, 121, NEWGATE STREET.

BATH:

Rev. Thomas Spencer, champion of the New Poor Law

Graham Davis

At a time of austerity and welfare cuts that have been dubbed 'the New Poor Law', it is no surprise to find the reappearance of the age-old tension in social policy between the stigmatizing of paupers and compassion for the poor. During the 1830s and 1840s, at national and local level, a major row erupted with the introduction of the New Poor Law following the Poor Law Amendment Act of 1834. National and local controversy featured the Rev. Thomas Spencer, who became the first chairman of the newly-created Board of Guardians of the Bath Poor Law Union in 1836.[1] Spencer was a prolific writer of pamphlets in which he roundly condemned the abuses of the Old Poor Law and became an enthusiastic advocate for the new system. His own period of office was also a time of fierce arguments among competing interests in the city.

The importance attached to the Poor Law as a sphere of influence was reflected in the fierce pamphlet warfare engaged in during elections to the Board of Guardians. The two sides represented the party rivalry of municipal politics. The poor, without a vote determined by a property qualification, were pawns in a political game. Behind the humanitarian rhetoric lay a political struggle for controlling the administration of the Poor Law. The politics of the Board of Guardians brought patronage and influence, and determined the level of rates to be paid by the citizens of Bath and district.

The Rev. Thomas Spencer, as curate of Hinton Charterhouse, near Bath [**fig. 1**], claimed to have already implemented the spirit of the new Poor Law, by applying a workhouse test to pauper applicants and to have reduced poor law expenditure in his own parish.[2] In March 1837, a new Board of Guardians was to be elected. Spencer produced a tract justifying the conduct of the first Board and attacked the 'mischievous meddling' of the City Magistrates in the administration of the Poor Law. This prompted one of the magistrates to reply in another pamphlet which castigated the 'inhumanity' of the Guardians in its first year of office.[3]

Spencer's pamphlet extolled the virtues of the 41 elected and 8 ex-officio Guardians while criticisms were directed at individuals. Nevertheless, country Guardians, who were mostly farmers, were less likely to attend Board meetings than those who represented Bath parishes.

S. JOHN BAPTIST, HINTON CHARTERHOUSE.—SOUTH.

fig 1: Church of St John the Baptist, south view, Hinton Charterhouse, 1876, steel engraving

Bath in Time - Bath Central Library Collection

Facing: Detail of Reasons for a Poor Law Considered. Title Page, 1843

Bath in Time - Bath Central Library Collection

77

'The feelings of the Board', Spencer claimed, 'are decidedly in favour of erring on the side of liberality….and although a senseless outcry is everywhere raised against Boards of Guardians, as though every man lost all the generous sympathies of his nature the moment he is elected a Guardian; yet notwithstanding this false and frequently malicious and <u>interested</u> outcry, the very reverse is the fact….The charge of cruelty, is misplaced even in the worst cases.' [4]

Spencer was equally critical of the interference of magistrates. The 27th section of the 1834 Act gave magistrates the right to interfere in cases of poor relief for those unable to work. Magistrates were accused of interfering beyond such cases:

'There have been perpetual messages from them to the Relieving Officer, requesting him to relieve able-bodied men; women with illegitimate children; or to give orders for medical relief or for coffins, and in cases where the very contrary had been decided by the Board after careful enquiry.' [5]

He argued that such interference undermined the authority of the Guardians, offered a premium to imposture, and stirred up ill-will among the poor towards the Guardians. 'So long as there is a court of discontent at the Guildhall', Spencer proclaimed, 'so long will there be no peace in Bath amongst the poor.' [6]

In reply, Augustus George Barretté, a local lawyer, denounced Spencer's pamphlet as 'obviously designed to promote the return of the same members of the Board at the next election; a thing most earnestly to be deprecated by everyone in whom a kindly feeling towards the deserving poor….has not altogether ceased to exist.' [7] The new act, he argued, had been brought into disrepute by the extreme measures taken by some Boards of Guardians, but 'in the Bath Union this tendency has been so excessive as to render the very name of Guardians an object of dislike.' 'Severity on the one hand', he continued, 'and disregard of the most sacred and most treasured feeling of the human mind on the other, have marked the entire course of their administration of the most trust confided to them.' Barretté defended the interference of the two

Administration of the Poor Laws.

THE liberality of the Public is solicited on behalf of MARY PRICE, whose parish-allowance has been discontinued under the following circumstances:

Her Husband having become chargeable to Walcot Parish during his last illness, she, after his death, continued to receive a weekly allowance of four or five shillings, on which, assisted by her own exertions, she maintained her young family, and also provided for an elderly woman, Ann Perry, of unexceptionable character, who having come to reside with the Prices about twelve years since, was afterwards sheltered by them when entirely past work, and a mere burden on her companions in poverty.—Soon after the election of the present Board of Guardians, the pay of Mary Price was reduced to one shilling and two loaves of bread. The distress thus produced having attracted the attention of one of the Parochial Clergy, he recommended an application on behalf of Ann Perry to the Board, who refused to grant out-door relief; and insisted on the removal of this decrepit and almost dying woman from the care and protection of her only friend; and her consignment, at the age of eighty, to the strict discipline and constant confinement of a parish workhouse.—The case having been reported to the City Magistrates, and appearing to be a fair sample of many others calling for their interference, an order for out-door relief was made, and served on the Board of Guardians; which after meeting it notwithstanding the remonstrances of a minority (of their own body) by a denial of the jurisdiction of the Magistrates, by temporary expedients and passive resistance, coupled with intelligible admonitions addressed to Mary Price by persons connected with the Board, respecting the possible withdrawal of her own pay, at length reluctantly obeyed—on the very eve of an intended application to the Court of King's Bench for a Mandamus to enforce compliance.—Ann Perry is since dead, having lived just long enough to be the instrument in procuring a result which has been followed, apparently as a consequence, by the allowance of out-door relief to several aged persons not previously so favoured. Mary Price, however, has been less fortunate, the Board of Guardians having, within the last week, *withdrawn her weekly allowance.*

Whether this event is to be considered as the execution of a threat, or merely as the fulfilment of a prediction, it must be considered as constituting a claim on those who sympathise with the aged poor in the struggle now carrying on in their behalf. It is therefore proposed to raise a moderate sum, by donations of not more than 2s. 6d. each, to be applied for her benefit, at the discretion of the MAYOR of Bath, Mr. BARROW, and Mr. SUTCLIFFE, who have undertaken to see the same properly applied.—*Subscriptions already received:*

The Mayor	2 6	W. A., Jun.	2 6
S. Barrow, esq.	2 6	Mrs. W. A.	2 6
W. Sutcliffe, esq.	2 6	J. R.	2 6
Willson Brown, esq.	2 6	M. D.	2 6
P. George, esq.	2 6	M. V.	2 6
Col. Bailey	2 6	E. D.	2 6
J. Shenstone, esq.	2 6	A. B.	2 6
John English, esq.	2 6	Mrs. Boultbee	2 6
Geo. A. Jones, esq.	2 6	John Lousada, esq.	2 6
John Stone, esq.	2 6	Mrs. John Lousada	2 6
Arthur West	2 6	Mrs. Brandon	2 6
G. H. Tugwell, esq.	2 6	Miss Barrow	2 6
B. Peach, esq.	2 6	J. Barrow, esq.	2 6
A. O. B.	2 6	J. R.	2 6
W. A.	2 6		

fig 2: Administration of the Poor Laws, Bath, 1837
Bath in Time - Bath Central Library Collection

city magistrates and argued that the law allowed appeals to be lodged 'in the controlling authority of the Magistrates.'[8]

Particular instances of inhumanity were cited as evidence of the cruel conduct of the Guardians. In July 1836, the use of the pall to cover a pauper's coffin was forbidden and when friends of the deceased had borrowed a pall for 'the maintenance of public decency. ....it was thrice dragged off the coffin by the Porter of the Workhouse.' The subsequent popular clamour obliged the Board to give way. Spencer's description of the Workhouse as 'comfortable lodging under a warm roof' was contrasted with the sick ward on November 8th and 'a Pauper in the worst condition of disease, is lodged in a wretched outer room and stone floor for an indefinite length of time.'[9] Here we have echoes of the current political row over NHS patients waiting on trolleys for a bed.

However, the case that prompted Spencer's pamphlet and fully featured in Barretté's reply was that of Ann Perry. It proved to be a test case for the control of the New Poor Law in Bath. [**fig. 2**],[10] Barretté obtained the original documents from the Mayor and city magistrates to reveal the full story and to cause maximum embarrassment to the Guardians. In other respects, the case was symbolic of the poverty issue in Bath. Ann Perry lived in Avon Street [**fig. 3**] whose notoriety shaped public attitudes to the treatment of the poor in Bath.[11]

Barretté gave a sympathetic description of Ann Perry's circumstances before condemning the action taken by the Board of Guardians:

AVON STREET BATH.

1872.

fig 3: Avon Street, Bath c.1872
Bath in Time - Bath Central Library Collection

The poor woman, who is upwards of eighty years of age, and infirm in the very greatest degree, has always borne an unexceptionable character. For these ten years past, she has been lodged and fed out of mere compassion by a widow named Mary Price, who, during her husband's lifetime, was able to do so without detriment to her family, but since his death about four years since, has become reduced in circumstances. Ann Perry was afraid of applying to the parish, lest by doing so, she would be forced into the Workhouse, and Mary Price also…..At length, however, Mary Price did, on her behalf, make application some time in October last, and her appeal was met on the part of the Relieving Officers by an assurance that if she made any further enquiries about Ann Perry, her own pay, should be taken off, and she and her family should go into the Workhouse. [12]

Friends of the pauper intervened and the case was brought to the Board, and again considered on November 2nd 1836. The only relief offered was in the Workhouse. Upon this application was made to the magistrates. Two of them, Mr. Barrow and Mr. Suttcliffe, having examined the case, served an order on the Board on November 9th. Spencer, as the Chairman of the Board wrote to the Poor Law Commissioners for directions. The reply came that the order must be obeyed. On November 14th, two of the Guardians persuaded Mary Price to withdraw her application on behalf of Ann Perry, and this was duly reported to the Board at the weekly meeting on November 16th.

On hearing this, Mr. Barrow, one of the interested magistrates, made enquiries and he and the Mayor, W.T. Blair, interviewed Mary Price two days later. Mary Price confirmed that she had been intimidated by the Guardians to withdraw her application for relief for Ann Perry under threat of her own relief being stopped.

She had put her mark to the withdrawal letter which had not been read to her. Ann Perry was then given a shilling by one of the Guardians with the farewell comment: "God bless you, I hope you will get more without applying to the parish." According to the *Bath Herald* of February 11th, Mary Price had her parish pay of 2s 6d. taken away despite assurances to the contrary although she had three children to support.

That same evening, the Mayor wrote to the Poor Law Commissioners in London charging the Board of Guardians with illegal interference and intimidation and enclosing Mary Price's testimony. On November 24th, in a meeting between a deputation from the Board of Guardians and the City Magistrates, it was agreed that the Board had no power to resist an order by the magistrates under clause 27 of the Poor Law Amendment Act. The next day, a letter was received from the Poor Law Commissioners that Assistant Commissioner, Mr. Weale, would come to Bath to investigate the case. This resulted in a letter from Edwin Chadwick, written on December 6th 1836, which took the Guardians' side in the dispute. The letter claimed that Ann Perry had resided and worked as a laundress with Mary Price for many years, and although now unfit for work, was still capable of minding the house and business during the absence of Mary Price 'as any other person who must have been employed for that purpose'. The application for relief had been withdrawn voluntarily and 'no intimidation was used to exact such withdrawal'.[13] The case was closed. Barretté concluded, bitterly: 'Thus was all hope of obtaining anything deserving the name of fair and impartial inquiry from that quarter put an end to.'[14]

However, a further initiative was taken by Mr. Suttcliffe, the other magistrate who had signed the order. He pursued the matter in law with an application to the Court of King's Bench for a rule to show cause why a mandamus should not be issued to enforce obedience to the order on Ann Perry issued to the Guardians on November 9th. The case awaited its time in court. On January 4th 1837, one of Mr. George's clerks wrote asking the Relieving Officer to investigate the particulars of the case. He reported on January 13th when the poor woman was visited and relieved. 'Thus', wrote Barretté, after three months of anxiety, and after the Magistrates had been put to considerable expense and much trouble, a simple act of justice was done in the individual case, and a great principle established for the protection of the helpless in future.'[15]

The benefit to Ann Perry was short-lived. While the Magistrates and Guardians and Commissioners argued over matters of high principle, while the rhetoric on justice and humanity poured forth unabated, Ann Perry, the victim, died on Sunday, January 31st. Barretté, after recording her death, moved swiftly to mark its significance:

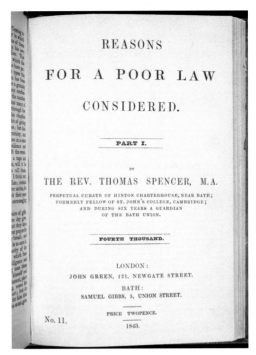

fig 4: Reasons for a Poor Law Considered. Title Page, 1843
Bath in Time - Bath Central Library Collection

'But the real evil in all this lay much deeper; whatever the Guardians in conference may say and whatever by certain late acts they may seem to imply, the real, though secret, object of all this is first to set aside the authority of the Magistrates, and then to compel every poor person thenceforward, asking relief, to come into the Workhouse…. But I warn the Rate-payers against being imposed upon any longer. I entreat all those in whom regard to the <u>deserving</u> poor, and reverence towards the appointment of God's law bear away (and who shall say these considerations do not influence HIM.'[16]

This is as frank a confession of motivation as one is likely to find. The case of Ann Perry highlighted the power struggle between the Magistrates and Guardians. The paupers themselves were merely the unfortunate victims in a propaganda struggle over the issue of the New Poor Law in Bath.

This process continued when Spencer returned to the attack in a pamphlet in 1838 that denounced the failure of the Bath Board of Guardians during its second year of office.[17] Following the Ann Perry scandal, he had seen the tough policies of the first year reversed. As Chairman, he had supervised a reduction in the poor rates from 19, 928 to 11, 520. The only difficulty, he claimed, had arisen from persons who lost fees, power or salaries. Some of the city magistrates, 'losing the power of hearing appeals and granting public pensions out of other people's money, and stirred up by clerks and paid overseers, were the most formidable.' In fact, according to Spencer, the interested parties brought back much of the previous pauperism within three years, as expenditure once more increased from 11,520 to 14,180. **[fig. 4]** [18] He berated the Board for reversing his policy:

> 'they have taken the smooth, the downhill course of complying with the desires of all that were formerly discontented ......In their desire to be thought compassionate, they overlook the thousands of burthened ratepayers, respectable widows with small incomes, tradesmen with large families, young men setting up in business, all of whom, by a little increase to their taxation, would be ruined.'[19]

In the competition for political influence, each side posed as champions of the poor. Barretté and the magistrates offered protection to the 'deserving' poor; Spencer and his Guardian supporters pointed to the plight of the poor ratepayers. The increased numbers of paupers receiving relief in 1837 were put down to a misguided policy. The number of inmates in the workhouse increased from 330 to 520 from Christmas 1836 to midsummer 1837, with a further 2,000 paupers in receipt of out-door relief, costing an additional 200.[20] Far from the workhouse being a place of dread, Spencer argued, people were queuing to gain admission. 'Such is human nature, that it is found that persons will prefer to live even on 2s. 6d. a week, received for doing nothing, than on four times that amount, as wages for labour.' The payment of out-door relief also provided the opportunity to obtain additional income deceitfully from charitable sources:

> 'In this idleness it becomes a great source of amusement to devise schemes of extracting money from private benevolence. Ladies of leisure, with no knowledge of the habits of the poor, and with more kindness than discretion, visit such persons: they conceal from them all favourable facts, and detail only such as are likely to obtain pity and a donation; they receive good clothing, which, if they wear, would prevent the next visitor from helping them – therefore, they pawn it and turn it into gin. They are then ready for fresh presents of clothing and money; they will always put on the appearance of rags, want, and wretchedness, by day, for these are the wares they deal in – this is their horrible trade; and in the evening, when their benefactors have gone home, they commence their mirth and festivity.'[21]

In using such terms, Spencer identified the essential political divide between factions on the Town Council – the leisured and professional classes residing in the upper part of the city, predominantly Conservative, versus the businessmen and tradesmen, predominantly Liberal, occupying the central business district and the lower part of the city. Posing as the true champion of the poor, Spencer believed that indiscriminate poor relief and charity not only allowed a dangerous extended influence for the benevolent classes, but undermined the spirit of independence among working people:

> 'The more intelligent of the working classes, however, have begun to discern this. They see that men who are so ready to bestow charity are most ready to deny justice; and that even their charity is not at their own cost, but at the expense of the ratepayers. They see that charity from the poor rates is but a mean substitute for prosperous industry; and that public injustice robs them of ten times as much as it gives them in charity…..[22]

Even when the New Poor Law had been established for some years, the controversy surrounding it continued.[23] Its critics argued most powerfully on the basis of anecdotal evidence. Spencer listed examples of alleged destitution, cases of infanticide and the starvation of children ascribed to the harshness of the New Poor Law.[24] The fiercest attacks were directed against the Union Workhouses, the hated 'Bastilles for the Poor'. Wild stories circulated in the anti-Poor Law pamphlets of the 1830s and 1840s about the evil practices that existed inside the new Workhouses. It was rumoured that the Workhouse bread was poisoned, that every third infant born inside the Workhouse was to be murdered, and young girls 'verging on womanhood have at times had their persons exposed to the most brutal and indecent manner by the Master, for the purpose of inflicting on them cruel floggings.'[25] The popular literature of the day, ranging from Charles Dickens's *Oliver Twist* to George Sims's ballad, *Christmas Day in the Workhouse* imprinted the 'cruel' spectre of the Workhouses on the public imagination.[26] The notably grim architecture of the early Union Workhouses reinforced the terrifying images created in propaganda pamphlets and contemporary literature.[27]

Spencer in defending the New Poor Law argued that the evils of pauperism had to be attacked and conditions inside the Workhouse were much better than people realized. He claimed the public were misguided and sentimental with regard to certain classes of pauper such as aged paupers:

> 'There is great scope for the exercise of discretion and compassion; at the same time the public feeling is far from correct on this head. In fact, on no class does the public mind require enlightening as much as on that of pauperized old age. Leaving out as exceptions, the afflicted and bedridden, the characteristics of the aged pauper are dirty and intemperate habits; begging and stealing to add to his parish pay; a discontented spirit, the result of an ill-spent life. Wherever he goes, he affords a living demonstration that youth may be profligate and manhood improvident, and yet old age be equally well provided for at the public cost.'[28]

Religious convictions easily slipped into moral condemnation supported by Divine truth: 'It is the will of God', Spencer proclaimed, 'that men should acquire habits of forethought and self-denial; and that if they prefer present ease to future good, they should suffer the consequences.'[29] When he surveyed the paupers inside the Workhouse he found them not only morally deficient but of six hundred inmates not one had any religion.[30] The advantage of the

Workhouse was that it provided discipline and religious instruction: ''the regulations favour a recovery from bad habits: where wholesome food, unaccompanied by intoxicating liquor, regular washing, decent apparel, daily prayers, and sermons on Sundays, should draw his attention to the serious realities of his situation.'[31]

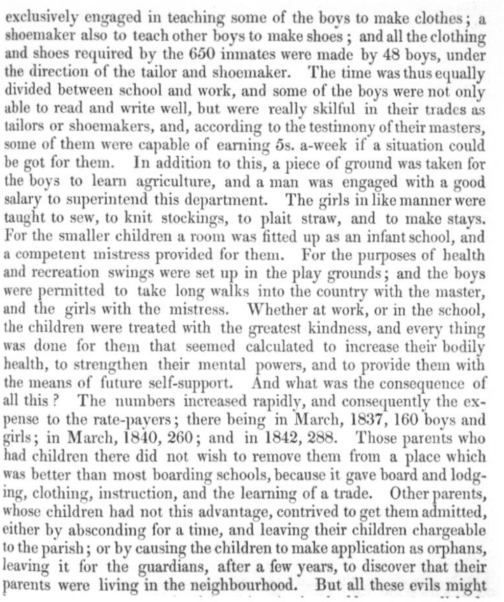

A disciplined regime, however, did not mean unmitigated austerity. Spencer claimed that conditions inside the Workhouse were superior to those available outside to the industrious poor. Children inside the Workhouse were instructed by schoolteachers in useful knowledge, had access to a library of 'useful and entertaining books', and received religious instruction from the Workhouse Chaplain. A tailor and shoemaker were engaged to teach boys their crafts and all the clothing and shoes required for 650 inmates were made by the 48 boys, the most skilful earning 5s. a week. The girls were taught to sew, knit stockings, plait straw and to make stays. For the younger children, an infant school with a competent mistress, was provided, and there were swings in the playground. The boys and girls were allowed to take long walks with their teachers in the countryside. Spencer claimed that 'whether at work, or in the school, the children were treated with the greatest kindness', and everything was done for their benefit. **[fig. 5]** [32]

exclusively engaged in teaching some of the boys to make clothes; a shoemaker also to teach other boys to make shoes; and all the clothing and shoes required by the 650 inmates were made by 48 boys, under the direction of the tailor and shoemaker. The time was thus equally divided between school and work, and some of the boys were not only able to read and write well, but were really skilful in their trades as tailors or shoemakers, and, according to the testimony of their masters, some of them were capable of earning 5s. a-week if a situation could be got for them. In addition to this, a piece of ground was taken for the boys to learn agriculture, and a man was engaged with a good salary to superintend this department. The girls in like manner were taught to sew, to knit stockings, to plait straw, and to make stays. For the smaller children a room was fitted up as an infant school, and a competent mistress provided for them. For the purposes of health and recreation swings were set up in the play grounds; and the boys were permitted to take long walks into the country with the master, and the girls with the mistress. Whether at work, or in the school, the children were treated with the greatest kindness, and every thing was done for them that seemed calculated to increase their bodily health, to strengthen their mental powers, and to provide them with the means of future self-support. And what was the consequence of all this? The numbers increased rapidly, and consequently the expense to the rate-payers; there being in March, 1837, 160 boys and girls; in March, 1840, 260; and in 1842, 288. Those parents who had children there did not wish to remove them from a place which was better than most boarding schools, because it gave board and lodging, clothing, instruction, and the learning of a trade. Other parents, whose children had not this advantage, contrived to get them admitted, either by absconding for a time, and leaving their children chargeable to the parish; or by causing the children to make application as orphans, leaving it for the guardians, after a few years, to discover that their parents were living in the neighbourhood. But all these evils might

fig 5: Extract from Reasons for a Poor Law Considered. Part II p.9, 1843
Bath in Time - Bath Central Library Collection

Moreover, the Guardians were concerned about the contaminating influence of long term stay upon Workhouse children, in mixing with the depraved and insane. Printed notices were circulated in shop windows listing the children ready for situations. Yet respectable families, conscious of the Workhouse stigma, did not want to take them.[33] The numbers of children inside the Workhouse increased rapidly from 160 in 1837 to 288 in 1842.[34]

Spencer argued that in food, clothing and medical care, inmates of the Workhouse enjoyed better treatment than the poor at large in the community:

> 'In the Bath Union Workhouse the aged and infirm, besides the usual visiting days, are allowed occasionally to go out for one, two, or three days, to see their friends. They enter the Workhouse at their own accord, and at any time, by giving three hours' notice, they can depart. When our applications were increasing faster than our accommodation, we offered to the aged inmates the full amount of out-door relief, but almost all of them refused the offer; and many of them said, "Where can we get the good food and clothing and fires and beds which we have here?"'

In refuting the charge of starvation of inmates, Spencer referred to the arithmetic of Workhouse expenditure:

> 'Without including rent, or the attendance of officers, the food, clothing, and fuel alone, bought at the wholesale price, amount each week, to 3s 1d for each inmate. I know a labouring man, a ratepayer, who has a wife and six children, and his earnings are nine shillings a week. After paying one shilling a-week for rent, there remain eight shillings to provide food, clothing, and fuel for eight persons; or a shilling a-week for each. If that labourer could even buy his goods at the wholesale price as the Guardians do, it would require 1 4s 8d a week to enable himself and children to live as well as the inmates of the Workhouse.'[35]

These glowing descriptions of life in the Workhouse were of course meant to counter the exaggerated charges of starvation and cruelty mounted against the Guardians. Both sides employed dubious anecdotal evidence quite shamelessly in support of their arguments, a trick not lost on modern politicians in attempting to manipulate public opinion.[36]

As a result of the conflict over the introduction of the New Poor Law, serious misunderstandings developed in the public mind that served to harden hostility to the poor. In the absence of a contemporary understanding of the causes and extent of poverty, despite a deep concern felt in the 1840s over the 'Condition of England' question, popular impressions remained unqualified without the systematic statistical evidence provided in the surveys of poverty by Booth and Rowntree later in the century.[37]

The bitterest criticisms among those who attacked the New Poor Law were reserved for the state of the Union Workhouses. The spectre of half-starved inmates at the mercy of a cruel Workhouse master became established. At Andover Workhouse in 1845, the stereotype became reality in the person of the odious M'Dougal. This was an extreme case of cruelty where the starved inmates grovelled in the dirt to obtain gristle from the bones thrown to them.[38] The attendant publicity on the Andover Scandal reinforced the bad, public reputation of all Workhouses. Defenders of the New Poor Law attacked the 'evils of pauperism' and the moral deficiency of the poor. Recipients of poor relief were labelled as lazy, filthy, drunken and dissolute persons who conducted their lives without forethought or sense of responsibility. Only the tough discipline of the Workhouse, it was argued, could wean such people away from the debilitating effects of pauperism and an unmanly dependence on the sentimental among the wealthy classes who dispersed charity without discrimination.

An alarming picture developed of a teeming mass of paupers who threatened the well-being of society unless they were either appeased or disciplined. In the 1840s, the existing social hierarchy and system of property rights looked to be under threat.

Yet two important qualifications should be made to the mental picture of the Poor Law produced by the two conflicting camps. First, the Workhouses only housed a small minority of paupers. The great majority receiving poor relief received it in their own homes.[39] As practical men, the Guardians, who mostly carried over into the new system, soon found it more economical to provide out-relief in most cases than to insist on paupers entering the Workhouse. Also, able-bodied paupers for whom the Workhouse Test was devised, formed only a small minority of pauper inmates inside the Workhouse. In practice, the sick and insane, the aged and young children, who formed the bulk of the Workhouse population, were the victims of the principle of 'less eligibility' designed to discipline able-bodied paupers.[40] Secondly, insufficient recognition was given to the influence of the trade cycle on the numbers of people applying for poor relief. These invariably increased during the winter months when employment was scarce, and in years of depression. What Spencer ascribed to lax administration and moral deficiency, could more properly be attributed to economic recession. The obsession with poverty as evidence of moral unfitness blinded most contemporaries to the inadequate incomes of the poor.

In contrast with the arguments over the Poor Law, it is instructive to examine the structure of the Workhouse population. The earliest snapshot picture available providing fullest information is in the 1851 census schedule. **[fig. 6]** [41] An analysis of the 724 pauper inmates of Bath Union Workhouse resident on census night 1851 points to the differences between pauper inmates, depicted in Poor Law propaganda, and as revealed under classification. Of the 384 males, almost a third (30.9 per cent) were aged ten years or less, and almost a quarter (23.0 per cent) were aged over 60 years. The next largest group, 11-20 years, formed just over a fifth of all males (21.4 per cent). Able-bodied male paupers, the supposed villains of the old Poor Law, formed a less than overwhelming proportion of the total. Less than half (46.1 per cent) of all males were aged 11 – 60 years. Not all of these were physically or

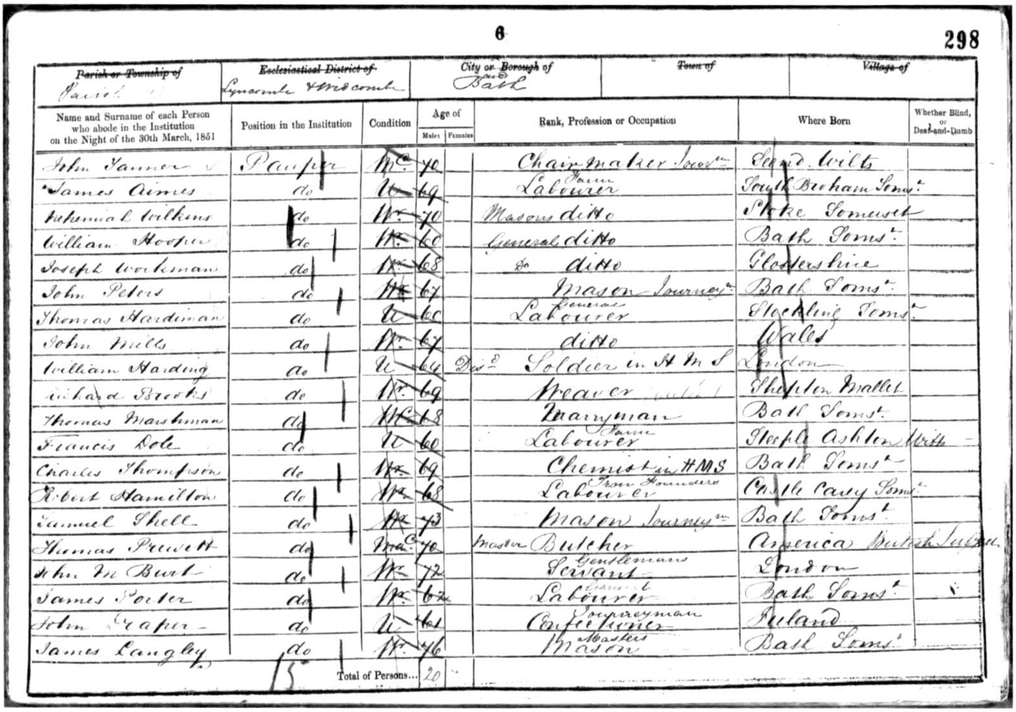

6 298

Parish or Township of	Ecclesiastical District of	City or Borough of	Town of	Village of
Parish	Lyncombe & Widcombe	Bath		

Name and Surname of each Person who abode in the Institution on the Night of the 30th March, 1851	Position in the Institution	Condition	Age of Males	Age of Females	Rank, Profession or Occupation	Where Born	Whether Blind, or Deaf-and-Dumb
John Tanner	Pauper	Mar	70		Chair Maker Journeyman	[illegible] Wilts	
James Aimes	do	U	69		Farm Labourer	South Brewham Soms	
Nehemiah Wilkins	do	Wr	70		Masons ditto	Stoke Somerset	
William Hooper	do	Wr	60		General ditto	Bath Soms	
Joseph Workman	do	Wr	68		do ditto	Glostershire	
John Peters	do	Wr	67		Mason Journeyman	Bath Soms	
Thomas Hardiman	do	U	60		General Labourer	Stockling Soms	
John Mills	do	Wr	67		ditto	Wales	
William Harding	do	U	64		Disd Soldier in H M S	London	
Richard Brooks	do	Wr	69		Weaver	Shepton Mallet	
Thomas Marshman	do	Wr	68		Marryman	Bath Soms	
Francis Dole	do	U	60		Farm Labourer	Steeple Ashton Wilts	
Charles Thompson	do	Wr	69		Chemist in HMS	Bath Soms	
Robert Hamilton	do	Wr	68		Iron Founders Labourer	Castle Cary Soms	
Samuel Shell	do	Wr	73		Mason Journeyman	Bath Soms	
Thomas Prewett	do	Mar	70		Master Butcher	America British Subject	
John M Burt	do	Wr	72		Gentlemans Servant	London	
James Porter	do	Wr	62		General Labourer	Bath Soms	
John Draper	do	U	61		Journeyman Confectioner	Ireland	
James Langley	do	Wr	76		Masters Mason	Bath Soms	
	15	Total of Persons...	20				

fig 6: Extract from 1851 census for Bath Union Workhouse
Crown Copyright courtesy of the National Archives, London

mentally fit for work. Fifteen males were classed as insane and many of those in the age group 11-15 years were listed as scholars.

An examination of specified occupations shows that the Workhouse did not merely claim the least skilled or most depraved among the labour force. Indeed, it is perhaps a surprising finding that craftsmen and tradesmen formed the largest occupational group with 43.4 per cent of the total. A further third (32.5 per cent) described themselves as labourers, and another tenth (10.8 per cent) were listed as servants or gardeners. A mere 2.4 per cent were styled as hawkers or costermongers, with the remaining 10.8 per cent classed as miscellaneous. Clearly, many skilled and intelligent workers, some of whom had been journeymen craftsmen or master craftsmen employing other men, had through sickness, old age or some misfortune of business, become pauper inmates of the Workhouse. This evidence does not support Spencer's strictures against aged paupers that he employed to attack the 'misplaced sentimentality' among the public. In fact, the occupational evidence presents a curiously respectable picture. Also, the itinerant poor were thinly represented among the inmates. It was the resident poor of Bath who predominated.

The higher proportion of male paupers compared with female paupers, despite a preponderantly female population in Bath, suggests that males were more adversely affected by economic recession. About a quarter of females, (24.5 per cent), were aged ten years or less and just over a quarter, (25.9 per cent), were aged over 60 years. Among those nominally in the working age groups, more than three-quarters, (77.2 per cent), were classed as domestic servants, laundresses or washerwomen. The only other group that formed above a tenth of the total was that of dressmakers or needlewomen (14.8 per cent). Bath was increasingly a service economy by 1851, suffering from the loss of trade and employment arising from fewer seasonal visitors to the city. Pauper inmates, male and female, were the victims of a surplus labour market at a time of recession in the city.

What contributed to the surplus labour market in Bath was the pattern of in-migration into the city. Inside the Workhouse, the proportion of Bath-born males was remarkably low, and there was a correspondingly large immigration from outside the city. More than a third of inmates, mostly children, had their birthplace recorded as 'not known'. These were most likely born outside the city and formed part of the substantial migration into the city in times of former prosperity. The evidence of pauper examinations suggests that migrants came from considerable distances, especially from south-western counties, in a long-standing pattern associated with the city's expansion since the late eighteenth century. [**fig. 7**] [42] A similar pattern existed for female paupers. Substantial in-migration occurred in search of employment opportunities in domestic service and other forms of service industry.

And what of the allegedly depraved inmates so vividly described by Spencer in his attacks on pauperism? What may be deduced from census data is limited but not without value. The unmarried mothers in the Workhouse were probably the target for Spencer's outburst about prostitutes using it as a lying-in hospital.[43] Yet the number was relatively small; eighteen mothers in total with twenty-three children between them out of 352 females resident in the Workhouse. Significantly, thirteen of the mothers were recorded as domestic servants. More than one authority has recognized that middle-class males commonly had their first sexual experience with female domestics employed in the home.[44] Servants were commonly regarded as fair game and if they became pregnant, they were unceremoniously thrown out of

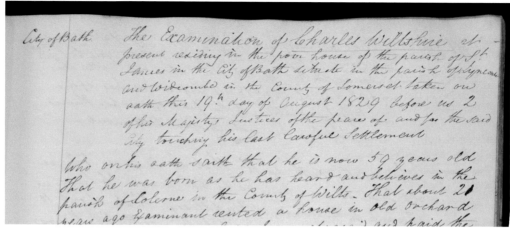

fig 7: Pauper Examinations, St. James's Parish, Bath, 1823-66, Walcot Parish, Bath, 1853-65
Bath Record Office - Bath & North East Somerset Council

employment. Without a reference, further domestic employment in a surplus labour market, was a remote prospect. Five of the women had more than one child, but the numbers involved offer less than convincing evidence of extensive immorality among female paupers. The low numbers of bastardy orders issued within the Bath Union support that conclusion. Between 1844 and 1885, for which period the records survive, a total of only 209 orders were issued for a population of 70,000, or an average of five a year.[45] The putative fathers were not all confined to the working classes. In addition to craftsmen, labourers and servants, army officers, tradesmen, and members of the professional classes were recorded.

The presence of inmates of Bath Union Workhouse can largely be explained in economic terms. The young and the old, the incapacitated and insane, without means of financial support, were added to those with occupations in which a surplus labour market operated against them. The insidious re-emergence of the language of 'the deserving' and 'the undeserving' poor, identified by Rowan Williams, the Archbishop of Canterbury in the rhetoric of modern political debate, suggests that the spirit of Thomas Spencer and the New Poor Law is alive and well in the twenty-first century.

Notes

1. Rev. Thomas Spencer, Fellow of St. John's College Cambridge, became perpetual curate of Hinton Charterhouse, near Bath (a living worth 90 a year) in 1826. Under his direction, parochial expenditure in Hinton Charterhouse was reduced from 950 in 1830 to 200 in 1836. Under the New Poor Law, he became Guardian for his parish and the first Chairman of the Bath Board of Guardians. A prolific pamphleteer on the Poor Law, he was also an advocate of education, thrift, temperance, and church reform. After a brief spell in the United States, he became Secretary to the National Temperance Society. He died in 1853, aged 56.

2. Rev. Thos. Spencer, 'The Working of the New Poor Law in the Bath Union or A Peep into the Board Room at Walcot', 1836, Bath Tracts.

3. Aug. Geo. Barretté, 'Few Plain Facts', 1837, Bath Tracts.

4. Spencer, 'The Working of the New Poor Law in the Bath Union', p.12.

5. Ibid, p. 14.

6. Ibid, p. 15

7. Barretté, 'A Few Plain Facts', p.3. Barretté was a lawyer who lived at 5 Claremont, Bath.

8. Ibid, pp. 3-4.

9. Ibid, pp. 9-13. This was not describing Bath Union Workhouse which was not built until June 1838, but one of the old parish poor houses. The Union Workhouse was built at Odd Down on the southern outskirts of the city.

10. See reports in the *Bath and Cheltenham Gazette,* January 24th, January 31st, and February 14th and 21st 1837.

11. See, Graham Davis, *Bath as Spa and Bath as Slum: The Social History of a Victorian City,* The Edwin Mellen Press, (Lewiston, Queenston, Lampeter, 2009).

12. Barretté, 'A Few Plain Facts', pp. 14-15.

13. Ibid, p. 18.

14. Ibid, p. 19.

15. Ibid, pp. 19-20.

16. Ibid, p. 25.

17. Rev. Thos. Spencer, 'The Failure of the New Poor Law: A Review of the Proceedings of the Board of Guardians during the second year.' 1838.

18. Rev. Thos. Spencer, 'Reasons for a Poor Law Considered', 1841, p. 5.

19. Op cit, Spencer, 'The Failure of the New Poor Law', pp. 4-6.

20. Ibid, pp. 8-9.

21. Ibid, pp. 11-12. For more examples of the initiatives and conditions of the poor, see Tim Hitchcock, Peter King, Pamela Sharpe, eds, *Chronicling Poverty: the voices and strategies of the English poor, 1640-1840,* (Macmillan Press, London), 1977.

22. Op cit, Spencer, 'Reasons for a Poor Law Considered', part III, 1843, p. 11.

23. See Rev. Thos. Spencer, 'The New Poor Law, its Evils, and their Remedies', 1843; 'The Outcry against the New Poor Law, or Who is the Poor Man's Friend' 1843; 'Reasons for the New Poor Law Considered', parts 1-4; 'Objections to the New Poor Law Answered'. Parts 1-4, 'The Want of Fidelity in Ministers of Religion respecting the New Poor Law'. Abuses listed by Spencer included the Clerk to the Union, Mr. Harrington, absconded

with £800 of parish rates; spirits carried into the Workhouse; drunken porters; paupers allowed out of the house unbeknown to the Governor and a former Governor enjoying splendid parties at the public expense. See 'The Failure of the New Poor Law', pp. 21-6.

24. Spencer, 'Reasons for a Poor Law Considered', p. 14.

25. G.R.W. Baxter, 'The Book of the Bastiles, or the History of the Working of the New Poor Law', 1841 from Michael Rose, *The Relief of Poverty, 1834-1914*, (Macmillan, 1972), pp. 109-20.

26. *Oliver Twist; or the parish boy's progress*, by 'Boz' first appeared in 24 monthly instalments in Bentley's Miscellany, Feb. 1837-April 1839; John Bowen, *A Refutation of some of the Charges preferred against the Poor*, 1837, James Withers Reynolds, *Written from Newmarket Union*, 1846; George R. Sims, *The Dagonet Ballads*, 1881.

27. John Bowen, *The Union Workhouse and Board of Guardians System*, 1842.

28. Letter by Spencer to Poor Law Commissioners, Aug. 1st 1836, 2nd Annual Report, p. 9.

29. Spencer, 'Reasons for a Poor Law Considered', Part III, p. 3.

30. Ibid, p. 7.

31. Ibid, p. 10.

32. Spencer, 'Reasons for a Poor Law Considered', Part II, p. 8.

33. Ibid, p. 9.

35. Spencer, 'The Outcry against the New Poor Law', pp. 10-11.

36. See Norman Longmate, *The Workhouse*, pp. 296-314 for further examples of anecdotal evidence.

37. In Charles Booth's survey of London, begun in 1886, he arrived at a figure of 30.7 per cent of the population living in poverty. B.S. Rowntree's study of York conducted in 1899, and based on different methods produced a comparable figure of 27.84 per cent living in poverty. Charles Booth, *Life and Labour of the People of London* (1 volume 1889; 2 volumes 1891; 9 volumes 1892-7; 17 volumes 1902-3); B.S. Rowntree, *Poverty: A Study of Town Life*, 1901.

38. See Longmate, chapter 10, Scandal at Andover, pp. 119-35.

39.

	No. of Paupers on in-relief	No. of Paupers on out-relief
1838	682	1704
1839	691	1687
1840	754	1765
1841	749	1518
1842	970	1648
1843	1,383	1,794
1844	1,119	1,816

Adapted from Stephen Williams, 'Bath and the New Poor Law', in J. Wroughton, (ed), *Bath in the Age of Reform*, (1972), p. 37, and John Bush, 'Bath Union Notes', 1865.

40. This was recognized as a national pattern by the Webbs:

'For instance, if any such classified statistics of pauperism had been made it might have revealed to the Commissioners, what Chadwick discovered a few years later, namely, that the bulk of the paupers were not, as the Commissioners seems to have imagined, either able-bodied men, or even wives and children of such men, but persons actually incapacitated by old age or laid low by sickness, with the helpless dependents of those impotent poor.' S. and B. Webb, *English Poor Law History, vol. 2, The last Hundred Years*, 1929, p. 88.

41. Bath Census, Workhouse Schedule, HO 1942 1- 363. The census Enumerator made some arithmetical errors which had to be identified before an analysis could be undertaken.

42. Pauper Examinations, St. James's Parish, Bath, 1823-1866, Walcot Parish, Bath, 1853-65.

43. Spencer, 'Failure of the New Poor Law', p. 20.

44. Steven Marcus, *The Other Victorians: A Study of sexuality and pornography in mid-nineteenth century England*, (Weidenfeld and Nicolson, 1966), p. 133; Frank Dawes, *Not in Front of the Servants: Domestic Service in England 1850-1939*, (Wayland, 1973), chapter 3, A Fate Worse than Death, pp. 35-45.

45. Bath Poor Law Union, Register of Orders in Bastardy, 1844-85.

The Rev.ᵈ Mʳ WILLIAM JAY, Aged 19.

William Jay: Evangelical Preacher

Stephen Waddell

In the novel, *Miss Mackenzie* (1865), Anthony Trollope (1815-82) parodies the city of Bath with the thinly disguised pseudonym of 'Littlebath'. As the story opens, the heroine, Margaret Mackenzie, is in London caring for her dying brother for fifteen years. Soon after his death, she inherits his substantial fortune. She is now a wealthy, 34-year-old spinster. With no close connections in London she decides indulge and move to prominent 'Littlebath'. She rents a home in the Paragon where 'the assembly rooms were quite close'.[1] Upon her arrival, she discovers she must make an immediate choice of with whom to align her allegiance; either the evangelicals who follow the clergyman Mr. Stumfold or those who don't. There was no middle ground. Trollope writes:

Mr. Stumfold at Littlebath had very special views, and was specially known for them. His friends said he was evangelical, and his enemies said that he was Low Church ... and he was always fighting the devil by opposing the pursuits which are the life and mainstay of such places as Littlebath. His chief enemies were card-playing and dancing as regarded the weaker sex, and hunting and horseracing-to which might be added everything under the name of sport-as regarded the stronger. Sunday comforts were also enemies which he hated with a vigorous hatred, unless three full services a day, with sundry intermediate religious readings and exercitations of the spirit, may be called Sunday comforts.[2]

It would be a mistake to assume that the clergyman was dark and dire. In fact, he was quite jovial and attractive. Upon her arrival, Mackenzie's neighbour asks the spinster, 'Have you known Mr. Stumfold long? Perhaps you have come here to be near him; a great many ladies do.'[3] From Trollope's parody, the question must be asked: What happened to the city of Bath that it became known not only for its pleasures but also as a bastion of Evangelicalism that opposed them? There are many reasons for the overall transformation of the city.[4] But the single greatest reason for the rise of Evangelicalism must be that Bath was the home to William Jay [**fig. 1**], the Evangelical attraction in a city full of attractions.

William Jay.

fig 1: The Revd. William Jay, c.1800
Bath in Time - Bath Central Library Collection

Facing: Detail from Revd. Mr William Jay aged 19, October 4th 1788.
Bath in Time - Bath Central Library Collection

The Early Life of William Jay

The rise to fame of the Argyle Chapel pastor might be viewed as either most fortunate or providential. Jay was born in Tisbury, Wiltshire to William Jay and Sarah Mead. His father was apprenticed unusually late in life to a mason at age twenty-one.[5] Shortly after his apprenticeship the elder Jay leased a cottage, land and quarry from Lord Arundel in 1765.[6] The *Autobiography* revealed the property was situated almost an equal distance from Wardour Castle, Pithouse, and Fonthill.[7] The younger William grew up helping his father as a mason on William Beckford's (1760-1844) estate at Fonthill. The editors of the *Autobiography*, in a footnote, incorrectly assumed that Jay had worked on Beckford's Fonthill Abbey, also known as Beckford's Folly. Construction on the Abbey didn't begin until 1796, five years after Jay was minister at Argyle Chapel. However, Beckford came into his majority in 1781 and hired a builder in Tisbury, Josiah Lane, to construct a romantic grotto on his estate in 1784 and no doubt Lane would have hired the Jay family for the masonry work with their quarry the closest to the estate. The young Jay would have likely remained a stone mason had it not been for the Evangelical revival sweeping through England.

The Revival began as early as 1740 through the influence of George Whitefield, and the Wesley brothers, John and Charles. All three were staunch Anglicans and sought to renew the spirit of the church by promoting the Evangelical criteria of conversion, (an experience of change or as described by the Evangelicals a 'new birth'), Biblicism (the view that the Bible was the absolute and infallible source of all religious authority), crucicentrism (an emphasis on the atoning sacrifice of Jesus Christ on the cross in order to have a right relationship to God), and activism (the desire to see the world transformed through the Evangelical witness).[8] Both the Wesleys and Whitefield had considerable influence in the south west of England; Whitefield through his tireless outdoor preaching and the Wesley brothers through the organisation of their religious

*Yours most affectionately
in H^t Jesus
George Whitefield*

fig 2: The Reverend George Whitefield
Bath in Time - Bath Central Library Collection

94

societies. Both were considered Methodist. Yet each promoted a different conflicting theological mind-set. Whitefield advocated Calvinism and the Wesleys advocated Armenianism. But it was Whitefield's ecumenical spirit that leapt the boundaries of Anglicanism into Nonconformity [**fig. 2**]. The Evangelicalism of Whitefield ignited the Revival fire in later-eighteenth-century Dissent. Preachers associated with Whitefield's connection began a strong itinerant ministry in Gloucestershire, Somerset, and Wiltshire.

As a young child, Jay had been deeply interested in spiritual things. He caught the eye of the pastor of the Presbyterian chapel in Tisbury. The lad was attentive in church but also quite restless and unsatisfied. Jay was under conviction of sin and felt what he called 'deficiencies in regard to duty' and 'dissatisfied with the state of my heart towards God'. It was at this time his minister placed a letter in his hands announcing the formation of a Calvinistic Methodist chapel in Tisbury. The chapel was a plant by Thomas Turner and his wife Joanna, of Trowbridge. Both were disciples of Whitefield. Thomas Turner was originally a native of Tisbury whose business removed him to Trowbridge and found modest success. Prior to her marriage Joanna (1732-84) and her cousin, Jonathan Clark (1745-1809), planted The Tabernacle in Trowbridge in 1771.[9] Joanna married Thomas Turner at age 38 and together the couple were led through prayer to plant a new work in Thomas' native Tisbury. They purchased a private dwelling and had it licensed for worship in 1781.[10] Thomas returned to Trowbridge to continue in his business affairs while Joanna his wife remained in Tisbury to superintend the work of the chapel, enlisting the aid of itinerant preachers from Whitefield's Tabernacle in London. Jay attended the first service held on a Saturday evening and was struck with 'the singing, the extemporaneousness of the address, and the apparent affection and earnestness of the speaker'.[11] He said it was like 'rain upon the mown grass, or cold water to a thirsty soul'. He attended the early service the following morning. The congregation met at seven a.m. so as not to interfere with the services of the Establishment. Joanna Turner who was opening the chapel met him at the door. From that point the two struck up a cordial friendship. She would meet him as he was returning home from work at Fonthill and the two of them would talk about the things of God. Turner enjoyed watching Jay's growth and recorded in her diary the zeal of the young man who, after hearing a sermon on family worship, confronted his father that he should be having devotions with his family. Through tears Jay's father confessed his inability to perform the function, so the son led the family in worship.[12] Jay was only thirteen years of age at the time.

One of the preachers itinerating at the new chapel was Cornelius Winter (1742-1807). He was the protégé of George Whitefield, even accompanying the evangelists on his final trip to America. Winter had opened a Dissenting academy in Marlborough to train young men for ministry. On his first supply to Tisbury he noticed the attentiveness of a young man who always attended the services in his white-leather mason's apron. While not knowing the identity of the boy it left an impression which led Winter to consider asking the boy to attend his academy. A year later he returned to Tisbury to preach again. When Joanna Turner met him, she said she wanted to introduce a young man for consideration to attend his school. When Jay was presented to him, he realised it was the same boy he had been considering and was moved to tears. Presenting the young Jay to Winter was most likely Joanna Turner's final service for God. She died of breast cancer at the end of 1784. Jay began his career as an Evangelical preacher under the guidance of Winter.

Jay entered the academy at Marlborough in the spring of 1785. Winter's school, as acknowledged by the editors of Jay's autobiography, was untypical of the academies of the day. The school was small and never had more than twelve students at a time. Winter's philosophy of education was based more on mentoring young men than lectures. The emphasis was on practical preparation for the ministry. Priority was given to providing opportunities to gain experience in preaching. But Jay still had instruction. He was required to learn Greek, Hebrew and Latin. Winter placed a high value on learning. He had his students even reading and reciting their lessons on horseback. But Winter also sent his students throughout Wiltshire to preach the Gospel in the villages. Jay estimated that by the age of eighteen he had already preached nearly 1,000 sermons. It was a time when itinerant preaching was not welcomed, particularly that of Dissenting preachers. But Jay met with little opposition when he preached in the villages. It also became apparent that Jay had a natural ability that others did not readily possess. He was known for

fig 3: Original Chapel at Christian Malford, Wilts where William Jay commenced his Ministerial career
Bath in Time - Bath Central Library Collection

his directness and style. On appearing in Melksham to supply the pulpit, a London gentleman informed him that beardless boys should not be preaching. Jay replied 'Sir, had my master supposed you wanted a beard, he would have sent you a goat.'[13] The young man remained under the tutelage of Winter for two years which Jay considered the most influential of his life. Jay developed a passion for preaching that would shape his identity for the rest of his life.

Winter had arranged for Jay to be the continued supply for the chapel at Christian-Malford [fig. 3]. Winter had planted a work there prior to coming to Marlborough. It was while Jay was here that Winter recommended the nineteen-year-old to fill Rowland Hill's pulpit in Surrey Chapel, London for eight weeks. Jay was such a success that, after his first sermon, people followed him to the house he was residing and would not disperse until he addressed the crowd from the windows. His preaching was so sensational it drew other Evangelicals of note. The Baptist, J.C. Ryland of Bristol (1723-92) and the Anglicans John Newton (1725-1807), of Amazing Grace fame, and Richard Cecil (1748-1810) from the Eclectic Society and perhaps most importantly Rev. Thomas Tuppen (1742-90) from the fledgling Independent chapel in Bath, all came to hear the young preacher during his eight week engagement. Rowland Hill immediately contracted him to fill his pulpit for eight weeks in late Summer for the next 40 years. Jay would have continuous access to a London pulpit for the remainder of his life.

Jay returned from the metropolis to complete a brief settlement in Christian-Malford. Through Winter's connections, the young man [fig. 4] had made the acquaintance of Lady Maxwell in Bristol. She recruited him to supply Hope Chapel in Hotwells, Clifton. Lady Maxwell was a devout Wesleyan Arminian. But in deference to the deceased Chapel patronesses, Lady Hope and Lady Glenorchy, she agreed to provide Calvinstic Methodist pastors in the pulpit. Jay supplied the chapel for 12 months with an offer to remain the chapel's full time pastor. This would have been quite a coup for the young pastor. In the last few decades of the century, the Hotwells [fig. 5] had become the most fashionable spa in England, even surpassing Bath in its exclusiveness. At the time, Jay had a good stipend, a place to build his reputation, and a fashionable audience with whom to preach. But Jay chose to leave Hope Chapel for the Argyle Chapel in Bath [fig. 6]. There appear to be two

fig 4: Revd. Mr William Jay aged 19, October 4th 1788
Bath in Time - Bath Central Library Collection

reasons for this. The first is when Jay preached to the good people at Argyle Chapel, he felt himself 'at home' and in the place he was designed to be. Secondly, and most importantly, Hope Chapel had a 'sub-governess' who kept trying to dictate doctrinal points to Jay.[14] Jay's son noted he could not tolerate 'female ecclesiastical rule, whether supreme or subordinate.'[15] Jay's obedience to his principles turned out to be providential. Within eight short years the Hotwells ceased to be the fashionable resort of the elites. Its famous hotels became deserted and abandoned.

Eighteenth-Century Bath

By the mid-eighteenth century, Bath had become a leisure city to indulge the senses. Every form of entertainment and vice was offered in Bath. Balls were regularly held at the assembly rooms in which visitors hoped to catch glimpses of those above their social station. When not at a ball, visitors might enjoy the theatre with performances by the famous actor Sarah Siddons. Or they might take in a concert to hear Handel or Paganini. Even as late as 1830, it was reported, 'the concerts were unrivalled, the theatre second only to London'.[16] Yet there

fig 5: Approach to the Hotwell House, Bristol, 1792
Bath in Time - Bath Central Library Collection

was also a seedy underside to Bath. Vices such as gambling, pornography, and prostitution were readily available. The Rev. John Skinner (1772-1839), a Somerset rector of nearby Camerton, commented 'I was a little astonished, as I walked through Bath, to observe the streets so crowded with prostitutes, some of them apparently not above 14 or 15 years of age.'[17] Charles Wesley (1707-88) called Bath Satan's 'head- quarters'. He ordered a Wesleyan society member to leave the city quoting the scripture text, 'Depart, I pray you, from the tents of wicked men, and touch nothing of theirs, lest you be consumed with their sins.'[18] Eighteenth-century Bath was the place to be seen. The total number of visitors distinguished enough to be listed in the *Bath Journal* rose from 510 in 1746 to 5,341 in 1801.[19] Historian R.S. Neale estimated that by 1800 there were some 40,000 visitors a year with an average weekly attendance of 8,000 over the season. The purpose of Bath was to offer pleasure to a British society beginning to be consumed with the concept of leisure. The city of Bath was its major supplier.

Not only were visitors increasing but the resident population grew. The resident population of Bath was around 6,000 in the middle of the century and nearly 34,000 by the century's end.[20] From that point its population rate increased an additional 20,000 by 1851.[21] The dramatic population change in the middle decades of the eighteenth century was not due to an increase of the elites but to an influx of genteel retirees mostly made up of spinsters, widows, clergy, admirals, generals and lesser pensioned officers. Bath became an attractive place which to retire not only due to the glamorous activities of the social elite, but also to a lower cost of living. Bath had lower municipal, water, and poor rates than London.[22] Magazine articles touted

Bath as not only a beautiful city for retirement but also providing the opportunity to be surrounded by the right sort of people.[23] It was the perfect place for Trollope's spinster, Miss Mackenzie to settle. Bath was the tenth largest city in England in the first half of the nineteenth century. Up till Jay's death in 1853, Bath was considered one of the greater cities of Britain.

The complaint against religious Bath was not necessarily its lack of activity, but its lack of sincerity in religion. The complaints came mainly from Evangelicals. George Whitefield (1714-70) [fig. 2] was welcomed into the city in 1737 and even allowed to preach at the Abbey Church on five different occasions. But two years later he found the pulpits closed to him.[24] The resistance to Evangelicalism seemed to stem from a fear of

Argyle Chapel, Bath.

fig 6: Argyle Chapel, Bath Exterior, 1841
Bath in Time - Bath Central Library Collection

upsetting the present state of affairs in Bath. Whitefield wrote, 'Many adversaries must be expected in so polite a place as Bath.'[25] When John Wesley (1703-91) [fig. 7] began preaching in Bath, he was confronted by Beau Nash (1674-1761) demanding to know what authority he had to be preaching in the city. Nash was concerned that Wesley's 'preaching frightens people out of their wits.'[26] Though the churches were filled to capacity it was obvious that the combined sittings of the four churches and two proprietary chapels (some 3,000) were hardly enough to meet the needs of the city's resident population (some 6,000 in 1750) plus the annual visitors to the city (some 2,500 in 1760). The best attended church, St James, did not have sermons but only read prayers till the early nineteenth century.[27] Wesley was disturbed by the complete lack of seriousness of the Christians that lived there. He was prompted to ask in his journal, 'Hath God left himself without witness?'[28] Both the Wesley brothers and Whitefield used the same word in describing Bath in their journals: 'Sodom'. Jay arrived in Bath at a time ripe for Evangelical influence. And unlike Hotwells, Bath maintained its popularity to both the upper and middle classes well into the nineteenth century. Whitefield prayed in 1739 that God would send Bath 'some faithful labourer'.[29] His prayer would be answered 50 years later in William Jay.

When Jay arrived at the Argyle Chapel, there were only three other evangelical causes in Bath. The Baptist had been the first to establish a cause in Bath as early as 1718 that would eventually evolve into the Somerset Street Chapel. But near the time of Jay's arrival there was a public dispute between the Pastor John Paul Porter and the previous pastor's son, Thomas Parson. Many of the church members left the Baptist Chapel transferring to Argyle Chapel shortly after Jay's arrival.

According to his journals, John Wesley made 100 visits to Bath over a span of fifty-one years.[30] While he had great success in attracting large crowds to his preaching, he made little progress in attracting people to the local Methodist society. Charles Wesley, on his visit in 1741, remarked, 'Satan took it ill to be attacked in his head-quarters … he raged horribly in his children.'[31] The first Methodist society met in a room on Avon Street, the poorest community in Bath. In 1755 the membership was no more than thirty-five.[32] Two years later a class list showed there were only seventeen members with all but three residing on Avon Street.[33] By autumn 1769 there were only eleven or twelve.[34] Wesley seemed to attribute the decrease to the opening of the Countess of Huntingdon's chapel in the Vineyards. He lamented in 1765 he had only the poor to hear him preach at Avon Street 'there being a service at the same time in Lady H's chapel.'[35]

The Countess of Huntingdon [fig. 8] had George Whitefield open her Chapel in the Vineyards in 1765. It appears the Countess tried to micro-

fig 7: The Reverend John Wesley A.M. 1792
Bath in Time - Bath Central Library Collection

manage her chapel and several members of the Vineyard seceded in 1783 to form what would become an Independent Chapel. The first full time pastor of this independent chapel was a convert of Whitefield, the Rev. Thomas Tuppen of Portsea, who accepted the pastorate in 1785. The congregation increased under his leadership and relocated from the premises of the old Roman Catholic chapel on St. James' Parade to a new Chapel being erected on Argyle Street in Bathwick just across the Pulteney Bridge. Tuppen became terminally ill and was unable to preach. Tuppen remembered Jay at Surrey Chapel and recommended the young man to fill the pulpit during his absence. Jay did such an excellent job that he was asked to open the Chapel in October of 1789. Tuppen died soon afterwards and Jay was unanimously asked to be the Pastor of the new Chapel.

Prior to being ordained, Jay courted Anne Davies, the daughter of Edward Davies, an evangelical clergyman in London. Davies had been in Wales and was well connected to the Calvinistic Methodist revival. Again, Jay met the family on his first visit to London when he preached at Rowland Hill's chapel. Edward Davies received a special dispensation to become the curate of St. Catherine's Church in Batheaston in 1790. Upon that news the couple became engaged. They were married on January 6, 1791 by Rowland Hill. They purchased a home at Percy Place, exactly one mile from the Argyle Chapel and the Davies' home in Batheaston. The couple maintained a residence at this address all their lives.

Jay was ordained Pastor of Argyle Chapel three weeks later on January 30 1791, and would continue as pastor until shortly before his death for a period of sixty-two years. The key factor that made relationship between the chapel and Jay so successful was the commitment of both to Evangelicalism. At his ordination at Argyle, he defined their mission, 'The glorious Gospel of the blessed God our Saviour is the great object of our attention as minister and people; this only am I allowed to preach, this only are you allowed to hear.'[36] Early in Argyle's ministry, Jay's friend William Wilberforce reminded him of the unique opportunity he had in Bath when people visit the chapel. 'Consider the situation in which you stand,' wrote Wilberforce, 'there was not another minister in Bath, whom any of *the poor wretched upper classes* are likely to hear, who preaches the Gospel.' *The Bath and Cheltenham Gazette* confirmed the 'Establishment presented few attractions' to those of its Evangelical members prior to Jay's arrival.[37] Argyle Chapel was in a perfect site between the shops in Bath and the new elite homes growing in Bathwick along Great Pulteney Street. The location of the Chapel offered a steady stream of 'sinners' crossing the Pulteney Bridge into town to whom Jay could preach and influence.

And the upper classes did come. The masses flocked to the Argyle Chapel not only on Sabbath Day services but also on the week night services. The guests included the upper strata of society. Sir Richard Hill (1732-1808), Lady Duncan (1748-1832), the wife of Admiral Lord Duncan, the Earl of Gainsborough (1781-1866), Sir William Knighton (1776-1836), physician to George IV all worshipped at the chapel.[38] He attracted visitors both far and near. Henry Johns (1803-59), chaplain of the United States Senate, reflected fondly on having the opportunity to hear Jay in his chapel.[39] Not unusual was the case of the successful clothier, William Henry Tucker (1814-77), who as a young man walked from Trowbridge to Bath, a distance of 10 miles, to hear the celebrated preacher.[40] Some visitors attended the chapel on a regular basis. The abolitionists, William Wilberforce (1759-1833) and Evangelical philanthropist, Hannah More (1745-1833) [**fig. 9**], attended

fig 8: Countess of Huntingdon, by Benjamin West. Pen and brown ink and (graphite?) on laid paper
National Gallery of Art, Washington, John Davis Hatch Collection

the chapel on their frequent visits to Bath.[41] When his own congregation became dissatisfied with his preaching, Thomas Haweis (1734-1820), a founder of the London Missionary Society, left the Countess of Huntingdon's Chapel to worship at the Argyle Chapel until his death. The Anglican clergy came as well. Bishop Walter Shirley (1797-1847) and Charles Simeon all came to hear Jay on their visits to Bath. Richard Cecil even rented a chapel pew for his daughter during the season she visited Bath. Other celebrities attended. The celebrated actor Charles Young (1777-1856) frequented the chapel.[42] Richard Sheridan (1755-1816) called Jay the most natural orator he had ever heard.[43] Jay had not only established Evangelicalism in Bath. He had made it fashionable to be seen in his chapel.

fig 9: Hannah More (1745-1833), by Henry William Pickersgill, Oil on canvas
National Portrait Gallery, London

Jay became nationally known for his preaching. The Argyle Chapel became flooded with visitors to hear the young preacher. The chapel had to be enlarged to accommodate the listeners. [fig. 10] [44] Even as late as 1851, the Argyle Chapel had the greatest attendance of any Chapel or Church in Bath on census Sunday. At 1,400 listeners it was filled to capacity. His sermons were well received in print. He published his first collection of sermons in 1804 and went on to publish an additional eleven volumes. In 1810, he was awarded an Honorary Doctorate from Princeton University for his publication, *Short Discourses to be Read in Families*. His services were engaged all over the nation. He was asked to preach numerous ordinations, chapel openings and collection sermons. He made preaching tours of Ireland and Scotland. He was the first Congregationalist to preach at the Baptist Missionary Society and at the Wesleyan Missionary Society. He is the only person to have to have preached on five occasions at the annual meeting of the London Missionary Society. On the last occasion, people arrived several hours early to make sure they had a seat and 'thousands' were turned away for lack of space.[45] Jay as a preacher was a national sensation.

The members of the Argyle Chapel are also not to be overlooked. The chapel roll listed the movers and shakers among Bath business men. Early in the chapel's history were men such as the Ironmonger, Samuel Whitchurch (1755-1817) who initiated the Bath Sunday School Union and was secretary of the Bath Penitentiary. Whitchurch and his partner were part of the elite few who were able to issue tokens during the small currency crisis of the first decade of the century. Thomas Parsons (1744-1813) left Somerset Street Baptist Chapel to join the Argyle Chapel. Parson was a founding member of the Bath and West Society and an outspoken pacifist.

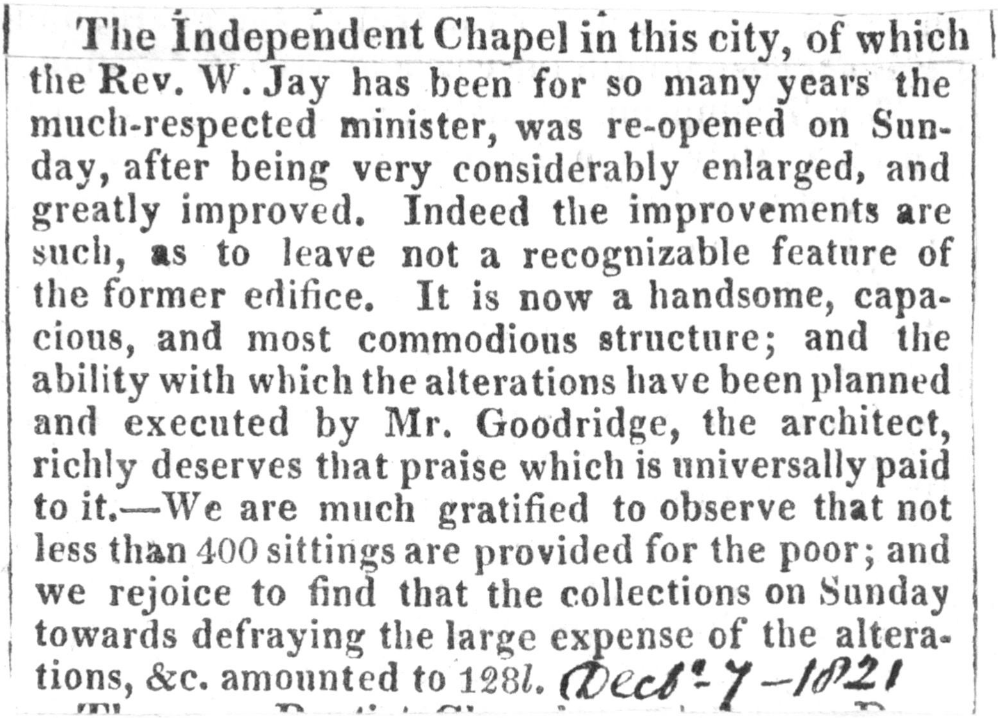

The Independent Chapel in this city, of which the Rev. W. Jay has been for so many years the much-respected minister, was re-opened on Sunday, after being very considerably enlarged, and greatly improved. Indeed the improvements are such, as to leave not a recognizable feature of the former edifice. It is now a handsome, capacious, and most commodious structure; and the ability with which the alterations have been planned and executed by Mr. Goodridge, the architect, richly deserves that praise which is universally paid to it.—We are much gratified to observe that not less than 400 sittings are provided for the poor; and we rejoice to find that the collections on Sunday towards defraying the large expense of the alterations, &c. amounted to 128*l*. *Decr 7 – 1821*

fig 10: Argyle Chapel reopens after being improved and enlarged, December 7th 1821
Bath in Time - Bath Central Library Collection

In its later years, the chapel could boast the membership of iron founder, Henry Stothert, architect H.E. Goodridge (1797-1864), and the bookseller Charles Godwin (who was also friends with William Wordsworth). The middle class membership of Argyle matched the prestige of their pastor.

The influence of the Argyle Chapel and its pastor was staggering. Together they led the way as Evangelical activity broke out en mass at the turn of the century. The Chapel began the first Dissenting Sunday School for Children in 1802 and jointly formed the Bath Sunday School Union in 1812 with the Methodists. Bath Adult Schools were opened to teach adults how to read the Bible in 1814.[46] Within the city, the Bath Tract Society was formed in 1827.[47] Together with Thomas Haweis of the Vineyard, Jay founded the auxiliary of the London Missionary Society in 1816 (later the Bath Missionary Society). Also, Jay was instrumental in the formation of the British and Foreign Bible Society in 1812 giving the church a wider scope for outreach beyond the city. Together with Somerset Street Baptist Chapel, the Argyle Chapel planted a dissenting interest in Widcombe and in Combe Down. Jay was also a founder of the Wiltshire and East Somerset Congregational Union having a wider effect of Evangelicalism in surrounding communities.[48] Even Jay marvelled at the transformation of Bath over forty years. As long as Evangelical conversion remained the focus, the church and pastor stayed in perfect harmony. 'The cause here,' Jay proudly proclaimed on his fortieth anniversary, 'having been a candlestick holding out the light to others.'[49] At the time of Jay's death, Argyle Chapel could boast no less than five evangelical organisations operating on the chapel premises. Both Jay and his congregation believed together they would accomplish great things for God in the spirit of Evangelicalism.

The effect of all this activity was apparent in its criticism and assimilation. The Rev. Richard Warner (1763-1853) of St. James' Church attacked Evangelical ministers 'for their want of humility and charity' in that they thought they alone were correct in their interpretation of scripture and that only the converted are saved.[50] But the adage of 'if you can't beat them, join them', came into play. In 1828 the Church Missionary Society invited the highly Evangelical clergyman, Edward Bickersteth (1786-1850), to speak at its Bath meeting.[51] A letter to the editor of the Bath and Cheltenham Gazette, signed 'A member of the Church of England', complained that unlike the Dissenting Chapels there were no churches that offered services on weekday evenings.[52] More Evangelical clergymen were appointed to Bath Anglican pulpits. By 1840, an open letter to the mayor complained, 'the clergy of this town for a long time past, but particularly more recently, by their preaching and exhortations, to endeavour to suppress the various amusements of this place; and indeed so comprehensive have been their denunciations, that scarcely an entertainment of public character of which the inhabitants were won't to partake, has escaped; concerts, balls, races, theatrical exhibitions, and even horticultural shows, have each of them in turn been the subjects of clerical vengeance and pulpit anathematisation. The clergy of this city, of nearly all denominations, but particularly

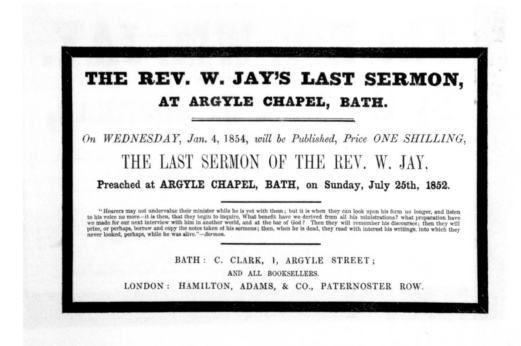

fig 11: Advertisement for the sale of Revd. W. Jay's last sermon, preached on July 25th 1852
Bath in Time - Bath Central Library Collection

those of the established church, have been unremitting in their exhortations to their various flocks to discountenance these entertainments ... the terrible condemnation to eternal punishment itself, has been held out as the consequence to all those who may give these scenes of pleasure their countenance.'[53]

The first meeting of the Evangelical Alliance of all denomination in Bath occurred in January, 1848. Yet, the following week, Francis Close, the Evangelical Rector of Cheltenham was advocating separation apart from the Dissenters who seemed to be reaping all the rewards.[54] Evangelicalism had become a formidable movement within the Established Church as well.

It is clear Evangelicalism was in the ascendancy in nineteenth-century Bath. Prior to 1780, the Evangelical movement had made little impact on the City. The catalyst for the change appears to be the arrival of William Jay. The young preacher had all the tools to make such a change possible. He was a local Wiltshire product who had deep connections to the Evangelicalism of George Whitefield. He was a gifted orator that even attracted the admiration of the theatrical community. He had direct connection to the influential London Evangelicals through his annual preaching engagements at Surrey Chapel. He was embraced by Evangelicals in the Establishment as well Dissent. He arrived at a critical moment as the population of Bath began to swell with the genteel class who would find great appeal in the activism of Evangelicalism. And while the Argyle Chapel had great financial resources and leadership within the membership, they had yet to make an impression among the fashionable elite. Jay bridged that gap. As Jay's celebrity grew nationally through his preaching and publishing, so did the chapels reputation. The Argyle Chapel became the Evangelical attraction in Bath. By the end of Jay's career [fig. 11] there was a distinct Evangelical presence in Bath to justify Trollope's nineteenth-century characterisation of the city.

Notes

1. Trollope, Anthony. *Miss Mackenzie*. (London: Oxford University Press, 1950), p. 17.
2. Ibid., pp. 19-20.
3. Ibid., p. 32.
4. See Jeremy, David. 'The Social Decline of Bath', *History Today*, 17 (1967): pp. 242-249, Graham Davis and Penny Bonsall. *A History of Bath: Image and Reality*, (Lancaster: Carnegie Publishing, 2006), pp. 217-245, and P.T.Phillips, 'The Religious Side of Victorian Bath, 1830-1870', *Social History*, 6 (1973): pp. 224-40.
5. Christabel Dale, *Wiltshire Apprentices and Their Masters, 1710-1760*. Devizes: Wiltshire Archaeological and Natural History Society, 1961, p. 83.
6. Lease grant of Lord Arundell to William Jay, Tisbury, February 9th 1765, WSHC 2667/1/13/285.
7. Redford, George and James, J.A. *The Autobiography of William Jay*. Edinburgh: Banner of Truth Trust, 1974, p. 17.
8. This article follows David Bebbington's quadrilateral theory of Evangelicalism found in David Bebbington, *Evangelicalism in Modern Britain*. (London: Unwin Hyman, 1989), p.3.
9. Mary Wells, *Memoirs of Mrs. Joanna Turner, as Exemplified in Her Life, Death and Spiritual Experience*. New York: John Midwinter, 1827, p. 120.
10. D.A. Crowley, 'Tisbury' in D.A. Crowley, (ed.), Victoria History of the Counties of England, History of Wiltshire, Vol.13, (Oxford University Press, 1987), p. 245.
11. Ibid., p. 23.
12. Wells, *Memoirs of Mrs. Joanna Turner*, p. 186.
13. Redford, *Autobiography*, p. 44.
14. Jay, *Recollections of William Jay of Bath*. (London: Hamilton, Adams and Co., (1859), p.12.
15. Redford, *Autobiography*, p. 65.
16. *Bath and Cheltenham Gazette*, January 12th 1830.
17. Coombs, Howard and Coombs, Peter, (eds), *Journal of a Somerset Rector*, *1803-1834*. (Bath: Kingsmead Press, 1930), p. 395.
18. Thomas Jackson, (ed.), *The Journal of Charles Wesley*. Vol. 1. (Grand Rapids: Baker Books, 1980), pp. 285-286; Biblical reference Numbers 26:26.
19. Davis, *A History of Bath*, p. 112.
20. R.E.Peach, *The Historic Houses of Bath*. (London: Simpkin, Marshall & Co., 1883). Xiv.
21. Davis, *A History of Bath*, p. 159.
22. Mary Ede, 'Bath and The Great Exhibition of 1851', *Bath History*, 3 (1990), p. 50.
23. Davis and Bonsall, *A History of Bath*, pp. 153-154.
24. George Whitefield, *George Whitefield's Journals*. (Edinburgh: Banner of Truth, 1978), pp. 82-84; p. 213.
25. Ibid., p. 232.
26. Richard Watson, *The Life of the Rev. John Wesley*. (New York: B. Waugh & T. Mason, 1836), p. 75.
27. Mitchell, *Letters from Bath*, p. 44.
28. Joseph Benson, (ed.), *The Works of John Wesley, Vol. 2*. (London: Conference Office, 1809), p.122.
29. Whitefield, *Journals*, p. 236.
30. Bruce Crofts, (ed.), *At Satan's Throne: The Story of Methodism in Bath over 250 Years*. (Bristol: White Tree Books, 1990), p. 13.
31. Thomas Jackson, (ed.), *The Journal of the Rev. Charles Wesley, Vol. 1*. (Grand Rapids: Baker Book House, 1980), p. 286.

32. Croft, *At Satan's Throne*, p. 25.

33. R.S. Neale, *Bath: A Social History, 1680-1850*. (London: Routledge & Keene, 1981), p. 29.

34. Croft, *At Satan's Throne*, p. 29

35. Nehemiah Curnock, (ed.), *The Journals of the Rev. John Wesley, A.M., Vol. 5.* (London: Charles H. Kelly, 1901), pp. 148-149.

36. Jay, *Autobiography*, p. 72.

37. *Bath and Cheltenham Gazette* January 4th 1854.

38. Jay, *Recollections*, p. 142 and Godwin, 'Reminisces of William Jay' Ms., Central United Reform Church, pp. 46-47.

39. Redford, *Autobiography*, pp. 221-224.

40. Helen Rogers, (ed.), *The Diary of William Henry Tucker, 1825-1850*. (Chippenham: Wiltshire Record Society, 2009), p. 22.

41. Jay, *Recollections*, p. 16 and Redford, *Autobiography*, p. 321.

42. Thomas Wallace, *A Portraiture of the Late William Jay of Bath*. (London: Arthur Hall, Virtue & Co., 1854), pp. 37-38.

43. Jay, *Recollections*, p. 346.

44. Mary Ede. *The Chapel in Argyle Street, Bath 1789-1989*. (Bath: Central United Reformed Church, 1989), p. 14.

45. *Missionary Magazine & Chronicle* (1844), p. 161.

46. *Bath and Cheltenham Chronicle*, December 13th 1815.

47. *Bath and Cheltenham Gazette*, January 15th 1828.

48. Wiltshire and East Somerset Association Minute Book, July 5th 1997, WSHC 2755/1.

49. William Jay, 'The Retrospect. A Sermon Preached at Argyle Chapel, Bath on Sunday Morning, January 30th, 1831, being the Fortieth Anniversary of His Ordination', *The Pulpit*, 425 (1831), p. 170.

50. *Bath and Cheltenham Gazette,* July 1st 1828.

51. *Bath and Cheltenham Gazette*, 1 April 1st 1828.

52. *Bath and Cheltenham Gazette*, February 12th 1828.

53. LUD HUDIBRAS. *A Letter to the Mayor of Bath, on the Causes of the Present Declining Condition of the City*, (Bath: Williams and Thorley, 1840), p. 11.

54. *Bath and Cheltenham Gazette*, January 19th and 26th 1848.

Green Park: Residence, Residents and Change in the 19th century

Alan Thwaite

Green Park Buildings – a micro study

Before it was bombed in 1942, number 6 Green Park Buildings displayed a bronze plaque telling us that essayist Thomas de Quincey had lived there. His mother, the relatively well-off, widowed Mrs Quinsey [*sic*] rented this new house from 1797 until 1801, while Thomas was a pupil at King Edward's School.[1] Three years later, in 1804, George Austen, his wife, and his two daughters, Cassandra and novelist Jane, moved into number 3. Who else lived in Green Park Buildings, for how long, and what residential changes took place? This essay aims to answer these and other questions through a micro study of social structural change from Georgian to late Victorian Bath, through the focus on the inhabitants in this street.

The view is set against the broader background of the city, particularly that described in Graham Davis and Penny Bonsall's *A History of Bath: Image and Reality*.[2] Chapter 5 looks at the city

fig 1: Green Park Buildings, Bath, pub. 16 July 1860. Steel engraving
Bath in Time - Bath Central Library Collection

Facing: Green Park Buildings, 1969. Photograph by Lesley Green-Armytage
Bath in Time - Bath Preservation Trust: Building of Bath Collection

between 1820 and 1910, as a place of 'Genteel Residence' and an emergent small-scale industrial city. Bath was undergoing significant change. The population increased by two-fifths from 1811 to 1851, suburbs were built, and there were changes to transport, including the arrival of three railways between 1840 and 1874. Abandoned by the aristocracy, it was no longer a fashionable place to visit and attempts at revival were largely unsuccessful. Increasingly, however, the wealthy upper class, and later the middle classes began choosing it for long-term residence.

At the time construction of Green Park Buildings commenced, Shropshire visitor Katherine Plymley recorded in her diary: 'Bath is on the whole a good retreat for elderly ladies, elderly gentlemen, widows, and single women'. She could have added retired military officers and clergymen. [3]

Numbers - Houses, Population, Males and Females.

Green Park Buildings was constructed on land known as Kingsmead, west of Bath city centre, outside the city walls and on the flood plain of the River Avon, not an ideal place to erect houses [fig. 1]. Building work began at a bad time; there was a severe financial crisis,

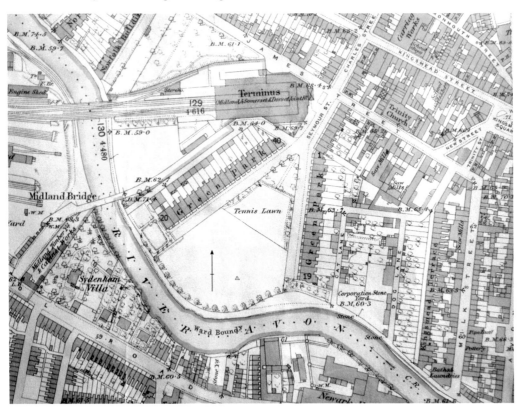

fig 2: Green Park Buildings, East and West (with numbers indicated in blue), 1881 Ordnance Survey
Bath Central Library Collection

which lasted for well over ten years. This bankrupted speculators, builders and two of Bath's banks. It is not surprising, therefore, that it took from c.1793 until 1809 before all forty houses were complete. A *Bath Chronicle* advertisement for a sale at the White Hart Inn in June 1794 exemplifies the problems: 'Property: Fennell bankruptcy, contd - lot 1/3, f/hold dwelling house being erected & known as 6 Green Park Bldgs, Bath …' [4] Early residents, whatever their status, lived adjacent to a building site for many years.

Originally, there were two uneven rows, diverging southwards from Seymour Street to the River Avon. Both rows had smaller and larger four-storey houses with basements and vaults. The eastern row (now demolished) was always consecutively numbered 1 to 19, from the north. The western row, initially 1 to 21 in the same direction, was renumbered 20 to 40, the opposite (present) way, in 1830. Here, the later numbers, are used as shown on the map, and the present name, 'Green Park'. [fig. 2]. [5]

From completion in 1809 to the 1841 census, rate books indicate that, essentially, all houses were continuously occupied. From 1841 to 1911 only the 1861 census, with 290 residents, the highest recorded, showed every house occupied. This accounted for approximately 0.5% of Bath's population. [6]

If population numbers in Green Park were similar at the beginning and middle of the nineteent-century, early totals would have been about 280. Table 1 shows the variations in population, the average numbers of people per house and information about the numbers of men and women. These figures hide large differences: for example, Ann Errington's 'Boarding Academy' at number 22, had twenty residents in 1851 while at number 4, in 1901, there was only a lone lodging-house keeper.

Table 1   Green Park Buildings   Census Data   Houses, Population, Males and Females

Census	1841	%	1851	%	1861	%	1871	%	1881	%	1891	%	1901	%	1911	%
Total Houses	40		40		40		40		40		40		40		40	
No. Houses occ	38		39		40		37		36		32		34		30	
Total population	262		266		292		260		255		232		186		157	
Ave per house	6.9		6.8		7.3		7.0		7.1		7.3		5.5		5.2	
FullHseEqiv (Ave x 40)	276		273		292		281		283		290		219		209	
Head of hshld (HoH)	39	14.9	46	17.3	54	18.5	41	15.8	39	15.3	32	13.8	31	16.7	28	17.8
Males (HoH)	21	8.0	22	8.3	24	8.2	21	8.1	25	9.8	18	7.8	23	12.4	21	13.4
Females (HoH)	18	6.9	24	9.0	30	10.3	20	7.7	14	5.5	14	6.0	8	4.3	7	4.5
Prportn Fem. HoH	0.46		0.52		0.56		0.49		0.36		0.44		0.26		0.25	
Males Total	56	21.4	52	19.5	62	21.2	61	23.5	63	24.7	50	21.6	49	26.3	47	29.9
Females Total	206	78.6	214	80.5	230	78.8	199	76.5	192	75.3	182	78.4	137	73.7	110	70.1
Married			23	8.6	29	9.9	27	10.4	23	9.0	21	9.1	22	11.8	26	16.6
% Married/All F				10.7		12.6		13.6		12.0		11.5		16.1		23.6
Widows			26	9.8	20	6.8	17	6.5	17	6.7	22	9.5	10	5.4	12	7.6
% Widows/All F				12.1		8.7		8.5		8.9		12.1		7.3		10.9
Unmrrd others			165	62.0	181	62.0	155	59.6	152	59.6	139	59.9	105	56.5	72	45.9
% Unmrrd others/ALL M+F				62.03		61.99		59.62		59.61		59.91		56.45		45.86
% Unmrrd others/all F				77.1		78.7		77.9		79.2		76.4		76.6		65.5
Ratio 1M:xF x=	3.7		4.1		3.7		3.3		3.0		3.6		2.8		2.3	
No. of Female-Only houses	9		11		10		9		2		8		6		7	

Rates and directory data from the earliest days indicate, and census data confirm, that females were always by far the greater proportion of residents. Until 1901, they outnumbered males by more than three to one, roughly twice the figure for some parts of Bath. [7] Almost 90 per cent of women, including widows and children, were unmarried. Unsurprisingly, we find that in five out of eight census years, one fifth or more of all occupied houses had only female occupants. Generally, they lived in the smaller properties. These high numbers of single women in Green Park would clearly reinforce any image Bath had as a place for 'maiden aunts' (though how many Green Park actually contributed to that idea is not obvious).

Residents and Residence

Information from directories, newspapers, deeds, wills and family histories gives helpful insight into the origins, backgrounds and occupations of early residents. A clergyman arrived in 1797, two colonels in 1799 and then more clergymen, including the retired George Austen. Other early arrivals were local printer and bookseller, Samuel Hazard, who took in lodgers; Sir William Addington, a retired London lawyer, and the earliest with a title; Lady Louisa Lennox, perhaps the most elevated of all Green Park residents; the Moncks, George and Lady Araminta, who had substantial lands and property in Ireland, and two local attorneys, both involved in transactions

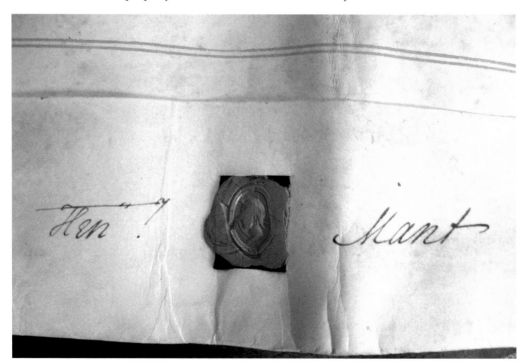

fig 3: The signature and seal of Henry Mant, Attorney, on a 'Grant Release and Assignment' dated 30th June 1802 relating to 4 Green Park Buildings.
Bath Record Office - Bath & North East Somerset Council

relating to properties in Green Park. One of them, Henry Mant, 'Gentleman' and Freeman of the city, owned land in Widcombe. **[fig. 3]**. He also had industrial interests.

Lack of adequate data means that durations of residence can only be determined very approximately. The following statements are, therefore, only indicative. Of 325 selected residents (or families) between 1797 and 1895, a quarter stayed less than two years, half less than five years, and almost three-quarters less than ten years.

Some, like the de Quinceys, moved away; others, like George Monck and the Revd. Austen, died soon after their arrival. Within seven months, after one of the shortest of all stays, the remaining Austens had to move to somewhere cheaper, whilst Lady Araminta and her daughter could afford to stay until Araminta's death in 1818.

In 41 cases residence appears to have exceeded twenty years. Relations succeeded earlier occupants. Henry Mant died in 1845, at the age of 70 after 44 years at number 4, and was followed by descendants. The Trails were next door for 45 years and their Wemyss relations for another fifteen. At number 34 lived the five Ladies Keith **[fig. 4]**, three sisters, a sister-in-law and her daughter, family of the Earl of Kintore, from 1817 until they died, the last in 1864. Other cases include those who lived in more than one house, each for long periods. Priscilla Rowe was there, in two houses, for a total of fifty years. But all were outdone by Cécile, youngest daughter of Roman Catholic, French Revolution refugees, the Marquis Auguste and Marquise Agathé de Sommery. The widowed Agathé, moved to 37 Green Park Buildings with her daughters in 1829. Seventy years later, aged ninety-five, Cécile died at number 35.

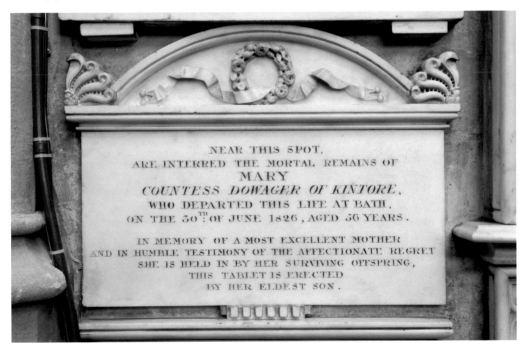

fig 4: Lady Maria (otherwise Mary) Keith-Falconar, née Bannerman, died at 37 Green Park Place, Bath, on 30 June 1826. Memorial Inscription, Bath Abbey

Photograph by Dan Brown

Other residents were well known in the local scene; for instance General Donkin, Henry Mant, and the de Sommerys, who made their mark as vigorous supporters of the new Catholic Church. Fanny Burney records the de Sommerys and the Ladies Keith in her diary, as her friends. [8]

As for Bath being a place for retired military men, Green Park certainly played its part. More than thirty, with ranks from naval captain to admiral and army major to general, lived in one or other of twenty-seven houses at sometime during the century. At the end of the first decade and in the 1840s and 1860s, as many as seven were in residence at a time, but in 1891 only one remained. The most notable may have been General Robert Donkin [fig. 5] and Sir William Napier. Aged 81 in 1808, Donkin became the first occupant of number 17. He died there thirteen years later; St Swithin's Church, Walcot, displays his memorial tablet. Briefly, during 1841, Napier, famous for his history of the Peninsular Wars, lived at number 19. In the 1880s. Surgeon Major T E Hale, awarded the Victoria Cross for Crimean gallantry, lived at number 15.

fig 5: Miniature of General Robert Donkin (1727-1821), born in Morpeth, Northumberland, who was the first occupant of house number 17 in 1808
Holburne Museum, Bath

Clergymen came to Green Park in similar numbers to military men, and lived in as many houses. Davis and Bonsall's *History* explains part of the story: before 1871 the number of clergymen increased as the city grew and new parishes were created. For much of the century, at least three clerics were in residence at any one time. The most erudite was the Revd Dr. William Trail, who, before taking the cloth, had been professor of mathematics at Marischal College, Aberdeen. He retired from the church through ill health then lived at number 3 until eighty-five years old, dying in 1831. Sadly, his memorial in Bath Abbey is obscured. His well-connected wife Lady Frances, daughter of the Earl of Wemyss, remained there until 1848. Two ministers were responsible for new parishes carved from Walcot parish. High-church priest, Father Sissmore, rector of Holy Trinity Church, James Street West, [fig. 2] lived at number 31, a small house, for two decades from 1890. At the same time, Angus Clerk, evangelical vicar of neighbouring St Paul's, on the corner of Monmouth Place and Chapel Row, lived in a larger house, number 12. Others were retired and some, like Morris Yescombe, had 'no cure of souls'. He lived at number 21 for over thirty years from 1854.

Bath had many lodging houses. Green Park sometimes had as many as eight, often run by women. Frequently, they accommodated more than one household. In the mid-century decades, the proportion of 'heads' who were women hovered around half [table 1]. By 1911, it was only a quarter. In 1851 and 1861, widows and unmarried women were practically equal in number (about a dozen of each), then the balance tipped in favour of widows.

A 'Useful Servant'

Throughout the century, the most common single occupation in Green Park was that of servant. Helpfully, Samuel and Sarah Adams' *Complete Servant* of 1825, lists 'the number of servants usually employed, according to income.' With an income of £100 or guineas a year 'a Widow or unmarried lady may keep a Young Maid Servant'. For £200 a year, a couple with no children may afford a 'professed Servant-Maid of All-Work'. A 'Gentleman', with a family and annual income of £500-£600, may have 'three Females and one Man', and so on. Male servants, on whom tax was payable, indicated wealth and status. [9]

At least two-fifths of the Green Park population appear as servants in the four census years from 1841, and it seems reasonable to assume that this was so from the 1790s. Table 2 gives the numbers of male and female servants, the average per house, and how many houses had how many servants, for each census year. There were governesses and housekeepers but most appear simply as 'servant', general or domestic. More specifically, there were house, kitchen, parlour, nurse and ladies' maids. One hopes that each was a 'Useful Maid', as Doctor James Wigmore described his 26-year-old servant Louisa Bray, in 1901. Roughly a fifth were described as 'cook', though others must also have had this responsibility.

The age-range of servants was wide. The four youngest included Annie Snook, aged fourteen, from Bath, Orpha Wilcocks from Durham, Sophy Ashley from Hertfordshire, and Thomas Stanafer from Nantwich, all aged fifteen. Thomas, a page, was one of five servants looking after Augusta Pennington, her two nieces and a nephew at number 19 **[fig. 6]**. At the other end of the scale were Mary Hudson, 73, Hannah Steeds, 77, and Miriam Cordery from Somerset. Employed since before 1851, Miriam was, twenty years later, at the age of 82, still a 'ladies maid' to Mary Pitman, a widow half her age.

Table 2   Green Park Buildings   Census Data   Servant Numbers

Census	1841	%	1851	%	1861	%	1871	%	1881	%	1891		1901	%	1911	%
No. Houses occupied	38		39		40		37		36		32		34		30	
Total GP Population	262		266		292		260		255		232		186		157	
% Srvts-ALL / GP ppln.	119	45.4	118	44.4	122	41.8	113	43.5	76	29.4	84	38.2	54	29.0	36	22.9
No. / House	3.13		3.03		3.05		3.05		2.11		2.63		1.59		1.20	
Male Servants / % GP Popln	15	5.7	16	6.0	9	3.1	7	2.7	1	0.4	1	0.4	0	0.0	0	0.0
Female Srvnts / % GP Popln	104	39.7	102	38.3	113	38.7	106	40.8	76	29.8	83	35.8	54	29.0	36	22.9
No./Hse	2.7		2.6		2.8		2.9		2.1		2.6		1.6		1.2	
% F-Servt/All Females		50.0		47.7		49.1		53.3		38.5		45.6		39.4		32.7
No. of Houses with																
0 servants	1		1		0		2		2		2		7		11	
1 servants	1		0		5		1		7		1		10		10	
2 servants	10		10		6		7		12		11		9		5	
3 servants	11		20		16		16		12		12		6		4	
4 servants	12		3		8		7		1		5		2		0	
5 servants	1		4		5		2		1		1		0		0	
6 servants	2		1		0		2		1		0		0		0	
No. of Vacant Houses	2		1		0		3		4		8		6		10	

Successive census data are revealing in measuring social change over the Victorian period and in the personal lives of residents. Mothers worked with daughters and sisters worked with sisters. Longevity of service also becomes evident. Sisters Ann and Elizabeth Mills worked for Priscilla Rowe for over ten years from the 1830s, then Elizabeth left when Priscilla moved from one side of the park to the other, in 1852. When Priscilla died in 1877, Ann, aged 70, was probably still there. Of all the servants, she was the one employed continuously in the same household for the longest time; over half her life. Next door, in 1861, at least five servants continued to serve the last of the five Ladies Keith. Three were there for more than twenty years: the housekeeper, Cecilia Brown, Scottish born like her ladies, George Cullen, the butler, from Westonzoyland on the Somerset levels, and lady's maid Ann Pinkett, from Bath. The de Sommerys had numerous servant changes over a much longer period, but only one appears with long service: Sarah Cordy was housekeeper to Cécile for over twenty years from 1871. In contrast, from before 1841 and for well over 30 years, Colonel John Potter Hamilton, at number 10, employed between three and five servants at a time, even as an 83 year old widower. They appear to have changed relatively frequently. In four consecutive censuses, no names recur.

fig 6: William & Anna Harriette Pennington, c.1861. After his sister-in-law, Augusta (alias Elizabeth) died in 1886, he became owner of No.19. Photograph.

Provided by and reproduced with the permission of Stephen Swaby

Many servants were women of marriageable age, which may be one reason why domestic staff changed relatively often. Others will have moved to better themselves. They worked long hours, with little free time to meet other people. When they did meet, few would have anticipated the experience of governess 'Mademoiselle' Louisa Koch. The Revd Morris Yescombe, her employer, accused 'a gentleman of fortune', John Roche of Queen Square, of abducting her. Roche lost the ensuing court case, which 'should never have been brought', paid a one-farthing fine and still got Louisa. [10]

Davis and Bonsall state that 'No full-scale study of servant-keeping in Bath has yet been undertaken' but a study of Northampton and Rivers Streets from 1851 to 1881, 'revealed that the lower-middle and professional middle-class homes of employed on average only one resident female servant'. This supports a view that 'many of Bath's genteel residents seem to have made economies by reducing the number of servants employed.'[11] This contrasts with an average of 2.8 resident servants in Green Park over the same period. Servant numbers in Green Park peaked at 122 in 1861. They made up over two fifths of the occupants. In the years to 1871, there were, on average, more than three servants per house. Numbers then dropped dramatically, clearly symptomatic of major changes taking place. These included less wealthy heads of household, a diminishing population, and houses used as offices and for other non-residential purposes. By 1911 there were only 36, a proportion marginally above one-fifth of residents and one-third of the female population. Almost all were English, mainly locally-born and half were under 30 years of age. The number of men servants was always low. There were none by the end of the century. Nevertheless, it seems that most of Green Park's residents, at least until 1881, were 'genteel' without being too poor.

Birthplaces

The attorneys Mant and Salmon, with printer Hazard, were locals. From the earliest days, however, 'outsiders' lived in Green Park. With diverse backgrounds, they came from far and wide, but where they were born is often unclear. Some brought servants with them. The de Quinceys came from Salford, the Austens from Hampshire, Sir William Addington from London and General Donkin from Northumberland. The Trails came from Scotland via Ireland, where the Moncks had ancestral property. The Marquise Agathé de Sommery was French, her daughter Comtesse Cécile, English.

Table 3 summarises information on where all residents and servants were born. In Green Park, if not Bath, the population of those locally-born (in Somerset, Gloucestershire, and

Table 3   Green Park Buildings Census Data   Birth Locations

ALL RESIDENTS	Numbers / Percentage of total population															
Census	1841	%	1851	%	1861	%	1871	%	1881	%	1891	%	1901	%	1911	%
Local (in Sset/Glos/Wil) * Sset only	69*	26.3	117	44.0	146	50.0	130	50.0	145	56.9	131	56.5	120	64.5	100	63.7
Othr Eng cnty (♦incl Glos + Wil)	156♦	59.5	95	35.7	83	28.4	77	29.6	66	25.9	63	27.2	43	23.1	27	17.2
Wales	0	0.0	9	3.4	12	4.1	5	1.9	7	2.7	7	3.0	9	4.8	5	3.2
Scotland	9	3.4	15	5.6	4	1.4	1	0.4	2	0.8	2	0.9	2	1.1	0	0.0
Ireland	23	8.8	17	6.4	23	7.9	15	5.8	10	3.9	4	1.7	3	1.6	2	1.3
Foreign	5	1.9	13	4.9	24	8.2	32	12.3	23	9.0	24	10.3	9	4.8	12	7.6
Others Unknown	0	0.0	0	0.0	0	0.0	0	0.0	2	0.8	1	0.4	0	0.0	11	7.0
Totals	262	100.0	266	100.0	292	100.0	260	100.0	255	100.0	232	100.0	186	100.0	157	100.0
SERVANTS	Numbers / Percentage of total population															
Local (in Sset/Glos/Wilt)	40*		74	27.8	81	27.7	79	30.4	59	23.1	62	26.7	48	25.8	26	16.6
Othr Eng cnty	u/a		34	12.8	26	8.9	26	10.0	15	5.9	17	7.3	2	1.1	5	3.2
Wales	u/a		1	0.4	5	1.7	3	1.2	1	0.4	1	0.4	3	1.6	2	1.3
Scotland	u/a		5	1.9	1	0.3	0	0.0	0	0.0	1	0.4	0	0.0	0	0.0
Ireland	u/a		3	1.1	7	2.4	4	1.5	1	0.4	2	0.9	0	0.0	0	0.0
Foreign	u/a		1	0.4	2	0.7	1	0.4	0	0.0	1	0.4	0	0.0	1	0.6
Others Unknown	u/a		0	0.0	0	0.0	0	0.0	0	0.0	1	0.4	1	0.5	2	1.3
Totals All Servants	119	45.4	118	44.4	122	41.8	113		76	29.8	85	36.6	54	29.0	36	22.9

Wiltshire) increased as the century progressed. In 1841, a sixth of the heads of household and a quarter of the whole population were Somerset-born. From 1851 to 1911, the proportion of locals increased, from 44 to 63 per cent. The contribution from 'other English counties' fell, correspondingly, from 36 per cent to half that figure. Similarly, the total from Ireland, Scotland, and Wales dropped from a mid-century high of fifteen per cent to less than five per cent. In contrast, the number born abroad peaked in 1871 before dropping more modestly. More details of the 'foreigners' and the Irish follow. Changes in the status of heads of household and residents are dealt with later.

Green Park had residents who were Irish or had Irish connections from the earliest days, for example the Moncks, in 1804, and the Revd. Morris Yescombe's wife in the 1850s. The Irish presence was more prominent than the Welsh or the Scots for most of the century and it is worth comparing the position of Green Park with that of Bath given by Graham Davis, in his article *Social Decline and Slum Conditions: Irish Migrants in Bath's History*.

The Irish in Bath formed part of a national pattern: 'Irish migration to Britain developed progressively in the first half of the century, reaching a climax during the famine years, 1845-52. In 1841, the number of Irish-born resident in Britain was over 400,000 and in 1861 a peak figure of 806,000 was recorded.' [12]

The proportion of Irish residents in Green Park did not mirror this pattern. The peak probably occurred in 1841, at 8.8 per cent (23 people in 10 houses, including eight heads of household), fell in 1851, rose again to 7.9 per cent (23 people) ten years later, then dropped to virtually nothing by the end of the century. Their backgrounds and status varied from those of the gentry to domestic servants (only a small proportion) and at least two female boarding school pupils.

Foreigners, those born outside England, Ireland, Scotland and Wales, made up seven-and-a-half per cent (144) of those registered in the 1841 to 1911 censuses. The largest groups, spread over the last five decades of the century, were from the East Indies (65), including 50 from India, and the West Indies (16), of which ten came from Jamaica.

Most of those from the West Indies lived in Green Park during the 1850s and 1860s. Some may have arrived following the decline in sugar production and diversification into other occupations, but this is not obvious. Only four were men: three 'fundholders' and a 'Lieutenant Colonel Army Retired'. Eight of the women were 'fundholders' or 'landowners', though it is not clear where their lands were. None were children.

The Indian Uprising of 1857-8 and the abolition of the East India Company could have contributed to the move to Bath of East-Indian-born British. However, only nine from there lived in Green Park in 1861. Of these, five were children and none were men. The only military officer recorded was the Welsh-born father of two of the young girls. The peak numbers of these residents occurred from 1871 to 1891; the total was 42. Seventeen were children under the age of fifteen years, overlapping eighteen described as 'scholars'. Only six were heads of household, including three widows and two men, the long retired Major-General James Kennedy and Lt-Col Charles Blair, who were both resident in 1891.

France, with fifteen, headed the places in which other foreigners were born. In much smaller, often only single figures, they came from America, Australia, Belgium, Canada, the Channel Islands, China, Germany, Malta, Singapore and South Africa.

From 1841, servants generally came from the three local and the next nearest counties.

118

They contributed significantly to the increasingly local bias. In 1851, only one third came from local counties; ten years later it was twice that. By 1901 it was 89 per cent. Few came from far afield. The Isle of Wight was one extreme, Essex and Kent to the east were others. In all, less than ten came from England north of Birmingham; Northumberland and Durham each contributed one. In 1851 there was one from Belgium (and another later, both employed by the de Sommerys), and three from Ireland. Of five from Scotland, three served their Scottish mistress Margaret Dalrymple at number 15.

Life expectancy

By 1840, the national norm of life-expectancy had just reached 40 years for both sexes, and it remained virtually the same until 1871. Then, expectancies rose slowly, reaching 48.5 years for men and 52.4 for women by 1901. People living in rural areas and non-industrial towns could anticipate a significantly longer life.

Data, from all censuses provides many examples of Green Park residents who, at birth, probably had a short life expectancy yet achieved longevity. [13] They include George Monck, who died at 68 and Revd. George Austen at 73. William Trail was 85 and at least two of the Ladies Keith were over seventy. Then there are the very old servants, already mentioned. Many residents were certainly past the 'meridian of life', but there was a 'continuous migration of young women into the city' and certainly into Green Park. [14] There were also newborn children.

The average age of heads of household in 1851 was marginally below 50 years and for the rest of the century to 1911 it is in the high fifties, indicating that many survived well beyond 60 years. Some, like General Donkin and Cécile de Sommery lived into their nineties, more than double national life expectancy. Through the second half of the century, the average age of all residents fluctuated around 35 years. The proportion of those aged 60 or more was, with little variation, a seventh. Residents' sons, daughters, and grandchildren under the age of fifteen made up roughly ten per cent of the total population from 1841, except for a low figure in 1851. The highest numbers occurred from 1861 to 1881, the maximum being 36 children. These figures suggest that while 'Bath's population [was] subject to a process of gentle ageing', an age-balance was being maintained in Green Park. [15]

A mid-century Cameo

A snapshot of some households in 1851 gives a fleeting view of Green Park. House number 1 was small with an unusual, kite-shaped plan. Its main occupant was a lodging-house keeper living with his wife, daughter and a 76-year-old servant. His lodgers were of two households. One included a 72-year-old widow, living on an army pension, with two of her daughters in their forties, one also widowed. In the second, a nineteen-year-old housemaid served another widow and her visiting friend, both in their seventies and living on annuities. In a conventionally shaped house two doors away was a single household of fifteen. Successor to Lady Frances Trail, Major General Thomas Wemyss lived with his much younger wife, his mother-in-law who was an 'annuitant' in her eighties, four unmarried daughters aged 15, 17,

20 and 23, and an older daughter, a clergyman's wife, with her two young children. A cook, housemaid and two house servants and a nurse looked after them. Less crowded but also in two of the smaller houses, numbers 34 and 37, were the Ladies Keith and the de Sommerys with their servants. Nine people lived at number 19. Widower and 'Fundholder', 74-year-old Madras-born William Taswell, was doing very well as his is the only family recorded with three male servants: a footman, groom, and coachman. William and his two visitors also received service from three more servants, the housekeeper, housemaid, and cook. The *Complete Servant* suggests his income was at least £1,000 to £1,500 a year.

At number 23, opposite, widow the Right Honourable Gertrude Tollemache presumably did nothing for herself; she lived 'alone', with her butler, his wife, a footman and three other servants. Two doors away, at number 21, 50-year-old widowed charwoman, Rosina Bond, was in sole charge; the family was away. Their neighbours included seven military officers and three clergymen, all with servants. The ratios of those above and below stairs in these homes highlight those of the 'quality'. As we shall see, the view 'over the garden wall' in Avon and Milk Streets was quite different, especially from the late 1840s. It may have been a contributing cause to the changes which took place in Green Park from the 1860s.

Owners and Tenants

At the beginning of the nineteenth century, only ten per cent of people bought their own house, rental was the norm. [16] In Green Park ownership was much higher; rates records show that more than a quarter of houses were owner-occupied in the 1840s. A contrary case is the de Sommerys' long-term whole-house rental. After renting number 37 for 26 years, they moved to and rented number 35 for another 44, from 1855. Others simply required rooms rather than a whole house, as lodging provision in Green Park demonstrates. The Bath Directory of 1854 shows one-fifth of the 40 houses in the 'List of Lodging House Keepers', all but one being smaller properties, mainly on the eastern side. Only at number 31 was the owner, Mr Aquila Pippen, resident.

At various times during the first 100 years, half the houses, including eight in the 1860s, were owned by one or other of at least 33 women; some had more than one. As Gillian Tindall says in her book *The House by the Thames*, 'owning a few houses had long been a popular way of securing an income, especially for respectable widows'. [17] Examples include widows Frances Wemyss and Harriet St Barbe, formerly of Lincoln, who owned and lived in numbers 3 and 18, respectively. Unmarried Priscilla Rowe first tenanted her deceased parents' abode, number 13, before buying numbers 32 and 33. She rented the first and moved into the second. Another case was spinster Ann Errington's academy, set up by 1830 at number 2, which she later moved to the larger number 13 and eventually to number 22, opposite. In 1851, she and her sister ran the school with two governesses and three servants. They educated thirteen girl pupils, born as far away as London, Liverpool, Colchester, Newcastle Emlyn and Ireland. [18]

The general picture is of ownership for longer rather than shorter periods, with many properties being retained and let by executors of a will, long after the owner's death. This occurred in at least eleven cases. The name of William Phillips, who died in 1804, was associated with number 1 for 62 years. It appears that, from first occupation in the period 1796 to 1809, 22 houses were in the same individual ownerships until 1860, then, between 1859 and 1864, for reasons not clear, thirty-six changed hands. Despite this, new purchasers also tended to hang on to their property for years. Morris Yescombe held his house for almost 30 years, until his death in 1883, when it passed to his son-in-law, James Baldwin. His family lived there into the 1940s.

All Change

Bath's population decreased by eight per cent from 1851 to 1901, then rose slightly by 1911. [19] The Green Park population dropped by nineteen per cent and further decline followed; in 1911, the number was only three-quarters of its 1861 maximum. Other indications of change become increasingly apparent, especially after 1871, when the number of houses standing vacant for increasingly long periods, grew. One cause may have been the 'migration of wealthy citizens to [the growing] suburban areas', which 'tended to increase the geographical segregation of the different social classes' in Bath, particularly so from 1880s into the earlier twentieth century. [20] Data relating to heads of household certainly tells us that the status of this group changed significantly. Until 1881, a quarter or less of heads came from the three local counties. Then came a rapid increase, to a half by the end of the century. Correspondingly, fewer came from the other English counties while the number of foreign-born residents decreased gradually from the middle of the century.

Of the 242 heads of household from 1851 to 1901 inclusive, 169 (70 per cent) were non-local and all but eighteen of these were of the gentry (those with a title, a private income, landowners, the clergy, army and navy officers, and 'gentlemen').. Of the 95 from elsewhere in England, approximately one third came from Middlesex (London) and two-thirds from 26 other counties between Cumberland and the South Coast. 27 were born abroad and the rest in Scotland, Wales and Ireland.

Early, pre-1851 data indicate that Green Park was favoured by significant numbers of the gentry but a dramatic change is visible in the last quarter of the century. The census data for 1851 shows that 37 of the 46 heads of household (80.4 per cent) may be classed as 'gentry'. From then onwards the proportion decreased continuously. In 1871 it was 71 per cent, a half in 1891, and only a quarter at the end of the century. In this period, never more than four 'locals', in any year, were of the gentry.

Heads in 'Trade' and others of lower-status had always been present, and their numbers gradually increased until about 1860, when the number of those locally-born rapidly increased. This and the previous point, emphasise a process of social descent. Those with the money either moved out to the new suburbs or did not come.

In 1851, residents included Charles Danvers, a wine-merchant, and William Whaite, a 'Photographic Artist', both at number 5. Ten years later, a 'Conveyancer', an 'Engineer' and a young upholsterer were in residence but Errington's academy had closed. By 1881 there were at least eleven cabinet makers, colliery proprietors, a grocer, a pianoforte vendor and a stone merchant, and another ten in 'professions' (legal work, teachers, surveyors and architects), as well as the usual lodging house keepers (eight). The types and figures for 1891 appear similar but are unreliable. In the census years 1841 to 1911, there was no recorded occupation for roughly twelve per cent of individuals over fourteen years of age.

Another indicator of social descent is the number of servants. From a maximum of 122 servants, when every house had at least one, we find that, by 1911, one-third of occupied houses had none. Even if all 40 houses had been occupied, there would then have been only about 48 servants. It was now reminiscent of the earlier situation in Northampton and Rivers Streets.

The trend was to business and other non-residential use and a lower class of resident, whose occupations became more commercially orientated. Early on, when Ann Errington's academy moved, Miss Strachan's 'Ladies Establishment' appeared at number 2. By the end of the century other teachers and schools had appeared, providing education in music, dancing and calisthenics. From 1880, the Somerset and Dorset Joint Railway Company used number 13 (later with number 14), as offices until 1930. Then, in April 1895, the 'Committee of [Bath Education Authority] Science, Art and Technical Schools' occupied number 19 [fig. 7]., pending construction of new buildings. [21] By 1900, the Free Church House had taken number 3.

Medical men had been occasional residents from the early days. From 1881, there was a continuous presence, often of more than one practice at a time. Surgeon Edward White's family successively practised at number 2 from the late 1880s until the 1950s and, opposite, Mr Pitt provided 'Electro-hydrotherapy' in 1895. Other occupations and 'professions' indicate the way things were moving. Architects and the City Corroner [sic] arrived, as did a colliery owner, draper, pianoforte vendor, stationer, wholesale druggists, railway workers and wine merchants. The retired still sought refuge here: they included a fruiterer, grocer, stonemason, surveyor and

fig 7: A tinted postcard, c.1902 of Green Park Buildings (West), looking south from Seymour Street, showing the park gate.
Bath in Time - Bath Central Library Collection

an innkeeper. Residents also included, an artist, a tailor, a silk mercer's apprentice, articled clerks and, at the end of the century, an undertaker. At the rear of a number of the western houses, stables were let to non-residents, for either their original purpose or conversion to a 'warehouse and shed'. [22]

The events that drove change or those that resulted from it have yet to be analysed, but the following may have influenced some transformations that occurred. Conditions in the adjacent area of Avon and Milk Streets had deteriorated since the 1840s. Twenty years later the area was described as 'a constant source of anxiety' having 'the most abject poor in the city - skewer makers, gipsies, beggars ... and loafers of every description'. [23] On the evening of January 18th 1853, Lewis Perran, an Avon Street lodger, murdered Honora Hanaford near Green Park ferry. Her body floated four miles down-stream. [24]

On the morning of Tuesday October 24th 1882, the sudden rise of water of 'The Great Flood' inundated the city centre and, at the end of Green Park, even 'Midland Bridge was impassable'. [25] This filled the basements and vaults of Green Park. Similar events, which spread water and noxious waste, occurred throughout the century.

In 1857, confirming that Bath was an increasingly industrial city, Stothert and Pitt built their new iron foundry and crane works on Lower Bristol Road, affecting the view from Green Park itself. The Midland Railway proposed a line to Bath from Mangotsfield; it received consent in 1864. Queen Square station ('Green Park' from 1954) replaced nine houses on Seymour Street, and opened in 1869. Traffic increased there when the Somerset and Dorset Joint Railway opened in 1874. [26] Residents also suffered from the building of the large area of sidings, timber and cabinet works, cattle pens, coal and goods yards as well as two smoky locomotive-sheds. Aggravating the effects further, Midland Bridge and a new road were built immediately behind the western row in 1870, for the transport of goods between the railway yards and the town. Another problem lay half a mile to the west. In July 1882, the Town Council heard 'complaints from Sion Hill, Green Park [and] St James's Square 'about the 'dreadful smells ... emanating from the Gas Works'. The gas works blamed the adjoining 'Scavenger's Yard'. [27] The inevitable traffic, noise and smells made the area a significantly less desirable place in which to live.

As we have seen, Green Park was a place of residence from the outset. For much of the nineteenth century, it fitted the general picture of Bath as a town to which the clergy and military men retired, and as a genteel place in which to live, especially for single and widowed women with some wealth and perhaps a title. For those of lesser means or only requiring a few rooms for residence, lodging houses were available, but not boarding houses for visitors. The lengthy durations of residence by some and moving house, yet remaining within the Park, by others, are significant indicators that Green Park was a favoured place.

The last resident with a British title died there in 1864, leaving only Comtesse Cécile de Sommery. Military personnel and clergymen lost interest in living there. Some, as already mentioned, migrated to the suburbs. For example, soon after 1891, Coroner Craddock moved to Greenway Lane, Widcombe and Col. John Doveton moved to Springfield Place, Lansdown. The location fell out of favour and the clientele and tone became evidently different from that of a hundred years earlier. [28]

Another pointer to substantial change was the huge drop in servant numbers in the last quarter of the century. This accounted for almost the whole reduction in the resident population, proportionately, a fall much greater than that for Bath. Green Park was not itself industrialised,

fig 8: Green Park Buildings on fire during the Bath Blitz, April 1942. Photograph
Bath in Time - Bath Central Library Collection

but was clearly affected by the proximity of industrial developments. These might account for the gradually increasing use of houses for purposes other than simple residence. Despite this, there were those who still aspired to the 'genteel', and probably hired one of the increasing numbers of charwomen in the city rather than pay for a live-in servant. [29] At the end of the century, educational provision grew in the city and Green Park certainly contributed to this. Similarly, the increase in Bath of wider opportunities in the commercial sector for merchants, clerks, accountants and medical men, was reflected in the occupations of Green Park residents.

It would be surprising to find exact correspondence between the changes in Bath and those in Green Park from 1790 to 1900, but there are clear parallels. The essential change in Green Park was from a place bordering on 'Upper Class' to one definitely tending towards the middle class. There was worse to come. Dwellings became warehouses, number 19 was replaced by a utilitarian single-storey building, and stables were used for a pickle factory and workshops. Then, in 1942, the eastern side was badly damaged by bombs **[fig. 8]**, subsequently demolished and a new road was built over the remaining vaults.

Notes

1   Mrs Elisabeth Quinsey (both spelt with an 's') temporarily changed her name to 'de Quincey' then, soon afterwards, to 'Quincey'.
2   Graham Davis and Penny Bonsall (D&B), *A History of Bath: Image and Reality*, (Carnegie, 2006).
3   Ellen Wilson, 'A Shropshire Lady in Bath', *Bath History vol. IV,* (Millstream Books, 1992), p.102.
4   *Bath Chronicle,* 5 June 1794 p.3
5   Bath Police Rate Book, Michaelmas, 1830, p.186, Bath Record Office. The name of the western row was also changed from Green Park 'Place' to 'Buildings'.
6   D&B, p.159. The population of Bath in 1851 was 54,240 and that of Green Park 266 (0.490 per cent).
7   D&B, p.163. In 1891 the highest ratios of females to males in the inner city were in St Michael's parish at 148:100; Lansdown, 251:100 and Bathwick, 210:100. In Green Park, it was 364:100.
8   Warren Derry, *The Journals and Letters of Fanny Burney,* (Clarendon Press, 1982), Vol. X, Index, p. 1026, Keith, and p.1036, Mesniel (the de Sommery family name).

9   Samuel and Sarah Adams, *The Complete Servant; being a Practical Guide to the Peculiar Duties and business of all descriptions of Servants*, (Knight and Lacey, 1825), pp. 5 and 6.

10   *The Times*, Tuesday Dec 30th 1856, p. 10; Tuesday Jan 06th 1857, p. 11.

11   D&B, p196-7

12   Graham Davis, 'Social Decline and Slum Conditions: Irish Migrants in Bath's History', *Bath History vol. VIII*, 2000, pp. 134-147.

13   Censuses of England, Bath, Walcot, from 1841 to 1901; Kent and Medway Public Health Observatory, Annual Report 2006; BBC History, Overview: Victorian Britain, 1837 – 1901. www.bbc.co.uk/history/british/victorians/ (Accessed: 31 October 2011).

14   D&B, p.162.

15   D&B, p.162

16   Maxwell Hutchinson, *Number 57 - The History of a House* (Headline Book Publishing, 2003), p.25.

17   Gillian Tindall, *The House by the Thames and the people who lived there,* (Pimlico, 2007), p.64.

18   Pigot and Co's National Commercial Directory, Somersetshire, 1830, pp. 672 and 682, Bath Library; Hunt & Co.'s Directory and Court Guide for Bath, Bristol, and Wells, 1848, p. 117, Bath Library. The 1841 census asked 'Whether born in same County', from 1851 censuses the question was 'Where born'.

19   D&B, p. 159.

20   D&B, pp.159-160.

21   Post Office Directory, 1895, p.639, Bath Library.

22   Poor Rate Book, October 1895, Bath Record Office.

23   Sissmore, T. L., *Annals and Records of Holy Trinity Church, Bath, from its consecration in 1822, down to the year 1890*, Bath 1893. www.holytrinitybath.org.uk, Accessed: November 2nd 2009.

24   *The Times,* February 3rd, p.6; February 7th, 1853, p.8.

25   Bruce Crofts, *Forgotten Year: News from Bath in 1882*, (Bath City Council, 1982), p.46.

26   The *Bath Chronicle* of 'August the 5th 1869' reported that the, 'far from complete' station, opened, with the railway line, the previous day. The Somerset and Dorset Joint Railway, www.sdjr.net/locations/bath_history.html Accessed: August 16th 2010.

27   Bruce Crofts *Forgotten Year*, p.5; Stuart Burroughs, 'End of an era for the Bath Gas Works', *Bath Chronicle*, March 3rd 2011.

28   Bath Post Office directory, 1895, p.75 and p. 91.

29   D&B, p.184.

Charles Dickens and Bath:
The Bicentenary 2012 Celebrations

Graham Davis

Charles Dickens was born in Portsmouth on February 7th 1812. In 2012, the world celebrated the bicentenary of his birth with a plethora of exhibitions, readings, new biographies, television programmes including dramas of his novels, and a host of other activities that commemorated the life and work of 'the inimitable' genius of Victorian literature.

Bath had good reason to join in the fun and a series of events took place driven by a wish to celebrate all things Dickensian. The actor Peter 'Doc' Watson in Dickens 200 gave a performance of much-loved excerpts on February 7th in the Pump Room, alongside a newly-refurbished bust of the author. An entire reading of his favourite novel, *David Copperfield,* was undertaken at St. Michael's Without Church by volunteers in fifteen minute stretches, led by the popular television personality, Alan Titchmarsh. A series of Dickens suppers, readings and dramatised scenes, was presented to the public on February 9th, 10th and 11th at the Mission Theatre. Historian Graham Davis teamed up with actors of the Next Stage Theatre Company. Pickwick, Oliver Twist, Miss Haversham, Micawber and Heep were among the Dickens characters re-visited **[fig. 1].** Toppings bookshop invited Simon Callow, actor, writer, and great Dickens performer, to appear at St. Swithin's Church on February 24th to promote his new book, *Charles Dickens and the Great Theatre of the World.* Finally, Claire Tomalin, the celebrated biographer, was at the Guildhall on March 3rd to talk about her much-acclaimed *Charles Dickens: A Life* that appeared in print in late 2011.

The associations between Dickens and Bath live on in the names of several characters in his novels. Quilp, the deformed dwarf in *The Old Curiosity Shop* was based on a character that hired out donkeys in Victoria Park. The famous death scene of Little Nell

fig 1: The Editor of Bath History Graham Davis in 'Dinner with Dickens' at the Mission Theatre, Bath
Photograph by Ann Garner

was written by Dickens at 35 St. James's Square when he was visiting his writer friend, Walter Savage Landor [fig. 2], whose birthday he celebrated regularly. Sam Weller was the name of the ostler at the York House Hotel where Dickens stayed [fig. 3] and a possible source for Pickwick's popular companion in *Pickwick Papers.* The name of Samuel Pickwick has been identified with Moses Pickwick, the coach proprietor, and Pickwick Mews off Avon Street. The visit of Pickwick in *Pickwick Papers*, published in 1836, contains a scene where Mr Dowler introduces his friend to the Master of Ceremonies, the delightfully named Angelo Cyrus Bantam Esq.

The friend was a charming young man of not much more than fifty, dressed in a very bright blue coat with resplendent buttons, black trousers, and the thinnest possible pair of highly-polished boots. A gold eye-glass was suspended from his neck by a short broad black ribbon; a gold snuff-box was lightly clasped in his left hand, gold rings innumerable glittered on his fingers, and a large diamond pin set in gold glistened in his shirt frill. He had a gold watch, and a gold curb chain with large gold seals; and he carried a pliant ebony cane with a heavy gold top. His linen was of the very whitest, finest, and stiffest; his wig of the glossiest, blackest, and curliest. His snuff was princes' mixture; his scent bouquet du roi. His features were contracted into a perpetual smile; and his teeth were in such perfect order that it was difficult at a small distance to tell the real ones from the false.

fig 2: 35 St James Square, c.1938. The home of Walter Savage Landor where Dickens stayed. Photograph by George Love Dafnis

Bath in Time - Private Collection

The description of this popinjay and the scene of faded glitter in the Assembly Rooms offers a wonderful satire on the pretensions of Bath society just at the time when the city was suffering its fall from grace as the mecca for the fashionable company.

Dickens came to Bath on a number of occasions. In 1851, he took part in a play, *Not so bad as we seem,* written by his friend Bulwer Lytton, along with other friends, including Mark Lemon. He came to the city as part of his reading tour performing to a packed audience in the Assembly Rooms. He also made a number of mischievous comments about Bath society. In *Bleak House*, Bath was described as 'the grass-grown city of the ancients' and in a letter to a friend in America in 1864, Dickens continued the theme with the comment that Bath looked as if people had risen up from the graveyard and were wandering abroad trying to look alive but with very little success.

fig 3: The York House Hotel, George Street, Bath, c.1870
Bath in Time - Bath Central Library Collection

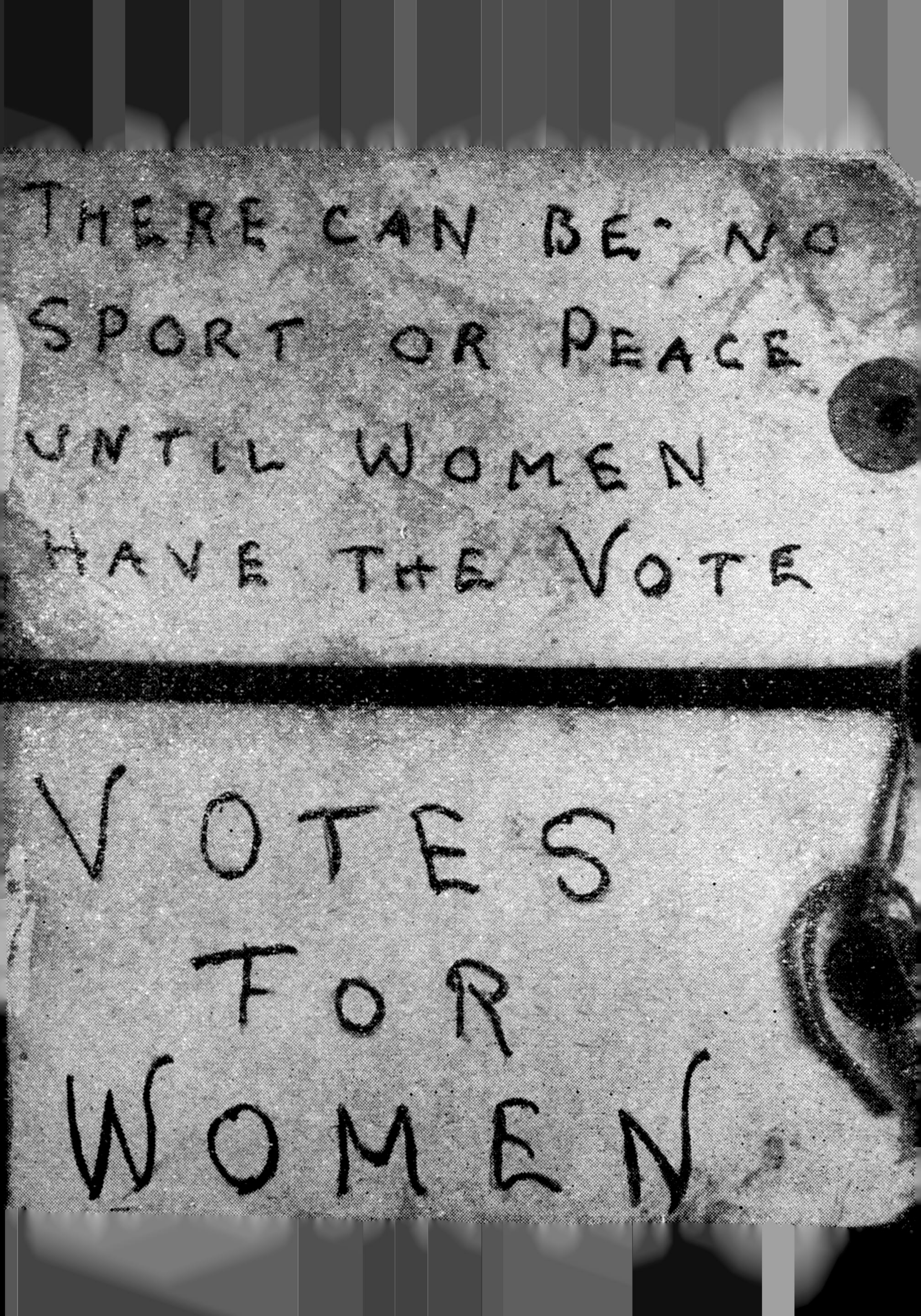

THERE CAN BE NO
SPORT OR PEACE
UNTIL WOMEN
HAVE THE VOTE

VOTES
FOR
WOMEN

Suffragette City: Spatial Knowledge and Suffrage Work in Bath, 1909-14[1]

Cynthia Hammond

Introduction: Beyond the Garden

On a late autumn Sunday afternoon in 1909, suffragist Mary Blathwayt (1879-1961) made an uncharacteristically short entry in her daily journal: 'have not been beyond the garden today.'[2] One might think of this Sunday as a pause in the rounds of activity in which this busy young woman was otherwise engaged, and likely it was, comparatively, a day of rest. But Blathwayt was referring to the generous lawns, flower beds, and arboretum found at her family home, Eagle House in Batheaston, a small suburb on the north-eastern periphery of Bath, Somerset. These grounds – this 'garden' – were one of several nodes in a vital circuit of suffrage activity in Bath in the years leading up to World War I, activity that made this village on the eastern reaches of Bath a key site in local, pre-war, feminist activism **[fig. 1]**.

If Mary Blathwayt did no more than walk through the lower garden and gaze at the late autumn flowers that she and her mother had grown – white, green, and violet, the official colours of the Women's Social and Political Union (WSPU) – she continued to participate, visually, in a field of political action. If she walked to the upper reaches of the garden, where the family and their gardeners had planted conifers and holly bushes in honour of women who fought for the vote, the 'suffragettes' wood', she would have immersed herself in a site of remarkable symbolic intensity. And if her movements that day kept Blathwayt mostly inside, there too she would have been immersed in the visual

fig 1: Portrait of Mary Blathwayt, 1911. Photograph by Col. Linley Blathwayt
Bath in Time - Bath Central Library Collection

and material culture of suffrage work: admiring photographs that her father had taken of visiting suffragettes; writing letters to fellow suffrage workers, doing up accounts for the Women's Social and Political Union (WSPU), or mending her green and white dresses, custom-made for suffrage processions.[3] As the day came to a close, Blathwayt would have planned

Facing: Detail of specimens of the luggage labels left by suffragettes at Bath Golf Links. March 3rd, 1914
Bath in Time - Bath Central Library Collection

with her parents whether she would take a tram into central Bath to greet the next suffragist visitor, or drive with her father. These visitors were often women who had recently been released from prison, and were in need of rest or even medical care.[4]

What might seem like a passing entry in a private diary thus can lead the reader directly to the larger spatial context of Edwardian feminism in the city of Bath.[5] In my previous work on the relationship between the city of Bath and early-twentieth-century women, I concentrated on the creation and significance of the Batheaston arboretum, and the beautiful collection of photographs that, having survived the arboretum's destruction in the 1960s, remain almost the only trace of that singular landscape.[6] What remained unexplored in my study, however, was the question of how early twentieth-century feminists used the larger space of the city for their cause. Beyond the garden, then, this essay seeks to make visible the spatial nature of suffrage activism in Bath. My goal is to understand how women, in search of the vote, deployed the built environment of Bath: its landmark buildings, private homes, city streets, and its centre and periphery as part of their daily movements on behalf of women's suffrage.

fig 2: Portrait of Annie Kenney, 28 March 1909.
Photograph by Col. Linley Blathwayt
Bath in Time - Bath Central Library Collection

The group of mostly women and some men that fall under the broader, pro-suffrage rubric in Bath prior to World War I was not homogenous. In addition to their political differences (there were by 1913 seven different pro-suffrage societies in Bath),[7] women's suffrage workers were different in terms of class and age[8] as well as gender. They also differed in their spatial relationships to the city. While a number of key figures were born in or made Bath their home, such as Mary Blathwayt, many others journeyed to Bath for symbolic or strategic purposes. Some stayed for a few hours or a day to give a lecture, while others criss-crossed the city every few hours, or the region, via Bath, every few days, such as Blathwayt's friend and frequent collaborator, Annie Kenney (1879-1953) [fig. 2]. Such journeys are themselves telling of the intensity of suffrage work in Bath and environs, but also speak to the interconnections between centres (London, Bristol) and peripheries in the suffrage campaign, and how divisions within the suffrage movement reconciled in a small town. In Bath there is plenty of evidence that militant and non-militant suffrage workers collaborated, supported one another's efforts, and would even stand in for one another when necessary. This sense of collaboration is beautifully manifested in the Blathwayts' arboretum, which despite its hierarchical nature, honoured different kinds of suffrage workers.

Bath is, further, an interesting site for a study of suffrage activism as its population was predominantly female and yet not particularly predisposed to the efforts of the suffragists and even less to those of the militant 'suffragettes' in the city.[9] Women constituted 65 per cent of the population in 1911, or 29,971 individuals. That majority was further concentrated between the ages of 20-44, in this grouping, Bath women outnumbered men 2-1.[10] A 1910 poll of more than one thousand women municipal voters in Bath found, however, that only 23 per cent were in favour of having the Parliamentary vote, despite decades of campaigning.[11] Bath was not a place, therefore, where suffrage work found a warm reception, but it was a place where the impact of suffrage for women would have been considerable. This essay aims, then, to contribute to the growing literature on the regional character of suffrage work.

Additionally, this essay situates its findings in relation to the history of women's spatial knowledge and practices. There are no primary sources that speak *directly* to women's accumulation, through suffrage work, of spatial capital in Bath. By spatial capital I mean not only familiarity but rather a particular knowledge of a given place, such as a city, and the ability to occupy or deploy various locations within that place to one's own ends, in a way that accumulates power, visibility, or effect. Although the Blathwayt family were prolific diarists, and the content of those diaries is enormously useful, the diaries do not, especially in the case of Mary Blathwayt, tend to recount motivations, reflections, or even opinions.[12] But the findings below, and the map that I have created to better understand women's suffrage work in Bath, collectively tell a fascinating story of sophisticated local knowledge and intelligence, likewise wit, courage, and bravado. They also speak to a broad range of spaces and locations in which these characteristics were practiced.

Understanding *where* suffragists and suffragettes worked illuminates the diversity of political positions among suffrage workers in Bath. Likewise, primary sources make clear that suffrage activists relied on their collaborators' and their audience's spatial knowledge of Bath, its spatial-symbolic register, for the effect and impact of their actions.[13] Geographer Caroline Knowles draws from 'mobilities' scholarship and spatial theory, which together see 'urban space and lives as co-productions so that people and places are made through the everyday social activities of urban citizens.' In particular, Knowles privileges the journey as an act by which 'city dwellers speak the city' and 'walk stories.'[14] What is significant about the journey is that it connects places on an itinerary, 'bringing them into a network of coming and going, so journeys are the very social practices that connect and constitute space.'[15] Points of arrival and departure are resonant, as are the means by which journeys are made, and the nodes within a journey: all speak to issues of access, class and power.

If place, network, and journey are significant, so too are the material objects that made the suffragists' journeys with them, enabled these journeys, or were left behind as a mark of their presence. Firstly, I discuss the sources and methods used in generating my map of suffrage work in the city of Bath, 1909-14. Then, I analyse the map for what it can communicate, broadly, about the geographical scope and classed nature of this work, touching upon the local contours of suffrage activity in Bath, in relation to major phases or moments in the national picture. Lastly, the essay divides into four brief motifs, 1) the Window, 2) the Bicycle, 3) the House, and 4) the Luggage Tag. They engage the reader in a journey perhaps not always of an individual suffrage worker, but of an object or piece of technology that speaks to the routes, access, and points of denial facing a suffragette in the city of Bath. Here, I address the *movements* of bodies, objects, and boundaries. Together, these suggestive but also concrete motifs speak to the relation of spatial knowledge and suffrage work in Bath, which I cannot resist designating 'Suffragette City.'

Sources and Method

A central focus is the review of Mary Blathwayt's daily diaries for the years in question, focusing on her entries from January 1st 1909 to December 31st 1910 and, more sporadically, those of her mother, Emily Blathwayt (1852-1940). The years 1909 and 1910 were important for Mary Blathwayt and the movement. During this period she removed herself from active campaigning in Bristol, where she had lived and worked with Kenney, turning her energies to the local effort. The WSPU had begun searching for a suitable storefront in Bath as early as March 1909.[16] Mary Blathwayt was instrumental in setting up and, after its inaugural event on September 14th 1910, running the shop at 12 Walcot Street. Her diaries are a wonderful record of the creation of this unique, feminist space within the city, but they also provide a wealth of information about the comings and goings of the many visitors to Eagle House, and the locations where suffrage work took place in Bath. Cumulatively they create a vivid impression of the intensely social, peripatetic, and detail-oriented life of a busy worker for the cause. While Mary Blathwayt's family frowned upon militancy, she did not – that she recorded – participate in the destruction of public and private property, which was an increasingly controversial feature of suffrage work in Bath, 1909-14.

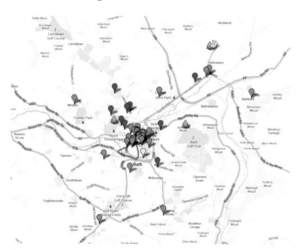

fig 3: Full view, Suffragette City map (Google), created 2012, also accessible as an interactive map via http://goo.gl/maps/kdpS

To learn more about militant and non-militant action in Bath, as well as the political shifts that often inspired them, I depended upon the city's daily and weekly print media, 1908-14, especially the daily edition of the *Bath Herald*, 1910-11.[17] I collected over 125 articles, letters, editorials, and a handful of advertisements regarding women's suffrage. Although Bath newspapers did comment upon major events elsewhere, such as the famous London suffrage procession of June 18th 1910, the majority of these items detail local events. These sources, alongside historic maps, photographs, and useful local publications such as the *Bath Directory* and Ordnance Survey maps, helped me to translate the details of feminist spatial activity in early twentieth-century Bath into what survives of the city today.

Part of my process has been to map this activity, with a view to understanding tendencies and patterns within this brief but potent period in Bath's feminist history. Using open-access mapping technology, I created an online, interactive map under the title of this essay,[18] identifying suffrage activity according to colour-coded location types [**fig. 3**] - **http://goo.gl/maps/kdpS**: these include private homes, public buildings and spaces such as streets and squares; landscapes and gardens; repeated itineraries and notable, singular journeys within Bath's cultural landscape of suffrage activism. Each location marker may be clicked for a pop-up window that identifies the site, explains its inclusion, and provides source material where quotations or paraphrasing has been taken from primary documents. In some cases, suggestions for further reading are provided, if a secondary source is known to have treated the events that took place at this location. In all but a handful of cases where buildings appear to have been demolished or an incomplete address was given, this cartographic exercise proved to be an effective register of key sites, and suggestive of the places where suffrage work was most resonant or recurrent in the city.

The Scope of Suffrage Work in Bath: Intensities

Even in its static form, the map generates some preliminary observations, primarily that the spatial scope of suffrage work in the city was broad; taking in its north-eastern extremity (Northend, Batheaston), its eastern limit (Bathford), its south-western point (Odd Down), and its western termination (Weston). It is clear that in 1911 suffrage work in Edwardian Bath exceeded the electoral limits of the city.[19] At the same time, however, there was a concentration of suffrage work towards the centre of Bath, particularly in the north-south axis between the Assembly Rooms [fig. 4] and the Guildhall, two of Bath's most significant sites of public and political gathering in the early years of the twentieth century. Here, suffrage events were often ticketed or sought a financial donation. Within this axis there is a further intensification in the Y-shaped pattern of streets incorporating Walcot Street, Broad Street, Northgate and High Streets, where several suffrage societies kept public offices between 1919-12. Near the groin of the Y, at the Post Office, is a further clustering of points of interest, to which I will return below.

fig 4: Interior, Tea Rooms, Assembly Rooms, after restoration, 1938. Photograph by George Love Dafnis.
Bath in Time - Private Collection

In addition, there are two, secondary axes of activity, both running roughly east-west. The first is a loose conglomeration of public and private buildings and spaces, stretching westwards from Pulteney Gardens, through Great Pulteney Street over Pulteney Bridge, and moving through The Corridor, a, covered Victorian shopping arcade, towards two public spaces, Kingsmead Square and the

Sawclose, where suffragettes held open-air meetings free of charge. An unbroken yellow line denotes the other secondary axis, running east-west from Batheaston to Walcot, where it moves southward into central Bath, terminating at the railway station. Colonel Linley Blathwayt (1839-1919), Mary Blathwayt's father, took this route almost daily in the family car when driving from Eagle House to Bath Spa Railway station, noted on the map with a yellow icon [fig. 3].[20] The station links Bath to the surrounding region and beyond; suffragettes, suffragists, and on occasion anti-suffragists[21] from other cities and towns to speak at the Guildhall, the Assembly Rooms, to address an 'At-Home' meeting in a private house, or to plant a tree or holly in the Blathwayts' arboretum.

The Scope of Suffrage Work in Bath: Class

Beyond this general snapshot, the map conveys another tendency regarding public and private space. 'Public' is for the purposes of this project broadly defined: churches and meeting spaces with regular opening hours, such as suffrage shops and offices, are considered 'public' as are commercial and retail venues normally open to anyone able to pay. The exclusions of such spaces along class lines should be noted, likewise the fact that not all pro-suffrage meetings and events were free to the public. Mary Blathwayt notes on October 27th 1910, for example, that the total collected in ticket sales for Mrs Pankhurst's lecture at the Guildhall that afternoon was £5-16-0. A ticket from the event in question, gives the price of one shilling. This price would have

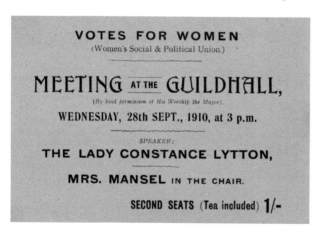

been out of the range of most working women and men in Bath, and may indicate the kind of audience sought for events in such prestigious locations. [fig. 5] [22] This tendency is not directly evident in the mapping described here; however another form of classed spatial activity is visible through the map. Readers will find a proliferation of violet icons outside the central core of concentrated activity. These indicate private homes, where a variety of activities on behalf of women's suffrage took place, such as 'At-homes', letter-writing campaigns, planning and membership meetings, musical or

fig 5: Ticket to Suffragette Meeting at the Guildhall, 28th September, 1910
Bath in Time - Bath Central Library Collection

dramatic rehearsals for up-coming events, and the all-important social calls that reinforced commitments and allegiances. The map's details reveal that these homes had elite addresses, including the Circus and the Royal Crescent, and in the newer and more fashionable neighbourhoods of Bathwick, Widcombe Hill and Lansdown. No private homes in the working-class districts of Twerton, Oldfield Park, or lower Weston were mentioned as sites of pro-suffrage activity in any of the sources consulted. The slum districts of Corn, Milk and Avon Streets seem to have been overlooked, save one journey by 'decorated wagonette' along the heavily industrial Lower Bristol Road on polling day in 1910.[23] The Dolemeads, the purpose-built, anti-slum project located due east of the Bath Spa railway station, appears to have been wholly ignored.

The map I have produced is possibly skewed by two factors. Firstly, Mary Blathwayt, was a devoted WSPU member until she resigned to please her family in 1913. Her diary therefore registers her immersion in the more militant world of that organisation. Secondly, local newspapers clearly relished the spectacle and outrage of the more militant WSPU. Reporting, for example, on a meeting of the Bath Liberal Women's Association, which was pro-suffrage but anti-militancy, one writer dutifully summarised the speeches but revealed his true feelings when he observed that, 'the proceedings were brightened considerably by an excellent musical programme.'[24] Even if Bath newspapers were, editorially, opposed to militancy,[25] there is little doubt that accounts of window-smashing sold papers. Reporters delighted in their time with militants, who confounded expectations and were often entertaining, as shall be seen below in my discussion of the WSPU's evasion of the Census in 1911. But, taking into account these potential imbalances, my mapping of the women's suffrage movement in Bath supports what historians have observed elsewhere. Where the WSPU undertook campaigns, there was a tendency to direct resources to middle- and upper-class women, and not their working-class counterparts.

Elizabeth Crawford observes, 'the WSPU never fell into the political trap of aiming to enfranchise all women.' After 40 years of active campaigning, women were still fighting stereotypical perceptions about womanhood. Crawford summarizes these stereotypes: 'Women

fig 6: Sawclose. View looking towards Westgate Buildings c.1912. Photographic postcard.
Bath in Time - Bath Central Library Collection

were, if middle-class, too noble, too sensitive, or too frivolous, and if working-class, too ignorant to cast a vote.' The other great fear over the notion of all women becoming enfranchised was that as a demographically larger group than voting-age males, they would overwhelm the electorate, control the House of Commons, and thus the future of England. A strategy of seeking limited female enfranchisement in this context is thus less elitist than it initially appears.[26] Nevertheless, class prejudices do emerge in this study of Bath, and these were spatially specific. Locations where the richer and poorer inhabitants of Bath encountered one another are points of intensity on the suffrage map. The aforementioned public spaces of the Sawclose and Kingsmead Square were located, for example, a walking distance from the slum and industrial districts of Edwardian Bath. [**fig. 6**] Such proximities likely inspired the choice of venue, but they also became part of the effect of these events for organisers. Mary Blathwayt, rarely one to offer an evaluative comment, wrote on June 11th 1910 of an un-ticketed public meeting in the Sawclose, 'The crowd was a very low class one, + rather noisy. But we made ourselves heard.'[27]

Gender, Space, Exclusion and Resistance

The Central Skating Rink at the Pavilion, North Parade Road, was another site of intensity, both for class prejudice on the part of suffrage workers, but also as a site where gender divisions and exclusions were powerfully enacted in what was, generally speaking, a public space [**fig. 7**]. Bath's Rink was host to a major event that speaks to the growing polarisation around women's suffrage between 1909-14. Located virtually on the dividing line between the richer Bathwick residents to the north, and the poorer residents of Dolemeads to the south, the Rink was an ideal location for a government seeking to consolidate its support across what they hoped would be a much wider electorate within the year. But that desired electorate did not include women. In 1911 the so-called 'Conciliation Bill' was up for its third reading in the House of Commons; if successful, it would have enfranchised approximately one million British women. Unexpectedly, however, in early November the Government dropped a bombshell. They planned to introduce a 'Manhood Suffrage' bill that would enfranchise all men above the age of 21, bringing the electorate from just over seven million male voters to eleven million.

Dismayed, women's suffrage workers recognised immediately that even if the Conciliation Bill still passed, their one million voters hardly would have the impact they had originally anticipated if the Manhood Bill moved through ratification as quickly as senior Liberals promised. They further doubted that a massive, male electorate would

fig 7: Bath Central Skating Rink (Bath Pavilion, on North Parade), built 1910
Bath in Time - Bath Central Library Collection

138

support the granting of the vote to any women at all. The Bath chapter of the WSPU saw the move to introduce the Manhood Suffrage bill as a direct attack on their efforts for political equality. Mildred Ella Mansel (1868-1942), WSPU organiser for Bath, observed that the government might just as well have said, 'We don't want to give any votes to women, we will give more votes to men!'[28] Mere weeks after the government's devastating announcement, the Liberal Federation advertised their Bath stop on their regional tour, in the Central Skating Rink on November 24th. Their large advertisement in the *Bath Herald* could only have added salt to the wound: 'Owing to the limited space and the tremendous demand,' it read, 'the Federation have decided that apart from the delegates, **Men ONLY can be Admitted**.'[29] The Manhood Suffrage bill, women's suffrage workers knew, was going to be discussed at this rally, as would votes for women. Yet women had been excluded from the very space in which these crucial issues were going to be explained and debated. There could have been no clearer indication that the Government had no intention of making political space for women in a larger sense. The Rink became an opportunity for Bath's activists to speak and act out.

Three days following Cabinet Minister David Lloyd George's address to a large crowd assembled inside the Skating Rink, the *Bath Herald* published a long article titled, 'Suffragettes and Mr Lloyd George: "What we Did and Why we Did it."'[30] A weary but triumphant Leonora Tyson (1884-1959), Secretary of the Streatham, London, WSPU, addressed a group of supporters at the Assembly Rooms. She described how, in the days leading up to Lloyd George's speech, 'she could not help smiling to herself, while watching the great preparations which were made to protect this Liberal gentleman' from a group of women who purportedly could not be trusted with the vote. But suffragettes had preparations of their own, including 'taking a house' near the Rink, and climbing to its roof. From that elevated position, she and her female collaborators (including Annie Kenney and 23-year old Mabel Capper) did everything in their power to rile the male crowd assembled outside the rink, so that the shouts of that crowd would disrupt the proceedings within. Tyson believed:

> … that the crowd was very much impressed by the fact that they were on top of the house, where the shouts, whether in favour or against them, could not do them the slightest injury They then left the house by creeping along the coping until they came well outside the house, and then they crawled down and over an adjacent garden, and made their way home. The police afterwards came into the house, and must have been astounded to see there was no one there. Did they imagine the Suffragists were going to wait until the crowd came up and did their sweet will upon them … ?[31]

This was not the first time that suffragettes had carried out acts of daring and ingenuity via the built environment. In May 1909, WSPU members Vera Holme (1881-1969) and Elsie Howey (1884-1963) astonished those assembled for a taxation meeting inside Colston Hall, Bristol, by calling out "Votes for Women!" from inside the hall's organ, where they had hidden overnight.[32] The spatial appropriation of city streets by suffragists and suffragettes in massive, planned spectacles is one of the best-known aspects of the early-twentieth-century suffrage campaign. But events of this nature were relatively unknown in Bath. Certainly the suffragettes' sense of political urgency conjoined with a very precise spatial awareness of Bath, leading them to strategically define the best place to carry out their plan, and to devise a conceptually elegant (if physically awkward) means of escape. Women shouting from rooftops, crawling along copings, and escaping angry mobs through back gardens, was almost unimaginable in this quiet city, where 'lady smokers' were enough of an aberration from feminine ideals that they inspired alarmed newspaper articles.[33]

But it was not the rooftop occupation during the Skating Rink rally that captured the press's most attentive reportage of that day. Instead, it was the work of Mabel Capper (1886-1956), visiting from London in order to disrupt Lloyd George's progress through the west country. As the *Bath Herald* recounted in the November 25th 1911 daily edition, Capper was 'charged with damaging four panes of glass in the windows of the New Bond Street Post Office, value £4' on the night November 24th. 'Miss Capper,' observed the reporter of her arraignment the following day, 'a good-looking young lady, was attired in green, and wore a Suffragette badge. She pleaded "Guilty" in a clear voice.'[34] Leonora Tyson told her audience that 'Miss Capper was … sentenced to a month's imprisonment for breaking a Post Office window in protest. But the men who smashed the windows of that private property for no reason at all, were not sent down for a month. It appeared as if men could smash as many windows as they liked.'[35]

Objects and Journeys: A Suffrage Cartography in Four Motifs

I now examine aspects of 'suffragette city' that static points on a two-dimensional map cannot communicate fully, on their own. These include passages and movements in the city, journeys taken once or often, and points of intensity that speak to the complexities within suffrage work in Bath. Drawing upon Knowles' model described above, as well as actor-network-theory, which assumes that material objects can inspire or enable humans to act,[36] the final section considers, in loosely chronological form, four motifs. These motifs suggest the itineraries of objects, and the effect of buildings and places that were an essential part of suffrage work in Bath prior to WWI.

The Window

Suffrage activity in Bath 1909-14 was marked by the tension between accepted modes of feminine decorum and what was, for many, a decidedly unladylike use of public space.[37] Crawford notes of Bath resident and member of the pro-suffrage Bristol and West of England Society, Lilias Sophia Ashworth Hallett (1844-1922) **[fig. 8]**, 'it required considerable courage [in the 1870s and 80s] for a woman to sit on a public platform and actually to speak from one was regarded as almost indecent.'[38] One generation later, Bath was still deeply shocked when, according to Police Constable Brown, he came past the sub Post Office in New Bond street, a few hours after the Liberal rally ended, only to find a young woman 'wilfully breaking panes of glass with [a] hammer.'[39] Capper defended her protest as a political gesture, in retaliation for the exclusion of women from the Rink: 'as they were refused admittance to the meeting where Mr Lloyd George was making a statement on woman suffrage she, as a voteless woman, took the only means for protest and smashed Government property.'[40] The window-smashing incident shocked Bath. Local newspapers recalled it on several occasions, even as late as July 1912, when the *Bath Herald* reported on a hatchet being thrown by suffragettes into a carriage containing Prime Minister Herbert Henry Asquith and the Home Secretary, travelling in Ireland.[41] This example of militancy, far removed from Bath, brought the spectre of Capper's gesture into the foreground once more. For Bath, the four broken panes of glass in New Bond Street spoke directly to the thousands of smashed windows across the country at the height of militant action.

My interest in Capper's window-breaking has to do with its location in Bath. This Post Office was, as Capper observed, Government property and thus, a logical site for her act of civil disobedience. As noted above, the Post Office was found at the junction of several streets in central Bath, including Walcot, Broad, Northgate and New Bond Streets [**fig. 9**].[42] The suffrage map shows that four women's suffrage societies located their public offices and shops near this junction. In 1908 the National Union of Women's Suffrage Societies (NUWSS) had a shop at 22a Broad Street, near the YMCA, while by spring 1912 their all-male counterparts, the Bath Men's League for Women's Suffrage, would take a space closer to the Guildhall at 3 Northgate Street, perhaps a five minute walk downhill. The WSPU shop was approximately equidistant from the Men's League offices at 12 Walcot Street (a location that no longer corresponds to present-day mapping, but was slightly north of St. Michael's without-the-walls) and opened in the autumn of 1910 [**fig. 11**].

Also visible on the suffrage map is the point where the walks between these three offices and shops would have converged: the very same Post Office where Capper left her mark in late autumn, 1911 [**fig. 9**]. What is not as immediately visible is the confluence on this site of tensions over militancy among pro-suffrage women. When Capper wielded her hammer against the Post Office windows, she also succeeded in attacking the very same building that the NUWSS had just occupied the

fig 8: Suffragettes Edith Wheelwright and Lilias Ashworth Hallett in the Suffragette's Wood, 1911

Bath in Time - Bath Central Library Collection

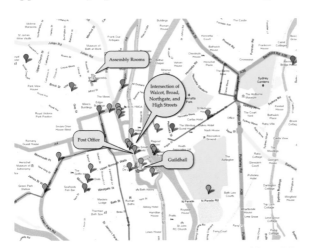

fig 9: Detail from the Suffragette City map (Google), created 2012, also accessible as an interactive map via http://goo.gl/maps/kdpS

fig 10: St Michael's Without the Walls, showing the former Bath Post Office chambers on New Bond Street to the left, 1904

Bath in Time - Bath Central Library Collection

month before. The October 12th 1911 edition of the *Bath Herald* reported on the opening of the NUWSS new offices in the Post Office Chambers, New Bond Street. The article included the opening hours: 'from 11 to 1, and from 3 to 5. On Thursdays and Fridays it would be open in the evenings also.'[43] Thus it is very likely that the offices of this non-militant suffrage society were open when Capper began to smash the building's windows. Inadvertently perhaps, Capper made the NUWSS the object of the very kind of action its members continually sought to discredit: a militant attack. Perhaps it was this acute proximity to militancy, and fears of an almost inevitable association between action and site, that prompted the Bath Society for Women's Suffrage (closely allied with the NUWSS) to publicly deplore militancy a few days later, in a document issued to the *Bath Herald* for printing. In it, the authors declare, 'such outbreaks injure women far more than anyone else, and that they are organised by one Suffrage Society only, and discountenanced by our own union.'[44] Perhaps the opening of the NUSWW affiliated men's offices within a few months of this statement, so close to the Post Office, was an attempt to consolidate, spatially, the non-militancy of this very small part of Bath, and to forestall any other violent action that might emanate, literally or figuratively, from the WSPU offices nearby.

2) The Bicycle

Physical vitality is not usually associated with suffragists and especially not suffragettes, whose public image remained, until recently, strongly tethered to their hunger strikes and physical maltreatment through force-feeding in prison.[45] Although she never went to prison, Mary Blathwayt suffered nervous tension and eye problems, apparently as a result of her hard work for the WSPU in 1908 and 1909.[46] Her mother, Emily, certainly did not see her daughter as having any particular physical potency. She wrote in her diary of March 14th 1911, '[Mary] is what her grandfather called "powerfully weak."'[47] Yet Mary Blathwayt's packed schedule, expertise in organisation, and remarkable commitment to the cause and spaces of suffrage may be found in a great number of her diary entries. She does come across as a timid person, not one to generate the legendary excitement and attraction of other, more charismatic suffrage workers. Mary herself comments on her struggles as a public speaker, and often notes her failure to sell the WSPU newspaper, *Votes for Women*, in comparison to her compatriots.[48] And one day, when attempting to sell flowers in the suffrage colours in Milsom Street to raise money for the WSPU, she notes sadly, 'I had to let a great many flowers go for a penny or people would not buy them.'[49]

fig 11: **Walcot Street looking north, with the entrance to St Michael's Cemetery, 1936. At the end of the railings is No. 12 Walcot Street, the former headquarters of Bath's WSPU.**
Bath in Time - Bath Central Library Collection

A striking feature of Blathwayt's daily diary is the frequent mention of apparently mundane articles such as her watch and her umbrella, both of which are cherished and, when lost or broken, occasion comment. But there is another object that has an even greater status in Blathwayt's life: her bicycle. The first mention of the bicycle is on February 17th 1909, not a time of the year when many would choose to cycle, but Blathwayt notes,'This morning I bicycled into Bath.' Later that spring, Blathwayt accompanied her neighbour, militant suffragette Aethel Tollemache (1875-1955) on their bicycles to the Guildhall, taking ivy and vases in their baskets to decorate the platform for a event the next day. The bicycle continues to be used in 1909 and early 1910, mostly for trips to Tollemache's home, nearby Batheaston Villa. In the summer and autumn of 1910, however, there is a dramatic increase in Blathwayt's use of the bicycle. Her primary destination is the 'Votes for Women' shop, as she calls it, in central Bath. Tuesday, September 27th 1910 was a typical day for this 31-year-old woman:

> I bicycled into Bath this morning. Miss Perkins opened the shop. I finished getting the literature ready for the meeting. Counted out some of the tickets. Had dinner + tea in the shop. This evening distributed handbills in Milsom Street. Bicycled home. …

The distance between the shop on Walcot Street and Blathwayt's home in Northend, Batheaston, is nearly 3 miles, and much of the journey homewards would have been uphill. That autumn, Blathwayt made this gruelling journey almost every day, apparently with relish, even when her day was quite literally full from morning until late at night; evening events normally began at 8pm. Even in the absence of declarative statements, these were clearly happy days. Although her parents were supporters of her work for the cause, and indeed initiated a number of projects of their own, the autonomy produced through the shop is evidently part of Blathwayt's pleasure. Blathwayt's daily journeys on bicycle to multiple destinations at the end of a long, tiring day, were worthy of comment. Perhaps it was the exhilaration of this autonomy, or the renewed purpose of the shop, or even the simple benefits of vigorous exercise: whatever the reason, Blathwayt begins to note her aptitude with people, particularly with selling shop items and encouraging new membership. On October 4th 1910, a month after the shop opened, Blathwayt records happily:

> … This evening I went into Bath … I took some strawberries to the Shop + sold them to a lady for 6d + also sold a 9d box of the Tollmaches' home made sweets. The lady took a membership card away with her. I arranged the flowers in the window. Neither Mrs Moger or Aethel had sold any thing all day.

The bicycle is a minor actor in the overall geography of feminist activism in pre-WWI Bath. But it does appear to have enabled this young woman, temporarily perhaps, to take greater charge of her daily movements, fortify her personal liberty, and to become a slightly different person, one who had greater ability to enact political change. These are all qualities that the suffrage movement wished to reinforce for women across a more explicitly political spectrum, but in the case of Mary Blathwayt and her frequent journeys on bicycle to and from central Bath, they became a reality, even without the vote, in the autumn of 1910.

3) The House

Eagle House, where Mary Blathwayt lived with her parents for most of the period in question, is likely the best known building in Bath in terms of suffrage history, and indeed it was a veritable hub of activity prior to WWI. But as the suffrage map indicates, at least ten other private homes were the site of multiple or singular events of significance to the women's suffrage movement. Whether these events were proactive, such as the use of Miss Johnston's home in the Royal Crescent in the winter of 1910 as a place to meet and rehearse suffrage songs for an upcoming event, or destructive, such as the burning by arson of Westwood Lodge in the exclusive neighbourhood of Lansdown Hill in December 1913,[50] that they took place in or deployed private homes had a particular charge in Bath, where the self-image of the city is closely tied to its iconic, predominantly residential architecture.[51] The third motif is also a private home that, like Westwood Lodge, is located on Lansdown Hill. This is where some of Bath's most famous and beloved works of Georgian architecture may be found: Somerset Place (John Eveleigh, begun 1790), a crescent which gives an southerly aspect over the centre of Bath, and Lansdown Crescent, designed by John Palmer, 1789-93 [fig. 12]. These graceful, neo-classical crescents, set high above the denser and more socially mixed parts of the city, signified an ideal of what Bath had achieved culturally and socially in its Georgian heyday. In the spring of 1911, the year of the census, WSPU organiser for Bath, Mrs Mansel took a one-week lease on

12 Lansdown Crescent, a building that she and a group of unnamed women would occupy for one night: Sunday, April 2nd.

As in Bath, suffrage groups across the country were gearing up for a major boycott of the census process as a means to thwart what they saw as the government's continuing intrusion into women's lives. Without constitutional recourse, they felt, women would have no control over the decisions the government might make with the information they were planning to collect.[52] To avoid the census, women gathered in skating rinks, restaurants, schools, theatres, and private homes such as 12 Lansdown Crescent. Mrs Mansel furnished the empty house with the help of an unknown number of suffragettes. In an early form of embedded journalism, a reporter was invited to witness the events, which were recounted, rather admiringly, in the April 3rd 1911 edition of the *Bath Herald.* Obviously delighted to partake in an all-night event of civil disobedience in the company of women, the reporter applauded 'the simplicity of the plan' in his article entitled, 'The Great Coup':

fig 12: Lansdown Crescent, Bath c.1916. Coloured sketch by Sylvia Gosse
Bath in Time - Holburne Museum, Bath

> There was nothing illegal … [in] obtaining a house and becoming the tenant for a week. Receiving a number of lady visitors was no crime. The events of the night, music, speeches, readings, and sleeping, offended against no laws. No offence, indeed, was actually committed until the 'head of the house' made a false return to the enumerator who called for the census paper today … the visitors, who are termed the 'evaders', could not be touched by the long arm of the law, even if their identity were established. And the damage would have been done, for by the time the call was made they would all have returned to their several homes … [53]

After commenting favourably on the furnishings, speeches, and refreshments, the author observed that the 'night was entertaining and pleasant, and the programme was well varied.'[54]

Of her experiences in Lansdown Crescent, Mary Blathwayt wrote, 'We had a charming room to hold our meeting, beautifully decorated and very comfortable.' Blathwayt gives the number that doubtless the reporter was urged not to reveal: 'There were 29 of us.'[55] But the reporter is more detailed than Blathwayt when discussing the great distances that some women had chosen to travel in order to participate in the evasion: 'They had come from far and near.

One lady had walked seven miles in order to take part; one had driven 10 miles, and they came from all over the city.' The *Herald* reporter also commented on the decor: 'the bareness of the walls effectively [was] broken by tastefully arranged tufts of foliage. Over the fireplace was a suffrage banner, and, in pride of place on the mantelpiece, for all to see, the fateful census paper which was going to mar the accuracy of the Bath figures.'[56] The author also recounted how, despite the provisions made for sleeping, 'astonishingly few took advantage … the 'evaders' found it quite easy to remain up; the excitement sustained them, and there was the primitive feeling abroad that they could go to bed any night, but might not have the opportunity to take part in such a meeting again.' Certainly the authorities knew that 12 Lansdown Crescent would be the site for this act of resistance. The reporter and the evaders both saw that detectives were watching the house from the end of the road.[57]

The 29 suffragettes successfully avoided the census, and greeted the dawn together with the reporter and the detectives, if with different feelings. By welcoming an outside witness into their temporary home, the women's suffrage movement invited the wider Bath community to reflect on the deeply-engrained tradition of associating femininity with a purportedly domestic realm, and showed, instead, how that very realm could be the site of radical, yet still 'entertaining and pleasant', political resistance.

4) The Luggage Tag

In stark contrast to the convivial events of April 2nd 1911, much of the remaining story of suffrage work in Bath is one of heightened tensions and violence, both against suffrage workers,[58] and on the part of suffragettes themselves: arson increased during these years, also hot tar attacks on letterboxes, and false fire alarms.[59] By April 1913 Emily Blathwayt, Mary Blathwayt's mother, writes, 'I am glad to say [Mary] is writing to resign membership with the WSPU. Now they have begun burning houses in the neighbourhood I feel more than ever ashamed to be connected with them.'[60] As opinions over militancy intensified, divisions among the pro-suffrage community in Bath began to show. The Blathwayts' more radical neighbours, the Tollemaches, stepped up their work and reduced what had been near-daily collaboration with Mary Blathwayt. Her mother, observing with no pleasure the destruction of Westwood in Lansdown in late December 1913, writes, 'of course one naturally suspects the Tollemaches.'[61]

I too suspect the Tollemaches in the case of the luggage-tag incident at the Bath golf course in the spring of 1914. Known informally at the time as the 'Sham Castle links', the Bath golf course was built in close proximity to the eighteenth-century sham or faux castle front on the western slopes of Bathampton Down. The Bath Golf Club first opened in the 1880s. At that time, a separate course 'for ladies' was situated to the north of the men's course. Over time, however, as demand for the men's course grew, 'the changes involved encroachment upon the ladies' course.' During this time 'the best' female players would be allowed onto the men's course, but it was not until after women got the partial vote, in fact, that 'ladies were finally admitted to Bath Golf Club' in 1920.[62]

The years of the encroachment of the men's course on the women's space were also the years of the most extreme militancy of the women's suffrage movement in Bath and elsewhere. On Monday, March 4th 1914, local papers reported on a strange act of vandalism on the men's course.[63] The *Herald* wrote:

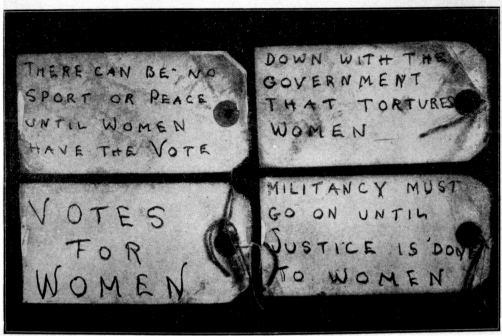

Suffragettes on Bath Golf Links.

THERE CAN BE NO
SPORT OR PEACE
UNTIL WOMEN
HAVE THE VOTE

DOWN WITH THE
GOVERNMENT
THAT TORTURES
WOMEN

VOTES
FOR
WOMEN

MILITANCY MUST
GO ON UNTIL
JUSTICE IS DONE
TO WOMEN

fig 13: Specimens of the luggage labels left by suffragettes at Bath Golf Links. March 3rd, 1914
Bath in Time - Bath Central Library Collection

The Sham Castle links were selected last night for wanton damage by suffragists … The first discovery was made by a green-man in the employ of the Bath Golf Club … He discovered that the 15th green, which is near the bridle path on Hampton Down, had been damaged. Between 30 and 40 holes were found in the green, and caustic soda had been scattered about, causing the grass to be discoloured. Further investigation revealed the fact that the 14th green and the 5th had also been similarly treated and very badly cut up.[64]

The *Bath Chronicle* provided further details through a photograph, quite rare in the press at this time except for coverage of sporting events, weddings of the peerage, or major political figures [**fig. 13**]. The image shows four paper luggage tags, slightly battered, with handwritten texts on each in capital letters. The caption to the photograph reads: 'Specimens of the luggage labels left by suffragettes at Bath Golf Links on Tuesday, last week, after their night raid when the turf and a number of greens was [sic] cut up. The labels were attached to the flags on the mutilated greens.'[65]

The writing on the four tags shown is clearly legible in the photograph, and the tags appear to have been inscribed on both sides. The texts read:

There can be no sport or peace until Women have the Vote'
'Down with the government that tortures Women'
'Votes for Women'
'Militancy must go on until Justice is done to Women'

Clearly relating these slogans to the place of sport where they were placed, the authors of this action must have wished to particularly target the well-heeled gentlemen who would have frequented the Bath Golf Club prior to WWI, the very same gentlemen who, in their appetite for their sport, had taken what had previously been available to women. (No doubt the parallels between this injustice and the withdrawal of the vote from women in the previous century were evident to those who visited the course that night.) But knowledge of the Bath Golf Club, even exclusion from it as a former female player, would have been specific to an equally well-heeled class of woman. The Tollemache sisters lived in a stately villa in Batheaston, like Mary Blathwayt, and while they did not leave diaries or any written legacy, by all accounts they did not work for a living. They were avid vegetarians, talented musicians, wonderfully creative in their radicalism,[66] and their names can be found over and over in the pages of Mary and Emily Blathwayt's diaries. They were at leisure to be fully devoted to their cause. When Grace Tollemache (dates unknown) served a prison sentence for breaking windows in London in 1912, Emily Blathwayt wrote drily, 'I wonder if she will come out madder than when she went in.'[67]

Someone was definitely mad, or angry, when they approached the Bath golf course on the night on March 3rd 1914. But whoever undertook the vandalism was also possessed of very specific spatial knowledge Bath in addition to some materials that spoke directly to gendered, spatial experience. The attackers, moving at night most likely through back roads and the unlit bridle path, knew exactly where to go to leave their literal mark in the tenderly cultivated turf; the fifteenth green mentioned in the first report was close to the former division between men's and women's spaces. The unwanted visitors to the course had also carried with them a sufficient quantity of caustic soda, a common and inexpensive household cleaning agent, one that would have been readily available and perhaps not missed in a large home with many rooms to clean. None of these details points unequivocally to Aethel or Grace Tollemache, but none points away from them, either. It is not so much my intention, however, to identify the actors in this unique act of political mischief in pre-war Bath as it is to think about the journeys that this act brings, tangentially, into representation. And in this sense it is the luggage tag that speaks most powerfully of the spatial capital of suffragettes prior to WWI.

One of the most remarkable aspects of my research has been to discover the intensity and frequency of suffrage-related travel in Edwardian England. My survey of Bath has provided rich evidence of an incredible mobility, not just of women, but also of objects, clothing, and printed materials. Packages of laundry and literature were in constant movement between houses, neighbourhoods, cities, regions, and even countries. It was not uncommon for Mary Blathwayt to travel to Bristol and back in order to consult with another WSPU member during a busy day that included seeing other suffragettes off, from Bath's two railway stations, on their own journeys.[68] For Blathwayt and other more mobile suffrage workers like Annie Kenney or Mrs Mansel, the luggage tag was an ordinary but necessary object, one that identified property, terminus, and less explicitly but no less powerfully, vocation. For any active suffrage worker, the luggage tag, inexpensive and sold in bundles at any stationary shop or post office, would have been readily to hand. It also offered the familiar practicality of something that could be attached to something else, to signal ownership, and to show the next destination. In calling for 'Votes for Women' on the Bath Golf course, the anonymous luggage tags found in March 1914 sent a clear message. It was high time for Bath to get on board.

Conclusion: To Find for Ourselves Our Own Place

In November 1912, one year after the contentious Liberal rally, organisers chose the Central Skating Rink on North Parade as the location for a talk by WSPU leader Emmeline Pankhurst (1858-1928). Doubtless the planners of this event chose to symbolically re-appropriate the building that had been the site of the Government's most audaciously anti-suffrage gesture in Bath. It was likely obvious to Bath's citizens as well that claiming this generous space for women's interests and concerns was a direct rebuttal to that event, for, as Emily Blathwayt recounted in her diary, assembled outside the building 'was a dense crowd and boys throwing fireworks into it.'[69] The violence that followed Mrs Pankhurst's lecture did not stop both Emily and Mary from judging the event to have been a great success.[70] The spirit of confidence that pervades accounts of this famous visitor's time in the Rink is perhaps best summed up in an exchange that took place between Mrs Pankhurst and a local, non-militant male supporter of women's right to vote. John Wynne Jeudwine (1852-1928), barrister, author and neighbour to the Blathwayts and the Tollemaches took the opportunity of Mrs Pankhurst's presence to call into question militant methods, and to underscore the direct thread between militant activism in Bath and elsewhere. Following her speech, he asked, "Are you aware that the Bath Men's League for Women's Suffrage was strangled at its birth by the women who broke windows in Bath and London?" In calm reply, "Mrs Pankhurst remarked that it must have been a very weakly infant."[71] What a far cry from the early discourse of women's suffrage this statement must have seemed. In this quick quip, the carefully cultivated image of women organising 'At-Home' meetings in tidy parlours, asking for entry into political life on the basis of their excellence as mothers and wives, vanished. Surely the setting for the quip, the very same vast stage that the Chancellor of the Exchequer had stood upon a year before, underscored the powerful shifts that had taken place since the beginnings of the radical suffrage campaign in the city.

But it is not the words of this famous suffragette that conclude this essay. I prefer to direct the reader into the suffrage map, to an event of far more modest proportion: in the weeks following the earlier meeting at the skating rink, when suffragettes had heckled their opponents from their rooftop safety. In the Assembly Rooms, which saw so much feminist activity, virtually every week, in Edwardian Bath, a woman named Mrs Montague addressed her audience. She was the secretary of a WSPU chapter in Exeter. She had journeyed to Bath for the day, and was 'a well-known West country supporter of the women's cause.'[72]

Mrs Montague spoke on the topic of 'Women's Place in the World', her words suggesting the intelligence, resilience and insight that must have been alive in many towns and villages across England, where so much of the battle for the right to vote, to count as citizens, took place. 'What we are fighting for,' affirmed Mrs Montague, 'is the right to work out our own salvation in our own way.'

We demand the right to try experiments and claim the right to all paths of labour … We demand the right to make failures and success. We ask to be allowed to work our own evolution, and find out for ourselves our own place in the scheme of evolving humanity. We do not want power over men, but power for ourselves. We are human beings first, and women afterwards.[73]

What has emerged from my mapping of women's suffrage work in Bath is a powerful image of politicised spatial activity, work, actions, events and patterns that served to remake the city, or parts of it, into a co-actor for women's rights. It also reveals something akin to what Mrs Montague called for in her consideration of women's 'place'. Rather than insisting on the rightness of one spatial or political sphere over another, Mrs Montague presented the idea that a world of political equality is not one in which women are infallible. Rather, she clarified that women deserve in all places and spaces to engage in a spirit of experimentation, to make mistakes, to try new things, to learn and judge for themselves. Above all, she said to her audience of Bath women, "we deserve to find for ourselves our own place." While neither the suffragists nor the suffragettes of pre-war Bath built any works of stone and mortar in this city of great architectural significance, they did transform and occupy its built spaces, effecting small but potent changes, using the city in ways it had never been used before. In short, women's suffrage workers staged their battle for political self-determination in and with Bath's built environment in the years before WWI. And in so doing, they created their own place: a veritable suffragette city.

Notes

1   My thanks to Professor Graham Davis for encouraging this topic, Dan Brown for his assistance with the images for this paper, the staff at the Bath Central Library and the Gloucestershire Archives for their help with my research, Thomas Strickland for edits and comments, and Dr Elaine Chalus for sharing her forthcoming work on historical women, diaries, and urban space. I owe particularly warm thanks to Anne Buchanan, Local Studies Librarian of the Bath Central Library, for making the original newspapers available for consultation.

2   This landscape is detailed in my book, *Architects, Angels, Activists and the City of Bath, 1765-1965* (Ashgate, 2012), which builds on the scholarship of June Hannam, 'Suffragette Photographs,' *The Regional Historian: The Newsletter of the Regional History Centre, The University of the West of England* 8 (2002): pp.17-19, and Beatrice M. Willmott Dobbie, *A Nest of Suffragettes in Somerset* (Batheaston Society, 1979).

3   All these activities are noted, most repeatedly, in the diaries of Mary Blathwayt, January-December 1909, and January-December 1910.

4   Many suffragettes visiting Eagle House were in need of rest, but in one case – Jennie Kenney (dates unknown), sister of Annie Kenney – had an operation at Eagle House. Mary Blathwayt, July 4th 1910.

5   I am using 'Edwardian' to include the years following Edward VII's death (1910), up until the start of World War I in 1914.

6   The collection of over 250 images was digitised in the early 2000s. Low-resolution versions of the images are freely available via the online photographic archive, Bath in Time, www.bathintime.co.uk.

7   The Bristol and West of England Society (founded 1868), with active members in Bath, was the longest-standing of these; in terms of its non-militant approach and non-party efforts it overlapped with the Bath Society for Women's Suffrage and the National Union of Women's Suffrage Societies. See Elizabeth Crawford, *The Women's Suffrage Movement: A Reference Guide 1866-1928,* (Routledge, 2001) p.259, and Elizabeth Crawford, *The Women's Suffrage Movement in Britain and Ireland: A Regional Survey* (Routledge, 2006) p.137. In addition, the Conservative and Unionist Women's Franchise Association, the Men's League for Women's Suffrage, the Church League for Women's Suffrage and of course the Women's Social and Political Union were all active in Bath in the years leading up to WWI.

8   Annie Kenney famously had worked in a cotton mill in Lancashire before working for the WSPU, but did not agree with the WSPU's characterisation of her as 'the Suffragette Mill Girl. Crawford (2001) p.313. Nevertheless, Kenney's financial circumstances did not resemble those of Mary Blathwayt, who did not need to work. Kenney, Blathwayt, and Clara Codd, another Bath woman active in Bath suffrage work, were in their early 30s at the start date of this study, 1909, and were not unusual in this respect. However, Mabel Capper, discussed below, was only 23 when she made her mark as a suffragette in Bath. To my knowledge the oldest of the local (non-militant) suffrage movement in 1909 were Lilias Ashworth-Hallet (65) and Colonel Linley Blathwayt (70).

9   'Suffragist' is often used as a blanket term by historians to include all those actively in favour of women's emancipation during this era. In Bath, newspapers generally used this term in the same way, but between 1909-14, as militancy gained in intensity and in public disapproval, non-militant pro-suffrage women began to insist upon the distinction, such as Emma Edbrooke Webb, who on November 23rd 1911 wrote to the editor of the *Bath Herald* (daily), saying

'although I am keenly anxious for women to have the privilege of Parliamentary suffrage, I am no 'Suffragette,' neither does our Bath Women's Liberal Association contain one … Most of us very much dislike the militant tactics',p.7.

10 Statistical information from the University of Portsmouth, 'Historical Statistics' for Bath CB/MB, Somerset, England, *A Vision of Britain Through Time* (web), 2009 < http://www.visionofbritain.org.uk/unit_page.jsp?u_id=10196930# > (Accessed June 15th 2012).

11 'Bath and Votes for Women: Result of a Canvass', *The Bath Herald* (November 28th 1910): 4. Women householders in Bath had the municipal vote by this time, as they did elsewhere in England.

12 Other scholars have noted this point; see Willmott Dobbie, p.9. June Hannam suggests that these diaries provide, nonetheless, valuable information. See 'Suffragettes are Splendid for Any Work: The Blathwayt Diaries as a Source for Suffrage History', in *A Suffrage Reader: Charting Directions in British Suffrage History*, ed. Claire Eustance et al. (Leicester University Press, 2000) pp.52-68. Blathwayt's diaries provided valuable details such as precise numbers (of *Votes for Women* sold, for example), times (of trains leaving or arriving for destinations where other suffrage work would be carried out), and costs (of furnishing and running the WSPU shop).

13 Other scholars have noted the close relationship between gendered identities and city spaces. Elaine Chalus understands elite women's relationships with one another through the expatriate British and cosmopolitan spaces of eighteenth-century Nice in 'Place, Space and Gender in *Le Monde cosmopolite*: A Female Household in Nice, 1855-7' forthcoming, while Jane Rendell explores the mutually constitutive character of early nineteenth-century London building types, such as assembly rooms and opera houses, and the growing female middle class in *The Pursuit of Pleasure: Gender, Space and Architecture in Regency London* (Athlone Press, 2002).

14 Caroline Knowles, 'Cities on the Move: Navigating Urban Life', *City* 15.2 (April 2011): p.137.

15 Knowles, p.137.

16 Mary Blathwayt, March 27th 1909.

17 Bath's newspapers have a rather labyrinthine genealogy; not all have been saved or microfilmed. The *Bath Herald* is held in remote storage in its original leather binding, and the daily version of this paper is only available for 1910 and 1911; the weekly edition may be consulted for the other years covered in this essay. The weekly *Bath Chronicle*, another popular paper of the era, was consulted via the 'local index', a partial subject record of items and articles in local papers held in microfilm format. The *Chronicle* was consulted on and around the dates of major events as described in the diaries of Mary and Emily Blathwayt.

18 The interactive, re-scalable map may be found at the following url: http://goo.gl/maps/kdpS.

19 The June 3rd 1911 edition of the daily *Bath Herald* includes a map of the electoral districts within Bath; of the districts mentioned, only Odd Down is not included within the boundary of Bath.

20 The frequency of these journeys would diminish in 1913, by which time both Emily and Mary Blathwayt had resigned from the WSPU.

21 A scrapbook in the Bath Central Library collection includes a newspaper clipping from 1908, detailing the visit of anti-suffragist Mary Dickens, granddaughter of the writer Charles Dickens, to Bath. Boodle Vol 30, p.44.

22 Graham Davis and Penny Bonsall note that 'as late as 1911 the largest single occupational group of women in Bath was the domestic service category', not a particularly well-paid profession p.201. 'On the eve of the First World War', Davis and Bonsall continue, 'a

'respectable' working-class family with a head of household in full time employment, at an average age of 'round about a pound a week' found it a constant struggle to make ends meet', p.216. A one-shilling ticket would have been a steep price for such a family. *A History of Bath: Image and Reality* (Carnegie Publishing, 2006).

23   Mary Blathwayt, December 5th 1910. This journey is represented on the interactive map with a purple line, originating in Milsom Street.

24   'Liberal Women and the Vote: The Coming of the Dawn, Women's Liberal Association Activity', *The Bath Herald* (weekly), (March 9th 1912),p.6.

25   The June 25th 1910 edition of the *Bath Herald* contains, for example, an editorial on 'Votes for Women'. The author, moved by the injustice of taxation without representation, writes nevertheless that 'one trembles at the idea of legislative business being controlled by persons of such hysterical temperament as those who have been taking the lead in the recent agitation', p.4. Similar accusations of hysteria, aimed at militant suffragettes, was peppered throughout the press in this period, but Bath newspapers did not generally indulge in the hypersexualisation or demonisation of militant women as was the tendency in London newspapers. See Lisa Tickner, *The Spectacle of Women: Imagery of the Suffrage Campaign, 1907–14* (University of Chicago Press, 1988).

26   Elizabeth Crawford, *The Women's Suffrage Movement: A Reference Guide, 1866–1928* (Routledge, 2001), p.727.

27   Mary Blathwayt, June 11th 1910.

28   'Suffragists and the Government. The Wrecking of the Conciliation Bill. Mrs Mansel's Challenge to Mr Lloyd George', *Bath Herald* (daily), November 11th 1911, p.3.

29   Liberal Federation, 'Visit of the National Liberal Federation to Bath, Great Demonstration In the Central Skating Rink, Bath. November 24th, at 8 p.m.' Advertisement, *Bath Herald* (daily), November 16th 1911, p.2. Emphasis in original.

30   *Bath Herald* (daily), November 27th 1911, p.4.

31   Ibid.

32   Crawford (2001), p.289.

33   Earlier that same year, 'lady smokers' seen on a train through Bath inspired a pained article in the *Bath Herald* (daily), May 12th 1911, p.6.

34   'Smashing the Post Office Windows; Suffragette in the Dock; Sequel to Mr Lloyd George's Visit: Preferred Prison to Paying Fine: Cheered in Court', *Bath Herald* (daily), November 25th 1911, p.7.

35   'Suffragettes and Mr Lloyd George: 'What we Did and Why we Did it.', *Bath Herald* (daily), November 27th 1911, p.4.

36   On actor-network theory (ANT) see Bruno Latour, whose book, *Reassembling the Social: An Introduction to Actor-Network-Theory,* (Oxford University Press, 2005), elaborates on the question of an object's 'agency'.

37   See Lisa Tickner, op cit, for her discussion of the suffrage movement using visual and material culture, including art and craft, to negotiate public opinions about feminist work.

38   Crawford (2001), p.260.

39   'Smashing the Post Office Windows …'

40   'Smashing the Post Office Windows …'

41   'Suffragist Outburst; Arrests in Dublin; Attempt to Burn a Theatre; Serious Police Discoveries', *Bath Herald* (weekly), July 20th 1912),;p.8.

42   This post office, located at 25 New Bond Street, was one of many "sub" or minor post offices found throughout Bath. Better known today is the old post office, designed by the Office of Works, which was built in 1927 on the same site as the older post office. Michael Forsyth, Pevsner Architectural Guides: Bath. (Yale University Press, 2003), p.129.

43   'National Union of Women's Suffrage Societies: New Bath Office', *Bath Herald* (daily), October 12th 1911), p.4.

44   'Militant Suffragists: Tactics Discountenanced; Statement by the Bath Society for Women's Suffrage', *Bath Herald* (daily), December 2nd 1911), p.5.

45   See Jill Liddington and Elizabeth Crawford, 'Women do not Count, Neither shall they be Counted: Suffrage, Citizenship and the Battle for the 1911 Census', *History Workshop Journal* 71.1 (Spring 2011), p.5.

46   Mary Blathwayt, January 7th 1910.

47   Cited in Willmott Dobbie, p.47.

48   When Blathwayt visited Swansea in October 1909, she recounted her struggle to sell issues of *Votes for Women* Sold Votes again this evening … I have sold 18 Votes today which makes a total of 60 since I have been here. Mrs Dove Willcox who was here before us sold 252. Altogether we have sold 503'. Mary Blathwayt, October 8th 1909. Of a meeting she participated in earlier that year she wrote, 'took the chair … but spoke very badly'. Mary Blathwayt, July 17th 1909.

49   Mary Blathwayt, May 2nd 1910.

50   The burning of Westwood, like the smashing of the Post Office windows, garnered lengthy press coverage. See 'Suffragette Arson in Bath: Lansdown Residence Burnt Down; Early Morning Blaze; Militant Literature found in the Grounds; Also a 'Cat and Mouse' Postcard', *Bath Chronicle*, December 27th 1913.

51   See Peter Borsay, *The Image of Georgian Bath, 1700–2000* (Oxford University Press, 2000); Ronald S. Neale, *Bath 1650–1850, a Social History; or a Valley of Pleasure Yet a Sink of Iniquity* (Routledge and Kegan Paul, 1981).

52   Liddington and Crawford's recent study of the census evasion is an insightful account of the motivations of and divisions among women's suffrage workers in the months leading up to April 3rd 1911, as well as the first attempt to assess the actual extent of the evasion. Not as many women appear to have evaded as would have been expected from accounts of the time. Emmeline Pankhurst, who publicly announced in *Votes for Women* that she had evaded enumeration, did in fact sign a census return, p.11.

53   'The Great Coup: Bath Ladies Evade the Census; An All-Night Gathering; How the Time was Spent', *Bath Herald* (daily), April 3rd 1911), p.6.

54   'The Great Coup …

55   Mary Blathwayt, April 3rd 1911.

56   'The Great Coup …'

57   Mary Blathwayt, April 3rd 1911; 'The Great Coup …'

58   The article, 'Mrs Pankhurst in Bath: Lively Scenes Outside the Rink; Women's War to Go On', describes how an angry mob attacked four suffrage workers (1 man and 3 women) outside the Central Skating Rink on November 7th 1912 after Pankhurst's lecture. One woman was hit on the head by a stone, *Bath Herald*, November 9th 1912, p.4.

59   See the diary of Emily Blathwayt, December 1912, for details of this activity, also Willmott Dobbie, p.53.

60   Cited in Willmott Dobbie, p.56.

61   Emily Blathwayt, December 20th 1913, Diary of Emily Blathwayt, January-December 1913, Blathwayt Family Papers, Gloucestershire Archives.

62   'History of the Bath Golf Club', *The Bath Golf Club* (web) www.bathgolfclub.org.uk/history.php (accessed June 4th 2012).

63   The *Herald* material was recounted in 'Fifty Years Ago: 4 March 1914', *Weekly Chronicle*, March 7th 1964, while the *Bath Chronicle* photographic and caption material, titled 'Suffragettes on Bath Golf Links' was pasted into Boodle Vol. 30, verso of p.44.

64   'Fifty Years Ago: 4 March 1914'.

65   'Suffragettes on Bath Golf Links'.

66   Mary Blathwayt describes the Tollemache sisters enlisting their dog, Baloo, in fundraising in Milsom Street: 'he had on a white collar which Aethel had made for him, it had on it in green + purple letters 'Please give Baloo something to help the woman's movement. Votes for Women' … Baloo had a little tin hanging to his neck. A good many people put in pennies'. May 3rd 1910.

67   Cited in Crawford (2001), p.688.

68   On September 8th 1910, Mary Blathwayt records: 'I went into Bath this morning by tram. Father drove Mary Howey to the Midland Station; I went there + saw her off. Then I went to see Miss Curtis about our shop opening cards, posters + handbills. Went over to Bristol + spent the afternoon with Miss Stewart learning about the way the accounts are now kept. To tea with Mrs Dove-Willcox + Mrs Dugdale. … I came home [to Batheaston] again this evening'.

69   Emily Blathwayt, November 7th 1912.

70   See note 58.

71   'Mrs Pankhurst in Bath …'

72   'Women's Place in the World: Will Work Out Their Own Salvation', *Bath Herald* (daily), December 4th 1911),p.4.

73   'Women's Place in the World …'

Madame Sarah Grand, 'Mayoress' of Bath

Colleen Denney

In 1896, Alfred Praga painted a half-portrait of Sarah Grand [**fig. 1**] which her son, Archie Carlaw Grand, gave to the city of Bath in 1943, the year of her death so that it could hang in Bath's Guildhall. It entered Bath's Victoria Art Gallery collection in 1984.[1] The city of Bath was interested in owning a portrait of Madame Sarah Grand because, in later life, she was Bath's Lady 'Mayoress' with the longest record of service. She took on this post under the mayoralty of Alderman Cedric Chivers who, as a widower, asked her to perform the duties that would normally fall to the wife of a Mayor. She held this position in 1922; and then from 1924-29. The Mayor died in 1929; ill-health in the last two years of his office meant that most of his duties fell to Grand. After his death, she was invited to stand for Mayor but she declined.[2] The purpose of this essay is two-fold: to use the acquisition of the portrait as a way of examining

Grand's time as Lady 'Mayoress' of Bath; and, within that assessment, to address Grand as an advanced Victorian woman, known as the 'New Woman,' and how that title influenced her public presentation of self as Lady 'Mayoress'.

Sarah Grand was born Frances Elizabeth Clarke in Ireland in 1854 but moved to Yorkshire with her family after her father's death. At sixteen she married widower David Chambers McFall, an army surgeon. They travelled extensively before settling first in Norwich, and then in Warrington, Lancashire, where he retired as honorary brigade surgeon. She left him in 1890, moving to London to pursue her writing career. Her twenty-year-old son, Archie, also stayed behind. In London she collaborated with the publisher William Heinemann on her novel *The Heavenly Twins* (1893); due to its immediate success, he produced ten editions by 1923. This collaboration made Grand financially independent. She extended her writing career to journalism, lecture tours and, eventually, to the suffrage platform. She never returned to her husband, who died in 1898. While she had a strained relationship with her son, her stepsons often visited her in London. Archie came back into the picture when she moved to Bath. He pursued an acting career in Bath and elsewhere.

fig 1: **Mrs. Frances Elizabeth McFall (Madame Sarah Grand 1855-1943), 1896 by Alfred Praga. Oil on canvas.**
Victoria Art Gallery BATVG.P.1984.47, Bath & North East Somerset Council

Facing: Detail from Madam Sarah Grand, Mayoress of Bath, 1925. Photograph by Lambert of Bath.
Bath in Time - Bath Central Library Collection

The Heavenly Twins dealt with men's sexuality and venereal disease for the first time in literary history and attempted to exert a new code of moral purity. Grand knew about venereal disease through her husband's work as an army surgeon at a Lock hospital, a place where the government sent prostitutes who had contracted diseases. Her knowledge base also came from Josephine Butler's work on behalf of the repeal of the Contagious Diseases Acts in the 1870s and '80s. That legislation had punished the prostitute and treated her while letting her male clients go free.[3]

In 1893, when her novel was published, she made the bold move of changing her name to Madame Sarah Grand, in part to alleviate her husband's anxiety over being associated with her radical views. By the time of his death in 1898, she had completed her feminist trilogy, *Ideala: A Study from Life* (1888) which she had self-published before leaving Lancashire, *The Heavenly Twins* (1893), and *The Beth Book* (1897).[4] Her writings established her as one of the key voices of feminist resistance to male profligacy. Grand asked, 'Why didn't the government treat the men?' She argued that such men eventually married and spread their disease to their wives and, inadvertently, to their children.[5] With thinking like this, Grand became an overnight *succès de scandal;* but, in terms of the public self she presents in the Praga portrait and in other portraits of the 1890s [**figs. 2, 3, 7**], Grand wanted to counter such criticism. To write boldly about such a forbidden topic aligned her with the most radical aspects of a new feminist figure, the New Woman. In doing so, she risked the charge of trying to behave like a man.

Sarah Grand and the New Woman of the Victorian Period.

The New Woman of Sarah Grand's novels as well as the actual New Woman of the 1880s and 1890s could, if she were middle or upper-class, take advantage of the new benefits of education and live an emancipated life, free of marriage. She was also helped by the 1882 Married Women's Property Act, which gave women the right to keep their own earnings. Victorian society's anxieties over this New Woman were real and they escalated in the 1890s. This fear was soon explained in the 1901 census of England and Wales which showed the 'surplus' of women to be over a million. David Rubinstein argues that contemporaries blamed the imbalance on the appearance of the New Woman, despite high levels of male emigration that contributed.[6] As a New Woman novelist herself, Grand came under continual scrutiny, finding herself at the centre of a gendered debate in which the New Woman acted as a symbol. This was so because Grand coined the term 'New Woman' in an 1894 essay where she said 'the new woman is a little above' the man and it was her duty to bring him up to her standard.[7] Literary critics viewed this New Woman, and Sarah Grand as its major representative, as personifying the culture's anxieties hence posing a threat to its stability. The New Woman acted as a symbol for and catalyst of the cultural boundary-breaking that was occurring in terms of gender, race and class in the 1890s.[8] Grand represented the New Woman's modern voice because she offered no easy solutions to the marriage question. Rather she attempted to 'subvert and redefine masculine values by exploring the complexities of women's lives' and her feminist stance meant she insisted on 'equal access to areas of masculine privilege - education, employment, legislation and government.'[9] To do so was to challenge the status quo of Victorian womanhood. Teresa Mangum has argued that the New Woman novelists, and the New Women alike, subverted this construction of the self-effacing, submissive wife, questioning the 'biological essentialism at the heart of ideal womanhood' such that '[t]he New Woman fiction emerged as one of the most powerful forms of resistance to this ideal.'[10]

The New Woman was doubly troubling. On one hand, she could be too full of rebellion to represent any real person; on the other, the culture, it seems, wanted her to be only a fiction because the ideals she represented posed such a threat to the gender structure. The New Woman was not a single, homogenous person; she often represented conflicting ideals at the end of the century. Some scholars have even gone so far as to suggest that the New Woman did not exist because she embodied too many contradictory ideals. The debate over her mirrors the arguments we still hear today over what constitutes a feminist. 'The New Woman was by turns: a mannish amazon and a Womanly woman; she was oversexed, undersexed, or same sex identified; she was anti-maternal, or a racial supermother; she was male-identified, or manhating and/or man-eating, or self-appointed saviour of benighted masculinity.'[11] Like her contemporary feminist counterparts, Grand chose to espouse certain ideals and to reject others. She was a feminist who knew that there was a politics of difference; that the women's causes and stances that she defended were not identical to those of other feminists working in England.

Photo: Elliott & Fry, Baker Street, W.

fig 2: Madame Sarah Grand c.1896. Photograph by Elliot and Fry.
Bath in Time - Bath Central Library Collection

The ways that Grand manipulated her own image and the way the culture constructed her, were at the centre of her masquerade of public self and reflected these contradictory ideals. In her portraits, she plays the part of a conservative, feminine woman who seeks to protect the lesser man (her husband and son) from embarrassment. Like other public women who were her contemporaries, such as the suffrage leader Millicent Garrett Fawcett, she fought resistance to her views by projecting a feminine stance. Her image practice reveals her public self, not her private one, just as it did for Garrett Fawcett who, like Grand, espoused her politics on public platforms and in other public forums.[12] Catherine Craft-Fairchild regards masquerade 'as the creation of an image or spectacle for the benefit of a spectator.'[13] Both of these women embraced a kind of subversive tactic, viewing masquerade as the inevitable female disguise 'as submission to dominant social codes,' but at the same time as 'disruptive and as resistance to patriarchal norms.'[14] Grand, as New Woman, resisted the dominant conversation but Grand as public figure in her portraits seemed to bow to such 'dominant social codes,' meaning that she, like Garrett Fawcett, created a shifting focus that allowed her to be in charge of her public presentation. We can see this shifting focus embodied in her portraits as Lady 'Mayoress' and, especially, in Praga's seemingly compliant public lady.

And, yet, it is more complex than that because Grand self-identified as a New Woman but she did not cross these borders without trepidation. When we look at her images for public consumption like the Elliot and Fry photograph **[fig. 2]** we see the way she sidestepped the manly stereotype of the New Woman by creating a soft-focus, romantic presence for her eager public. Here, as well as in Mendelssohn's photograph **[fig.3]**, Grand made concerted efforts to resist the transgressive label by masking it with a cloak of femininity, the camera's soft focus

fig 3: Madame Sarah Grand, c.1896. Photograph by H. S. Mendelssohn.
Bath in Time - Bath Central Library Collection

playing up her beauty. Grand reverted to an over-exaggerated feminine appearance in such imagery, in part, to compensate for her public role that not only identified her as stepping outside the bounds of femininity, but also, in her writings, challenged masculine patterns of philandering behaviour.

Yet she embraced the bicycle as a mode of transport, **[fig. 4]** and as a symbol of women's new-found freedoms, aligning herself with the key tenets of the New Woman's cause. She, like the suffragists, had to resist the damaging caricatures of the press, ones that positioned feminists as ugly harridans who, because cultural forces deemed that they lacked sufficient femininity, could not snare a man and hence agitated for their rights out of sheer unhappiness. [15]

While struggling to maintain an image of feminine respectability in her public presentation of self, Grand was aware of her position as one of the leaders who voiced the need for women's autonomy 'in everything from etiquette to employment.'[16] The suffrage woman had to resist the media construct of the 'shrieking sister,' which identified her as a hysteric who could not possibly vote rationally due to her excess of emotion. Like her, Grand had to soft-pedal her public image to downplay the extreme caricature of the New Woman that appeared in the press, and who herself was a 'wildly skewed, reductive media construct which did not represent the real lives and work of those people it purported to describe.'[17] Of course not; like any stereotype, it reflected the dominant narrative of the patriarchal culture, one that had to defend its ideologies against powerful women who were moving forward in education, government, and in a renegotiation of the domestic sphere. Such a threat inevitably produced a backlash, and the media representation of the New Woman appeared to deflect and discredit the real causes for which women like Grand were fighting.

According to Teresa Mangum, Grand felt secure in creating, a 'feminist fantasy' in her novels.[18] But she herself took a more middle-of-the-road feminist stance of 'liberal feminist personal rights philosophy.' Lucy Bland argues that she stressed 'a woman's right over her own person, her right to choose, and her claim to equality with men,' but she also embraced 'a changed standard of morality which not only demanded a change in male sexual behaviour, but also necessitated highly "moral" sexual behavior in women'[19] As Barbara Caine asserts when examining the lives of feminists, we must determine the character's development of a 'feminist consciousness'.[20] Grand, in this context, articulated it through her politics and presentation of self. The portraits are the conduit through which she created this consciousness and hence informed her later appearance as Lady 'Mayoress' of Bath. How did her civic and urban identity stem from her previous career and how did she make use of that earlier career to tap into the historical precedent of the Lady 'Mayoress'? How did her role as part of the 'corporate body politic' extend or negate her more radical self of the 1890s?[21] To ask these questions is to beg a further examination of the traditional structure of Bath society. A Lady 'Mayoress', if she wanted to pursue making a difference, had to move beyond a presence and practice that traditionally was construed as 'intermittent and ornamental.'[22]

fig 4: Sarah Grand in Cycling Attire, 1896. Photograph by Richard Williams Thomas.
Bath in Time - Bath Central Library Collection

Bath's Introduction to Madame Sarah Grand.

These questions are crucial if we try to position ourselves as those Bath citizens who knew none of this history in 1922 when Grand moved to Bath from Tunbridge Wells with her friends, Rachel Mary and William Tindall. Quakers about her age, they settled at Crowe Hall on Widcombe Hill with Grand as their permanent guest. When that house burned down in 1926, she moved into 7 Sion Hill Place with her sister Nellie, a retired nurse; meanwhile the Tindalls rebuilt their home and remained close friends. When Bath was bombed in 1942, Grand left Bath and died a year later at The Grange in Calne, Wiltshire.

The city of Bath into which Grand immersed herself is revealed in a guidebook description of the 1920s: 'Bath has its value as a health resort, particularly to invalids in the winter time; for the air is peculiarly sweet and fresh, and the encircling hills protect the city from cold winds. It is justly claimed that scarcely any other English town is graced with suburbs so bracing as these air-swept heights.'[23] She had entered a resort town that was somewhat on the decline but which entrusted itself to its alderman and councillors for protection and charity.

In 1922, at the age of 68, Grand received an offer from Cedric Chivers to be his Lady 'Mayoress'. Many years separated her from her work on suffrage platforms, but as Grand's biographer Gillian Kersley explains: 'In a close-knit society like Bath, Mr Chivers would have met Sarah at social gatherings, and her grace, charm and past experience on any platform would have marked her as an invaluable consort.'[24] It is ironic that a woman so famous would be unknown in this 'close-knit' culture, but not surprising, especially since her novels were out of print at that time. The only thing she had written while in Bath was an appreciation of the city as a newcomer for the local paper.[25] But the journalists began to do their work, calling her 'Madame Sarah Grand, the Distinguished Novelist,'[26] one journalist for the *Glasgow Herald* exclaiming: 'Who knows but a new work of fiction may result, and a new Jane Austen rise in Jane Austen's city, one hundred years after the first.'[27]

fig 5: **Mayoress Madame Sarah Grand posing on the Bandstand at Royal Victoria Park with the Mayor Cedric Chivers and others, 1920s.**

Bath in Time - Bath Central Library Collection

Grand did not know what was in store for her. Alongside Chivers, she would experience the longest running Mayoralty in Bath's history, reason enough to find her portrait hanging in the Guildhall. She stepped into the position naively, stating: 'I feel that, as Mayoress, I am just taking the responsibility for the little things that are not suitable for the Mayor to do, and that a woman ought really to do. The Mayoress is a sort of *aide-de-camp* to the Mayor.'[28] Such sentiments are a far cry from her former agitation for women's rights. Yet they show how cognisant she was of the conservative presentation she would have to create as Lady 'Mayoress'. This statement declares that she saw gender roles as traditional ones, but it is more likely that she was masking her true feelings. Grand was always diplomatic, able to speak both to conservative and liberal audiences on women's issues in a way that would not alienate them. This statement may reflect the old Sarah rising to the moment. But, it may reveal her understanding of the role of Lady 'Mayoress' as nothing more than that 'intermittent and ornamental' one. In one respect a Lady 'Mayoress' was like the Lady Bountiful, performing the duties expected of her, based on her gender and class. The work she was doing as 'Mayoress' was similarly charitable and hence it was work for which she needed to project an image of a proper, deferential lady. Also, according to Helen Meller, some educated women in England played up their biological essentialism of the nurturing role to create more visible positions of power for themselves in their communities.[29] Grand's statement suggests that she saw such a nurturing role as a similar place of power.

In addition, she became Mayoress at a powerful time for British women. In her political aspirations she was part of a new force of womanhood that acted on the new-found opportunities of leadership and citizenship. County and borough councils opened to women in 1907 with Elizabeth Garrett Anderson becoming the first woman mayor in her home town of Aldeburgh; local government was becoming a significant employer of women.[30] During Grand's time as Mayoress, there were at least three women councillors for Bath. Meller remarks:

> 'Undertaking "good works", caring for the poor of particular urban localities or whole cities and encouraging support for the wholesome influences, especially cultural activities such as music, literature and art, were socially acceptable roles for women.... It offered social status and gave women a public role that could be defined as citizenship. . . which became a loaded word, imbued with a meaning covering both concern for the public sphere and altruistic concern for society's well-being.[31]

Grand's career as Lady 'Mayoress' included many social highlights that reflected such 'cultural activities,' ones for which she had to act as elegant hostess, as well as perform the role of charitable lady, such as:

> 'Apart from entertaining the Sanitary Engineers from seventeen countries, organized by the League of Nations, opening Bath's first Lending Library . . and donating pictures to brighten the classrooms of local schools, the Mayor and Mayoress welcomed 250 doctors to a BMA Conference when the city became, in gaiety and colour, like a scene from the Arabian Nights. Balls and banquets, fairy lights and roses all over the Abbey churchyard and the Roman baths; concerts, plays, processions: all this was enjoyed as much by the citizens as by the visitors.'[32]

fig 6: Mayoress Madame Sarah Grand and Mayor Cedric Chivers at a Ceremony at the Pavilion, Sydney Gardens, Bath. 1920s
Bath in Time - Bath Central Library Collection

Lady Bountiful or no, such elaborate events spoke to her great success alongside Mayor Chivers, their imposing appearance reflected in photographs that document various civil ceremonies [figs. 5 and 6]. Chivers was a munificent man who had had a financially lucrative career in book-binding. His personal dedication to the city knew no bounds, first as an Alderman, then embarking on the longest running Mayoralty Bath would experience.

But matched with Chivers philanthropic attitude, one reflected in the above events and hence implied in the role he expected of Grand, we have to keep in mind Grand's passionate commitment to causes. Beyond the usual round of civic duties, involving official dinners, opening bazaars and flower shows, the 1927 *Evening Standard* reported, for example, that she was 'one of the rare examples of a literary light to whom social sovereignty in civic life appeals . . .' At the time she was President of the National Women Citizens' Association and worked with the Church of England Temperance Society.[33] Yet she was capable of using her reputation as a writer to forward such causes, a case in point being the book of Grand's quotations, edited by her admirer, Gladys Singer-Biggar, that raised funds for the Mayoress Fresh Air Fund for poor city children.[34] Grand's public images reveal this ability to appeal to many audiences whose ideals might, at times, conflict with each other. Most prevalent in this regard is the Praga portrait itself.

The Praga Portrait, 1896.

When Grand became Lady 'Mayoress' of Bath, she began an intense friendship and correspondence with Singer-Biggar, who provides a record of the Bath portrait [**fig. 1**] when she first saw it at the 1927 Autumn Exhibition of the Bath Society of Artists:

> 'Your portrait . . . there is a distinctive quality about it which is arresting-
> you must always have stood out in a crowd-but not with quite the still
> power you exercise today'[35]

The portrait's inclusion at this exhibition of local artists is somewhat unusual,[36] the Director of the Victoria Art Gallery, Reginald W. M. Wright, having asked Praga to exhibit the work, hoping to sell it to a Bath resident.[37] Prominent Bath citizens then worked with Wright to get up a subscription to buy the portrait in order to present it to Grand in recognition of her role as Lady 'Mayoress' of Bath.[38] In the event, however, Chivers bought it so that he could give it to Grand himself.[39] She asked the Gallery to house the painting but her family objected. It appears that her son Archie kept it, since he was in possession of it when he presented it to the city of Bath in 1943. His decision was probably based on a long-standing tradition of giving portraits of local politicians to the city so that they could hang in the Guildhall.[40]

This information suggests that Bath citizens approved it as an appropriate representation of their Lady 'Mayoress'. Praga said of the sale to Chivers: "It would be very gratifying to me to know that my portrait of Mme. Sarah Grand had found a permanent home in the City of Bath with which she is so actively and honourably connected."[41] He was aware of Grand's success as Lady 'Mayoress', otherwise he would not have tried to sell the work.[42]

It is somewhat ironic that we have a portrait of Madame Sarah Grand from 1896 that honours her as 'Mayoress' in the 1920s. There was talk of a painted portrait of her as Lady 'Mayoress' but no painting has emerged.[43] There are, however, several photographic portraits of her as 'Mayoress', one in which she wears the elaborate chain of office that the Mayor had created for her [**fig. 7**]. The photograph reveals her regal bearing and her ability to wear this new mantle literally. Singer-Biggar reported one of her appearances as 'Mayoress': 'A woman I spoke to at the Memorial said: "And Madame Sarah Grand - Oh! She's a grand lady!" So you see you live up to your adopted name all right!'[44]

The Praga portrait reveals the conflicting sides of the New Woman, Madame Sarah Grand, which, in later life, made her successful as a crowd-pleasing Lady 'Mayoress'. Grand's scholars readily admit that she is hard to pin down ideologically and she herself admitted her own contradictions. As Ann Heilmann explains, 'In her effort to mediate between her traditional and progressive female audiences, Grand feminised the feminist, impressing on her readers that, however 'modern' her views might be, [she] felt at home with the latest fashion and was, in fact, the standard-bearer of stylishness.'[45] Grand's careful self-presentation and self-promotion to two women's markets was mirrored both in Praga's portrait [fig. 1] and in Thomas's cycling picture [fig. 4], in which she appeared in a very in-style gown with leg-of-mutton sleeves, beaded detailing and a large, feather-filled hat. While she was very conventionally dressed, in the height of fashion, the reason she was being painted and photographed was because of her sensational reputation. Her scandalous representation was reinforced by her interest in cycling, a real mark of the New Woman, and by having her portrait done, it was a sign of her arrival in society. But there was another side to sitting for one's portrait. As Jill Ker Conway explains, 'The mere act of sitting down to write an autobiography broke the code of female respectability, because doing so required a woman to believe that her direct experience, rather than her relationships with others, was what gave meaning to her life.' Similarly, for a woman to collude in the act of portrait-making of a public self, meant that she walked a dangerous line in relation to respectability, that she, like her autobiographical sisters, was involved in a 'conscious act of rebellion.'[46] Grand committed such an act by leaving her husband and changing her name. Praga's portrait symbolizes that significant revolt hence it is puzzling to witness the Bath citizenry embracing this portrait of Grand as symbolic of her being one of their own. A woman politician, like a radical woman writer, was new on the horizon and subject to numerous discourses about a woman's proper place. Yet, it seems Grand and Praga's goal was to counter such discussion through a conservative presentation of a well-dressed, demure, attractive lady.

If we are tempted to think such an intention is inaccurate, we need only review Grand's views on women's dress in relation to advanced ideas in 1893:

> 'We women would have had the suffrage long ago had not, unfortunately, some of the first fighters for it - some of the strong ones - been unprepossessing women.. . . These two or three were held up everywhere as an awful warning of what the whole sex would become if it got the suffrage, . . . [T]he phrases most commonly employed to damage the cause are altogether significant of this: "The shrieking sisterhood," for instance. . . If you just saw them. Their dress! Their manners! If women are to look like that when they get the suffrage, then defend me from it!"'[47]

Grand desired to win over the conservative flock and to appear to be on their side when, in fact, she was heavily on the side of suffrage. We have already seen her calculated words along the same lines upon her election as Lady 'Mayoress' of Bath. She was a diplomat extraordinaire in this regard. Such diplomacy was necessary for any public political figure and one reflected in her portraits where she walks a fine line between conformity and resistance.

Grand's view of the New Woman was

> 'one who, while retaining all the grace of manner and feminine charm, had thrown off all the silliness and hysterical feebleness of her sex, and improved herself so as to be in every way the best companion for man, and without him the best fitted for a place of usefulness in the world.'[48]

We could not have a better argument for her desire to become Lady 'Mayoress'; 'usefulness' could be construed by conservatives as her wish to be charitable, by radicals to challenge the limited roles of women in her culture. Such contradiction was already well in place in her position as New Woman. As Lucy Bland explains:

> 'The 1890s contributed an important heritage to early-twentieth century feminism; it also raised issues of contradiction which still leave present-day feminists uncertain and confused. Can sexual "freedom" ever be an equivalent freedom for women as for men? In demanding equality, and declaring our "sameness," how are women to argue simultaneously for recognition of *difference*: our different procreative capacity and our different experience of sexuality?'[49]

fig 7: Madam Sarah Grand, Mayoress of Bath, 1925. Photograph by Lambert of Bath.
Bath in Time - Bath Central Library Collection

This dilemma is embedded in the various Sarah Grands before us in these images. A proper lady seated for her portrait [**figs. 1 and 3**], represented her difference, while her cycling acumen, combined with her dress of proper lady [**fig. 4**], symbolised the forced conflation of Bland's attributes: her *difference* was signalled in her dress, while her desire for the same sexual freedom a man had is explicit in the cycle itself and her active engagement in the sport.

But, further, her very efforts to maintain the fashionable attire of a proper lady signal her difference from men, her different experience of her sensuality and sexuality, her pleasure in clothes and her simultaneous understanding of those clothes as markers of conservatism which a public would read and approve. This careful sartorial regard made her acceptable, even though she lived at a time when a woman politician was still suspect. This self-scrutiny made her popular and contributes greatly to her lasting legacy, one readily evident through the purchase and display of the Praga portrait for Bath.

But wasn't Grand taking significant risks by presenting her public self in a feminine guise? Ellen Lambert argues, 'in feminist thinking, from Mary Wollstonecraft in the late-eighteenth century, on down to Naomi Wolf in the late- twentieth century, beauty has been associated with women's traditional powerlessness.'[50] However, Grand's beauty seemed to be more in alignment with her feminism, her celebration of her beauty and the media's response to it serving to counter the disreputable attacks against her. Key examples are the images here, all of which create a compelling feminine image. She was in good company, such as that of Millicent Garrett Fawcett and Emmeline Pankhurst who, while they undertook more radical feminist work, equally sought a safe, feminine guise to deflect criticism from their suffrage causes.[51]

Grand's goal was to protect women from profligate men; dressing like a woman, appearing womanly, worked in her favour to get people to listen. And those efforts translated well when she presented herself as Lady 'Mayoress' of Bath. Grand took the stance that dressing well was somewhat of a political act, her body and her adornment of it the most visible statement of her desire to masquerade as a more conservative woman than her feminist politics would suppose. Her clothing became her armour, a way to disarm her critics, who often noted her considerable charm, a characteristic we have seen followed her in her later role as Lady 'Mayoress'. She was in constant masquerade, seeking to deflect criticism by playing up her femininity. As I have discussed, while Grand was the woman who created the New Woman, she also invented a new self to go with that creation, Madame Sarah Grand. She helped to popularise the New Woman in literature, but she became her in real life. At the same time, she was obsessed with dressing appropriately so as not to gain adverse attention. It was her ability to keep her audience off-guard that kept her in the limelight, a purpose revealed in the visual images she has left us.

Some information in this essay first appeared in Colleen Denney, Women, Portraiture and the Crisis of Identity in Victorian England: My Lady Scandalous Reconsidered (Ashgate, 2009). I thank Ashgate for allowing me to reproduce the material here.

Notes

1. I thank Katharine Wall, Collections Manager at the Victoria Art Gallery, Bath, for help with this information (E-mail from Katharine Wall to Colleen Denney, May 17th 2010). On the gift of the painting see the correspondence held in the Victoria Art Gallery, Bath.
2. Gillian Kersley, *Darling Madame: Sarah Grand and Devoted Friend* (Virago Press, 1983), p.125.
3. See Lucy Bland, 'The Married Woman, the "New Woman" and the Feminist: Sexual Politics of the 1890s,' in *Equal or Different: Women's Politics 1800-1914*, ed. Jane Rendall (Basil Blackwell, 1987), pp.141-164.
4. On her life and publications see Joan Huddleston, *Sarah Grand [Mrs. Frances Elizabeth McFall, née Clarke]: A Bibliography* (Department of English/University of Queensland, Victorian Fiction Research Guides I, 1979); and Kersley, *Darling Madame*. See also Jane Eldridge Miller, 'McFall, Frances Elizabeh Bellenden (1854-1943,' *Oxford Dictionary of National Biography* (Oxford University Press, Sept. 2004) www.oxforddnb.com/iew/article/39086, accessed October 15th 2010, where, however, she inaccurately claims that *The Heavenly Twins* was the first New Woman novel. Many authors had written them in the 1880s and early 1890s, but none of them had addressed the issue of venereal disease.
5. See Huddleston, *Sarah Grand*; and Kersley, *Darling Madame*.
6. David Rubinstein, *Before the Suffragettes: Women's Emancipation in the 1890s* (Harvester Press, 1986), p.12, and p.12 n. 1.

7. Sarah Grand, 'The New Aspect of the Woman Question,' *North American Review* 158 (1894), p. 271.

8. Linda Dowling, 'The Decadent and the New Woman in the 1890s,' in *Reading Fin-de-Siècle Fictions*, ed. Lynn Pykett (Longman, 1996), pp.47-63. See also Sally Ledger and Scott McCracken, 'Introduction,' in *Cultural Politics at the Fin-de-Siecle*, ed. Sally Ledger and Scott McCracken (Cambridge University Press, 1995), 1; and Sally Ledger, 'The New Woman and the Crisis of Victorianism,' in *Cultural Politics*, 22-44.

9. Marilyn Bonnell, 'The Legacy of Sarah Grand's *The Heavenly Twins*: A Review Essay,' *English Literature in Transition 1880-1920* 36 (1993), p. 472; 469. This debate is also prevalent in Jessica Cox, 'Gender, Conflict, Continuity: Anne Brontë's *The Tenant of Wildfell Hall* (1848) and Sarah Grand's *The Heavenly Twins* (1893),' *Brontë Studies* 35 (March 2010), pp. 30-39; and, in terms of fuelling the debate, see Andrea L. Broomfield, 'Eliza Lynn Linton, Sarah Grand and the Spectacle of the Victorian Woman Question: Catch Phrases, Buzz Words and Sound Bites,' *English Literature in Transition 1880-1920* 47 (2004), pp. 251-72.

10. Teresa Mangum, *Married, Middlebrow, and Militant* (The University of Michigan Press, 1998), p. 2.

11. Lynn Pykett, Foreword, in *The New Woman in Fiction and in Fact,* ed. Angelique Richardson and Chris Willis (Palgrave, 2001), p. xii. The authors of this volume argue that the New Woman did not exist but rather was a media construct only.

12. See Colleen Denney, '"Voiceless London": Millicent Garrett Fawcett's Embodiment of the Common Cause, or, Resisting the Scandal of the Platform,' in *Women, Portraiture and the Crisis of Identity*, pp. 125-178.

13. Catherine Craft-Fairchild, *Masquerade and Gender* (Pennsylvania State University Press, 1993), p. 7.

14. Kathleen Woodward, "Youthfulness as a Masquerade,' *Discourse* 11 (Fall-Winter 1988-89), p. 125.

15. See Lisa Tickner, *The Spectacle of Imagery* (Chatto and Windus, 1987/University of Chicago Press, 1988); and Deborah Cherry, *Beyond the Frame* (Routledge, 2000).

16. Talia Schaffer, '"Nothing but Foolscap and Ink": Inventing the New Woman, 'in *New Woman in Fiction and in Fact*, p. 39.

17. Schaffer, '"Nothing but Foolscap and Ink,"' p. 49.

18. Mangum, *Married, Middlebrow, and Militant*, p. 7.

19. Bland, 'The Married Woman,' p. 164.

20. Barbara Caine, 'Feminist Biography and Feminist History,' *The Women's History Review* 3 (1994), p. 256.

21. See Rosemary Sweet, "On the Town," in *Women and Urban Life in Eighteenth-Century England*, ed. Rosemary Sweet and Penelope Lane (Ashgate, 2003), p. 25.

22. Sweet, "On the Town," p. 25.

23. Cited in Barry Cunliffe, *The City of Bath* (Yale University Press, 1987), p. 167.

24. Kersley, *Darling Madame*, pp. 124-125.

25. *Bath & Wilts Chronicle*, May 27th 1922, cited in Kersley, *Darling Madame*, pp. 125-126.

26. *Bath & Wilts Chronicle*, October 20th 1922, cited in Kersley, *Darling Madame*, p. 124.

27. *Glasgow Herald*, January 3rd 1923, cited in Kersley, *Darling Madame*, p. 124.

28. *Bath & Wilts Chronicle*, October 20th 1922, cited in Kersley, *Darling Madame*, p. 126.

29. Hellen Meller, 'Gender, Citizenship and the Making of the Modern Environment,' in *Women and the Making of Built Space in England, 1870-1950*, ed. Elizabeth Darling and Leslie Whitworth (Ashgate, 2007), pp. 13-32.

30. See Patricia Hollis, ed., *Women in Public 1850-1900: Documents of the Victorian Women's Movement* (George Allen and Unwin, 1979), pp. 228, 272-274.

31. Meller, 'Gender, Citizenship,' p. 14.

32. Kersley, *Darling Madame*, p.131.

33. *Evening Standard* (October 3rd 1927), cited in Kersley, *Darling Madame*, p. 132.

34. Printed locally as *The Breath of Life: A Short Anthology of Quotations for Days and Months, from the Works of Sarah Grand*. See Kersley, *Darling Madame*, pp. 195-197.

35. Gladys Singer-Biggar to Sarah Grand, November 9th 1927, Sarah Grand Papers, Bath Central Library. See also the Sarah Grand correspondence, Victoria Art Gallery, Bath. I would like to thank the staff at the Bath Central Library and the Victoria Art Gallery, Bath, for sharing these materials with me. Thanks also to Colin Johnston, Principal Archivist at the Bath Record Office, for his assistance.

36. E-mail from Katharine Wall to Colleen Denney, May 17th 2010.

37. Director of the Victoria Art Gallery, Reginald W. M. Wright to Alfred Praga, March 24th 1928; Alfred Praga to Reginald W. M. Wright, October 26th/27th 1927, Sarah Grand Letters, Victoria Art Gallery, Bath.

38. Thanks to Nicky Sugar and Colin Johnston at Bath Record Office who, though they searched, found no evidence of the subscription fund. This could be due, in part, to the fact that the Mayor's office files were salvaged for re-use during WWII (E-mail from Nicky Sugar, Assistant Archivist, Bath Archives, to Colleen Denney, December 21st 2010).

39. Sarah Grand to Mr. Colterell, May 14th 1930, Sarah Grand Letters, Victoria Art Gallery, Bath.

40. E-mail from Katharine Wall to Colleen Denney, May 17th 2010. There is no record of the portrait in Grand's will, so it appears the portrait was already in her son's possession at the time of her death. See Kersley, *Darling Madame*, pp. 334-335; and *Copy Will and Grant-Frances Elizabeth McFall Otherwise Sarah Grand*-probate 1943, Principal Probate Registry, England.

41. Alfred Praga to Director of Victoria Art Gallery, Reginald W. M. Wright, March 29th 1928, Sarah Grand Letters, Victoria Art Gallery, Bath.

42. We don't know, however, who commissioned the work in the first place. It was certainly not Grand herself, otherwise it would have been in her possession rather than being up for sale.

43. Reginald W. M. Wright, Director of the Victoria Art Gallery, to Alfred Praga, March 27th 1928, Sarah Grand Letters, Victoria Art Gallery, Bath, England: 'I have learnt that there is a project underfoot for the painting of a fresh portrait of Madame Sarah Grand as "Mayoress of Bath." . . . [T]his matter is in hand . ..'

44. Gladys Singer-Biggar to Madame Sarah Grand, November 13th 1928, Sarah Grand Papers, Bath Central Library, Bath.

45. Ann Heilmann, ed., *Sex, Social Purity and Sarah Grand* (Routledge, 2000), p. 5.

46. Jill Ker Conway, *Exploring the Art of Autobiography* (Vintage Press, 1999), p. 87.

47. *Humanitarian*, 1893, 3, pp.87-93, cited in Heilmann, *Sex, Social Purity and Sarah Grand*, p. 26.

48. Sarah Grand, 'The New Aspect of the Woman Question,' *North American Review* 158 (1894), p. 271.

49. Bland, 'The Married Woman,' p.141.

50. Ellen Zetzel Lambert, *The Face of Love: Feminism and the Beauty Question* (Beacon Press, 1995), pp.14-15; cited in Elaine Showalter, *Inventing Herself* (Cambridge University Press, 2000), pp. 321-322.

51. On Garret Fawcett see Denney, '"Voiceless London,"' and on Pankhurst see June Purvis, 'A Pair of Infernal Queens? A Reassessment of the Dominant Representations of Emmeline and Christabel Pankhurst, First Wave Feminists in Edwardian Britain,' *Women's History Review* 5 (1996), pp. 259-80.

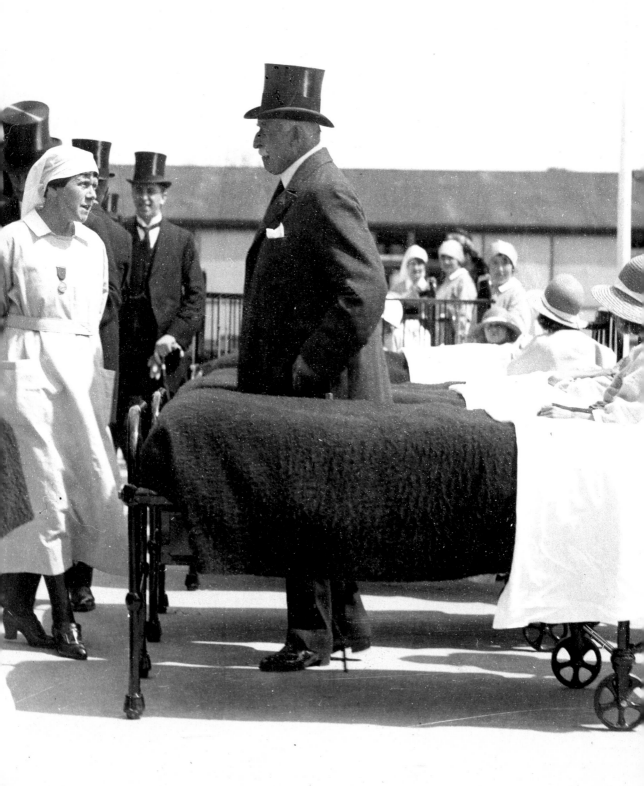

Maud Forrester-Brown (1885-1970), Britain's First Female Orthopaedic Surgeon

John Kirkup

By any standards, Maude Forrester-Brown was a remarkable woman [fig. 1].[1] Not only was she the first female orthopaedic surgeon in Britain – a physically demanding specialism – but, virtually single-handed, she consolidated a series of clinics for crippled children throughout the counties of Somerset, Wiltshire and Dorset. In the process, she elevated the Bath and Wessex Orthopaedic Hospital to national prominence. Her important published research, extending over fifty years, and strong links with distinguished orthopaedic surgeons in Europe and America, ensured she kept abreast of innovations beneficial to her patients.

Born in Enfield, north London on November 15th 1885, the daughter of James Samuel Brown, civil engineer and his wife, Emma Laetitia, she spent part of her childhood in India before attending Bedford High School from 1898 to 1906, where she was remembered as a brilliant and well-balanced scholar. At the age of 20, she applied as M. Forrester Brown (later hyphenated) to the London School of Medicine for Women, and was awarded a scholarship. There she achieved excellent examination results culminating in the London M.B. B.S.

fig 1: Portrait of Maude Forrester-Brown, c.1930s. Signed Photograph.
Bath in Time - Royal United Hospital

with honours in Pathology and Forensic Medicine. Postgraduate courses followed in London and Newcastle upon Tyne. A Gilchrist studentship from London University enabled her to study in Berlin where she took courses in surgical anatomy, and operative gynaecology, and after obstetric experience, she gained an MD (London) in gynaecology in 1914. [2]

Junior clinical experience.

Junior hospital posts were taken up in Dundee, London and Edinburgh, where she was house surgeon to Sir Harold Stiles at the Royal Hospital for Sick Children and Senior Resident at the Royal Infirmary Sheffield. Her stay in Sheffield was cut short in October 1916 and her subsequent career shaped by an invitation from Sir Harold Stiles to join him as orthopaedic resident at the Edinburgh War Hospital, Bangour, where he established a unit treating injuries

Facing: Detail of HRH The Duke of Connaught opens the Bath, Somerset & Wilts Central Children's Orthopaedic Hospital, 1924
Bath in Time - Bath Central Library Collection

171

sustained by soldiers in the Great War. Sir Harold was a pioneer paediatric surgeon familiar with fractures and dislocations incurred in peacetime. At the War Hospital, he was challenged by complex gunshot wounds, including nerve injuries. With the able assistance of Maud Forrester-Brown, Stiles undertook a special study on the subject which led to their joint publication, *Treatment of Injuries of the Peripheral Spinal Nerves.*[3] When Stiles resigned from the War Hospital in 1919, Forrester-Brown was Surgeon to the Edinburgh War Hospital, being responsible for 300 beds with the assistance of the Royal Army Medical Corps officers whom she supervised.

In 1920, she published *'Difficulties in the diagnosis of nerve function'* [4] and *'The possibilities of end-to-end suture after extensive nerve injuries'.*[5] In the same year, she also passed the Primary Fellowship Examination of the Royal College of Surgeons of England, and although she never proceeded to the Final Fellowship, she obtained her MS (London) with a thesis entitled: 'The results of operations for peripheral nerve injury'. Further publications followed in 1921 based on the experience at Bangour of open fractures complicated by sepsis, demonstrating that her responsibilities had not been restricted to nerve trauma.

fig 2: The Bath, Somerset & Wilts Central Children's Orthopaedic Hospital, Combe Park, Bath c.1927
Bath in Time - Royal United Hospital

After the war, Forrester-Brown worked in Dundee, one of her appointments being Visiting Surgeon to Fairmuir Specialist School. Lectures and further publications followed including 'Sacro-iliac strains' and 'Some modern methods in the treatment of bone and joint tuberculosis'. [6] In June 1923, she was awarded the William Gibson Research Scholarship (exclusive to women doctors) of the Royal Society of Medicine, London, which she held for three years. The scholarship enabled her to visit orthopaedic clinics in the USA, France, Italy, Scandinavian countries and many centres throughout Britain. Detailed reports of these visits were compiled which described many of the methods and equipment subsequently introduced into her practice in Bath.[7] She was particularly interested in the appliances and splints used by Vittorio Putti of Bologna and J.E. Goldthwait of Boston, USA, in sunlight methods for bovine tuberculosis used in Switzerland and gymnastic exercises employed in Swedish and Danish hospitals. After her scholarship had finished, she continued with regular visits abroad, spending one vacation every year visiting orthopaedic clinics.

The Bath and Wessex Children's Orthopaedic Hospital.

Until 1924 orthopaedic patients in the West Country were under the care of general practitioners. In-patient treatment was conducted by general surgeons who were interested in what was still an emerging speciality. At Bath an orthopaedic clinic was established in 1922 supervised by two general surgeons, WG Mumford (1870-1955) and JS Levis (1888-1943) of the Royal United Hospital who became the first surgeons to the Children's Orthopaedic Hospital. This was opened officially by the Duke of Connaught in May 1924 with 20 beds [**figs. 3 & 4**].

Specialist orthopaedic experience was provided by Sir Robert Jones and GR Girdlestone appointed as Honorary Consultant Surgeons. They had been promoting a national scheme of orthopaedic hospitals via the Central Council for Crippled Children. It is probable that they were instrumental in the appointment of Forrester-Brown as Resident Surgeon in 1925.[8] She lived across the road from the hospital at 22 Combe Park [**fig. 5**]and later rented rooms in the Circus and Queen Square for private consultations. Forrester-Brown shared the number of beds with Mumford and Lewis and increasingly took charge of the

fig 3: HRH The Duke of Connaught opens the Bath, Somerset & Wilts Central Children's Orthopaedic Hospital, 1924
Bath in Time - Bath Central Library Collection

major proportion of them when they increased from the original 20 to 72 beds by 1926. In addition, she had responsibility for a growing number of children's clinics throughout Somerset and Wiltshire: Taunton, Weston-Super-Mare, Bridgwater, Yeovil, Radstock, Frome and Glastonbury, and Corsham, Salisbury, Trowbridge and Swindon.[9]

During 1924 only 51 operations were performed, increasing rapidly to 140 by 1926 and 237 by 1927. Expansion continued with the addition of Dorset to the Hospital's responsibilities and by 1930, Forrester-Brown was designated Visiting Surgeon to Bath, Somerset and Dorset Central Children's Orthopaedic Hospital, and to the Clinics predominantly in Somerset and Dorset. [**fig. 6**][10] Former staff recall how she would disappear into Dorset for a week at a time, allegedly on horse back visiting Dorchester, Weymouth, Bridport, Sherborne, Wimborne, and the Red Cross Children's Hospital in Swanage.[11] In 1931, the original title was shortened to The Bath and Wessex Children's Orthopaedic Hospital and a special unit of 20 beds for infants was opened. Throughout the three counties, monthly or quarterly visits by surgeons to 14 minor clinics were established with follow-up from after-care sisters and later by orthopaedic physiotherapists.[12] In 1934, Mumford retired followed by Levis in 1935. They were replaced by John Bastow (1906-65), and Forrester-Brown became Senior Surgeon and Visiting Surgeon to

Bath and the Wessex clinics. Although she never dealt with acute traumatic cases, she gradually took increased responsibility for adult orthopaedic cases, especially former children under her care. During 1935 Capt. Ronald Wills provided an annexe to the babies ward in which a remedial pool was housed. Forrester-Brown donated to the new facility and dedicated it to Sir Robert Jones who had died in 1933.[13]

With the outbreak of World War II, the Orthopaedic Hospital was designated as suitable for acute surgical and medical cases under the Emergency Hospital Scheme. Extra beds were used by military personnel in the gymnasium, board room, and out patients' room until 1942 when the requirement ceased. In the meantime, the demand for children's beds intensified and extra accommodation was arranged at South Stoke House, near Bath. During the Baedeker air raids on Bath in 1942, patients were placed under their beds, reported to be 'nearly as robust as Morrison shelters'. Fortunately, the Hospital was only slightly scarred during the raids, and no one was injured despite considerable damage and loss of life inflicted elsewhere in Bath.[14]

After the war, the number of Visiting Physicians increased to four and Visiting Anaesthetists to five. Meanwhile Forrester-Brown and John Bastow were attending 21 children' clinics periodically, and performing more operative surgery as emerging antibiotic cover diminished risks and improved cure rates of bone and joint diseases. Ten clinics were also undertaken by after-care sisters. [15] Robert Robins, appointed House Surgeon in 1947, has vivid memories of Forrester-Brown's operating sessions:

fig 4: HRH The Duke of Connaught opens the Bath, Somerset & Wilts Central Children's Orthopaedic Hospital, 1924
Bath in Time - Bath Central Library Collection

She was a dab hand with a Thomas wrench for relapsed club feet: 'mush it up' was her advice. She never picked up a vessel unless it could be done with Ochsner's forceps and ligated with chromic catgut of her own manufacture. Before closing a hip operation she would empty a galley pot of neat iodine into the wound. She would not allow her patients to have a blood transfusion, even after a Hibbs' fusion for scoliosis ('overlap the bones like "shlates" on a roof') or an arthrodesis of the hip but the surgeon of today may be unaware of the efficacy of a plaster spica in securing haemostasis and counteracting shock. [16]

The passing of the National Health Service Act, and its implementation in July 1948, was coupled with an appeal for supporters to continue subscriptions and donations until the new arrangements were in place. Forrester-Brown was then termed Consultant Orthopaedic Surgeon until her retirement in December 1950 at the age of 65. In retirement she returned to Edinburgh to assist Sir James Learmonth's investigations into the repair of peripheral nerves and she was a frequent visitor to the Princess Margaret Rose Orthopaedic Hospital, contributing to discussions and ward rounds. In 1954, she worked as a locum in Huddersfield, in Kirkcaldy and other orthopaedic centres. She then went to South Africa as temporary orthopaedic surgeon at the Holy Cross Hospital, East Pondoland in the Transkei, where clinical problems resembled those she had experienced in her early career. Retaining Edinburgh as her base, she continued to travel and to attend meetings and conferences. At a congress of the British Orthopaedic Association, when in her later 70s, the writer recalls one session when she stood up to question, or more often to instruct, practically every speaker.

Clinical experience and further publications.

The annual reports of the hospital are largely concerned with financial matters, but also contain brief statistics of clinic, physiotherapy and dental attendances. These statistics do not separate new cases from readmissions. For example in 1936, when of 82 cases of poliomyelitis admitted, 25 were new ones requiring an average stay of 174 days.[17] Most years, congenital deformities formed the largest diagnostic group followed by surgical tuberculosis and infantile paralysis (poliomyelitis). Rickets remained a lesser problem as late as 1947, surprisingly so for an essentially rural area where children were exposed to sunlight and fresh milk enriched with vitamin D. Osteomyelitis was a significant cause of admissions and spastic paralysis, scoliosis, tumours, old bone and nerve injuries formed an important part of the remainder. Today, by

fig 5: Combe Park, Bath c.1910s. Postcard.
Bath in Time - Bath Central Library Collection

contrast, all these conditions produce very few admissions to orthopaedic units in Britain.

Forrester-Brown's experience of congenital skeletal deformities was prodigious. In 1929, she published *Diagnosis and Treatment of Deformities in Infancy and Early Childhood*, with a foreword by Sir Robert Jones.[18] This was aimed to assist early diagnosis by general practitioners and child welfare staff for, as she lamented, too many congenital defects were established and untreated before late referral, often when walking, the child being then considered by the family and practitioner 'strong enough' for treatment. She emphasised the importance of thorough examination with the patient naked except for a 'fig-leaf'.

In 1933, she co-authored *Paralysis in Children* with R.G. Gordon (1889-1950), Neurologist and Physician to the Orthopaedic Hospital.[19] The authors believed they had filled a gap in the literature by combining neurological and orthopaedic standpoints in order to obtain an accurate diagnosis and enhance surgical management. In 1935, she assessed 152 personal cases of congenital equinovarus (club-foot),[20] an experience accumulated over a mere 10 years that dwarfs that of today's surgeons, even many specialising in foot surgery. She emphasised the crucial importance of early and vigorous conservative care and the necessity to intervene surgically when progress was halted. Her paper listed additional appointments as Honorary Surgeon, Eastern Dispensary, Bath and Honorary Consulting Orthopaedic Surgeon, Swanage Red Cross Hospital and Walker-Dunbar Hospital, Bristol. In 1947, she lectured at the Royal College of Surgeons on 'Operative procedures in poliomyelitis' reported in the Annals of that year.[21] It is evident her personal experience of poliomyelitis was formidable and her advice full of common sense. Recognition of this and her many other contributions should have led to the award of an Honorary Fellowship of the College but the opportunity was overlooked.

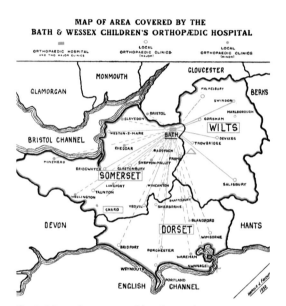

fig 6: Map of are covered by the Bath & Wessex Children's Orthopaedic Hospital, 1932
Author's Collection

Professional responsibilities and leisure pursuits

Maud Forrester-Brown was an assiduous supporter of professional associations and served as an officer in many of them. A member of the British Medical Association for over fifty years, she was Honorary Secretary of the Section of Orthopaedic Surgery at the Annual Meeting in 1931 and a member of the Association's Physical Education Committee formed in 1935 to report on the cultivation of physical development by the civil population.[22] In 1921, she

176

was elected an active member of the British Orthopaedic Association, joining the Committee of Physical Education in 1936, becoming Hon. Secretary in 1937, an Executive Committee member in 1948-9 and an Emeritus Fellow in 1961. When the B.O.A. held their first visit abroad in 1924, Forrester-Brown was in the party. She was again with the Association in 1956 when meetings were held in Rome, Florence and Bologna, and at further meetings in France and Scandinavia.[23] In addition, she joined SICOT, the International Society for Orthopaedic and Trauma Surgery, later being elected an Emeritus Member, and also the Medical Women's International Association, attending their Ninth Congress in the Philippines in 1963, where she insisted on a personal bed-to-bed tour of patients in the National Orthopaedic Hospital.[24]

As a result of her friendship with Vittorio Putti, the leading orthopaedic surgeon in Bologna, and her knowledge of Italian, she produced many English summaries for the journal *Chirurgia degli Organi di Movimento*, and translated his book *Historic Artificial Limbs* in 1930. Putti described medieval iron prostheses in the Stibbert Museum, Florence, that were designed for battle field aristocrats on horseback.[25] Maud Forrester-Brown was fluent in five languages, including Spanish which she first studied in her sixties, but her interests went beyond foreign languages:

She had a keen interest in all classical forms of drama, sculpture and painting; a wide knowledge of old masters, especially those of the Italian schools; a catholic knowledge of literature. Indeed her retentive memory and critical abilities made discussion of literature with her a formidable task.[26]

She was also not only keen on healthy physical activity but practiced it herself:

Bodily fitness was not only a sermon to be preached to others; it was a goal to which she strove all her life – by skiing, skating, riding, golf and swimming. She took a vacation each February for winter sports, usually in Norway. Many associates must remember the twinkle in her eyes when she slipped away from a congress session with murmur: 'I have an appointment with a horse.'[27]

Three years before her death, she was still riding once a week and swimming twice a week in the local baths. Despite this physical activity, she may have suffered from osteoporosis for she sustained at least four fractures after the age of sixty. She had a fracture-dislocation of an ankle in 1947 for which she refused an anaesthetic, insisting on a skin tight plaster which she cut down to a below knee plaster the following day and resumed horse riding with an excellent result.

In November 1948, a local newspaper reported her fall from a horse that caused a fractured collar bone. Then in 1960, she fractured the neck of a femur that was nailed successfully in Edinburgh. This was followed by a convalescent voyage to Cape Town on a ship with a gymnasium and mechanical horse offering suitable exercise for riders. On her return she informed surgeons at Bath how the mechanical horse had speeded her recovery and why she considered this a breakthrough in rehabilitating elderly ladies with hip fractures. She even offered to buy such a machine for the hospital, but was politely persuaded this would be inappropriate, even dangerous, for fragile patients who with few exceptions were unfamiliar with horse riding. Lastly in 1962, she sustained a comminuted fracture of an elbow joint which was reduced and plastered briefly. She insisted on her own rehabilitation, and within two months was swimming and driving her own car. Maud Forrester-Brown lived in Edinburgh after she retired from Bath. She died in the Edinburgh Royal Infirmary on January 12th 1970, aged 84 years after a cerebrovascular accident.

Conclusion.

Maude Forrester-Brown had an impressive career as one of the pioneers of British orthopaedic surgery in the twentieth century; the first female surgeon in Britain, and probably worldwide. Her life was dedicated to an emerging speciality in which she made significant contributions to its science and literature, and she spared no effort to keep in touch with developments at home and abroad. In an age before modern air transport, her international connections sustained over decades were extraordinary, and the fruits of best practice were brought back to her work in Bath. It was principally due to her knowledge, energy and dedication that a vast network of clinics was established throughout three counties for the treatment of neglected crippled children. This great endeavour helped to forge the favourable reputation of the Bath and Wessex Orthopaedic Hospital in treating surgical tuberculosis, congenital deformities, poliomyelitis, rickets, scoliosis and osteomyelitis, at a time when most preventive and therapeutic remedies had yet to materialize. Everyone who remembers her when she was 78 years of age, including the writer, recalls a formidable personality with firm opinions based on prodigious experience, yet a lady who combined compassion with an enquiring mind.

fig 7: Present day sign at the Forrester Brown Ward at Bath's Royal United Hospital, 2013
Photograph by Dan Brown

An entry for Maud Forrester-Brown has now been published in a volume of the Dictionary of National Biography. Locally, one of the wards at the Royal United Hospital in Bath bears her name [**fig. 7**], but her achievements deserve a wider recognition. Bath can be proud of her inspirational work, both nationally and in the city.

Notes

1   This is an edited version of an article published in the *Journal of Medical Biography* vol. 16 Nov. 2008, pp. 197-204.

2   Examination results of M. Forrester-Brown, Royal Free Archive, London, Royal Free Hospital, School of Medicine for Women, Registry records, School Examinations Record book, 1900-1911. H.J. Stiles, MF Forrester-Brown, *Treatment of Injuries of the Peripheral Spinal Nerves*, (London: Froude, Hodder & Stoughton, 1922).

4   M. Forrester-Brown, 'Difficulties in the diagnosis of nerve function', *British Journal of Surgery,* 1920: VII, pp. 495-5011.

5   M. Forrester-Brown, 'The possibilities of end-to-end to suture after extensive nerve injuries', *Journal of Orthopaedic Surgery*, 1920: XIX: pp. 277-87.

6   M. Forrester-Brown, 'Sacro-iliac strains', *Edinburgh Medical Journal,* 1924; pp. 392-98; 'Some

modern methods in the treatment of bone and joint tuberculosis', *Forfarshire Medical Association*, January 1925.

7   M. Forrester-Brown, 'Reports on William Gibson Research Scholarship, 1924-6 in MS Archives, Royal Society of Medicine, London.

8   First Annual Report of the Bath, Somerset and Wiltshire Central Children's Orthopaedic Hospital to 31 Dec. 1924.

9   Second Annual Report of the Bath, Somerset and Wiltshire Central Orthopaedic Hospital to 31 March 1926.

10   Sixth Annual Report of the Bath, Somerset, Wiltshire and Dorset Central Children's Orthopaedic Hospital to 31 March 1930.

11   RHC Robins, 'An Orthopaedic original', *British Orthopaedic News,* Autumn 1992; 6: p.17.

12   Seventh Annual Report of the Bath and Wessex Children's Orthopaedic Hospital to 31 March 1931.

13   Tenth Annual Report of the Bath and Wessex Children's Orthopaedic Hospital to 31 March 1935.

14   Eighteenth Annual Report of the Bath and Wessex Children's Orthopaedic Hospital to 31 March 1943. For further information on the Bath Blitz, see John Penny, 'Nazi Eagles over Bath: An analysis of German air Operations during World War II' and George Scott, 'Firebomb Fiasco: Civil Defence in World War II' in Graham Davis, (ed), *Bath Exposed!: Essays in the Social History of Bath, 1775-1945,* (Sulis Press, 2007).

15   22nd Annual Report of the Bath and Wessex Children's Orthopaedic Hospital to 31 March 1947 (final report).

16   R.H.C. Robins, 'An Orthopaedic original', *British Orthopaedic News*, Autumn 1992; 6: p.17.

17   Eleventh Annual Report of the Bath and Wessex Children's Orthopaedic Hospital to 31 March 1936.

18   M.F. Forrester-Brown, *Diagnosis and Treatment of Deformities in Infancy and Early Childhood,* (Oxford, Milford, 1929).

19   R.G. Gordon, M.F. Forrester-Brown, *Paralysis in Children,* (Oxford, Milford, 1933).

20   M.F. Forrester-Brown, 'The treatment of congenital equinovarus (club- foot)', *Journal of Bone and Joint Surgery,* 1935; 17: pp. 661-70.

21   M.F. Forrester-Brown, 'Operative procedures in poliomyelitis', *Annals of the Royal College of Surgeons of England,* 1947; 1:pp. 204-18.

22   R.I .Stirling, 'Obituary of Maud Frances Forrester-Brown', *Journal of Bone and Joint Surgery,* 1970; 52B: pp. 578-9.

23   British Orthopaedic Association, Minute book in MS, 1921; Annual Reports, 1937, 1949 and 1961.

24   R.I. Stirling, 'Obituary of Maud Frances Forrester-Brown'.

25   V. Putti, *Historic Artificial Limbs,* trans. M Forrester-Brown, (New York, Hoeber, 1930).

26   R.I. Stirling, 'Obituary of Maud Forrester-Brown'.

27   R.I. Stirling, 'Obituary of Maud Forrester-Brown'.

Professor R. Angus Buchanan OBE

Interview by William Hanna

My wife and I first met Angus and Brenda Buchanan in 1966. They were hosts at a University of Bath function for new Honorary Graduates, of whom my mother was one. Since then we have met regularly at history based events, for - dare I use the phrase - kitchen suppers, and as members of a winning team in a Holburne Museum quiz. Within the overall context of the interview I wanted to bring out particularly the national and international contribution Angus has made to the history of technology. He has been a patient interlocutor; any errors are mine.

WH. *Yours is a 'history family'; you and Brenda [Dr Brenda J. Buchanan] and your two sons all have PhDs in historical subjects, but you have different interests?*

AB. Yes. Brenda as an economic historian has, amongst many other interests, edited two volumes on the History of the Technology of Gunpowder; Tom, at Oxford, has written on the impact of the Spanish Civil War on Britain, and is about to publish on China and the British Left, while Andrew, who also read history at Oxford but has been in computerised engineering, gained his PhD in 2011 and now lectures in global and military history at the University of Vermont. Both boys attended Beechen Cliff School in Bath. We've never formally collaborated on any scholarly subject, but mutual support has been of great value.

WH. *In your own background you have family links with Scotland, Yorkshire and Gloucestershire?*

AB. That's right. My paternal grandfather was born in Dumfries, and worked there as an agricultural labourer. He moved south some time about 1890 and established a business in Huddersfield. My father was born there and he and his brothers all received a share in the family business. My father moved to Doncaster and that's where he met my mother who was a Gloucestershire girl; her family came from around Stroud. She was a school teacher; teaching jobs were scarce in the south and she moved north to Doncaster. My parents settled in Sheffield where I was born in 1930 in a nursing home on the very edge of the city just on the right side of the border with Derbyshire, so I'm a Yorkshireman.

WH. *You went to school in Sheffield?*

AB. Yes, High Storrs Grammar School, about 4 miles from where I lived, across the western suburbs; you went up and down up to get there so I got into the habit of walking and haven't lost it [**fig. 1**]. It started as a central city school at the beginning of the century, which then moved into the western outskirts in a new school - a very nice art deco building on a farm called 'High Storrs'. There were two quite distinct schools, separate but adjoining, for the boys and the girls. We didn't meet until the sixth form, when there was an Inter Sixth Form Club. Brenda and I met on an Inter-Sixth Form hike over the moors. She had only joined the school in the Sixth Form. She lived at the other end of the city in the eastern industrial part. You have to remember that Sheffield was heavily bombed during the war and Brenda's father was very anxious about her crossing the city to get to school, so she didn't transfer to High Storrs until after her School Certificate.

Facing: Angus, contemplative in a city square, while attending the ICOHTEC Symposium in Prague, 2000.
Author's Collection

WH. *Did you begin to concentrate on history at High Storrs?*

AB. Yes, I found that I was a complete duffer at languages, and not very good at maths - which was a pity. I always had a hankering to be an astronomer - and the two subjects I did well at were history and geography. I concentrated on history in the Sixth Form, where our teacher was Mr. Hamilton - he advised us "you should read big books" in the library. So we did, and it was a good habit to get into. I did well at Higher School Certificate and got an offer from St.

fig 1: **Angus and Brenda on the summit of Whiteface Mountain in the Adirondacks, New York State, 2011**
Author's Collection

Catharine's College, Cambridge of a Commoner's place two years ahead on the understanding that I would do my military service first. I was subsequently made a Scholar of the College on the strength of my performance in the History Tripos.

WH. *How did you find National Service - you were in the Army and went to the Far East?*

AB. I wasn't looking forward to it. I was against conscription, I didn't want to be told what to do, I had a feeling of 'we've won the war and ought to be able to do what we want', but I was called up for eighteen months into the Royal Army Ordnance Corps as a clerk.

I was posted to FARELF - the Far Eastern Land Forces. For an eighteen year old the journey was memorable. We were on an old British India Steam Navigation Company ship which was very crowded, but discipline was relaxed. Because there was little room there wasn't much the Army could do with you - physical jerks in the morning and hymns on Sunday. But you could read - there was a good library on the ship. And we stopped at Gibraltar, Port Said, Aden and Colombo, with a chance to go ashore and look around, all quite leisurely. Coming back was a bit different, the 'Devonshire' was a faster vessel, and there wasn't any time ashore. That didn't matter as our minds were very much on demob. So it was back to Liverpool, straight to Aldershot and I was demobbed on the spot and that was the end of my Army service. There are good memories of those days; I made a lot of friends, one of whom became my Best Man and I'm still in touch with him.

WH. *So then it was Cambridge; history and Judo?*

AB. St Catharine's was well known for rugby and geography. Neither was for me, but I did represent the University at Judo and was awarded a half blue in the sport. History was under Professor Rich, who later became Master. He recruited someone to do the basic tutoring, Oliver MacDonagh, who had been at Trinity College, Dublin. The undergraduates were paired up and my pair was tutored by MacDonagh for three years.

WH. He wrote on Victorian government, I think?

AB. Yes, and on Irish history, and biographies of Irish politicians. He also developed a theory that changes in government and society around the 1830s and 1840s were not the result of ideological preparation by, for example, Jeremy Bentham and J.S. Mill, but rather that historical change came about fortuitously as people re-acted to what they saw about them. I thought that was ungenerous to the thinkers. But he was a very good tutor, I did well in the History Tripos and was invited to research for a PhD.

WH. What was your research topic?

AB. As a social historian I chose to work on 'Non-Conformity and the Labour Movement'. That was too broad and I narrowed it down to 'Trade Unions and Public Opinion 1850-75'.

WH. You completed your PhD after leaving St Catharine's while you were working in Stepney ?

AB. Yes, I was invited to join The Royal Foundation of St. Katharine in Stepney which engaged in adult education and social work and was a centre for study and conferences. It was an idealistic choice which derived from my encounter through Brenda with the Sheffield Industrial Mission in which we had both been very involved.

WH. Would you like to say something about the Mission?

AB. The Industrial Mission had been set up in 1944 by The Bishop of Sheffield, Leslie Hunter who had very strong ideas about getting the church involved in the community and especially to improve the engagement of the church with the working people of the city. His key appointment was Ted Wickham who as Industrial Chaplain visited the big steel works and other factories and had meetings and discussions. The Mission was very successful, and at one time was in touch with many of the industrial workers in its area. We had visiting speakers too - one was Father John Groser,

fig 2: The founders of Industrial Archaeology at the Bath Conference in 1967. l-r Neil Cossens, Michael Rix, Angus Buchanan, Frank Atkinson, Robert Vogel and Marie Nisser
Author's Collection

a powerful, charismatic parish priest from Poplar, who was involved with St Katharine's, so I met him again there. Unfortunately, Ted Wickham left to become Suffragan Bishop of Middleton and when Leslie Hunter retired his successor as Bishop disapproved of the Mission's approach and it went downhill rapidly. Another interest Brenda and I shared was the Iona Community that we visited for the first time in 1952, staying in a Youth Camp. It was run by the Revd. George MacLeod who had been a parish priest in Govan. He founded the Community in 1938 in an attempt - rather like the Sheffield Mission later - to close the gap he saw between the church and working people. The Community rebuilt the Abbey on Iona as an ecumenical place of study and contemplation. It was another place which influenced the choice of working at St. Katharine's.

WH. You mentioned Father John Groser earlier. He seems to have been quite a controversial figure: against the advice of his Bishop he left his parish to become a Chaplain to the Forces in the Great War - and very much a front line Chaplain, decorated with the Military Cross for staying with wounded soldiers under fire. When he returned to his parish in Poplar he was seen by some as 'that turbulent priest'?

AB. Yes, he was certainly turbulent in the 1930s. He was devoted to his parishioners and to East London as a whole: he led rent strikes, and took part in the Cable Street troubles, with Mosley and his supporters coming up from one end and the people from Poplar coming from the other. He moved to a parish in Stepney and was invited to revive the Foundation, which had been founded near the Tower in the twelfth century.

fig 3: The cover of Industrial Archaeology of The Bristol Region, published 1969
Author's Collection

WH. What was your role at St Katharine's?

AB. I was the Adult Education Officer. We ran courses for apprentices, who would come for a week to courses that I set up. We needed to get permission for them to come, so I had a lot of leg work going round firms to get them to release their young people. It was good training for me and I think the young men and women enjoyed it. That was what took most of the time. There was also an evening class for the Workers Educational Association (WEA). and some extra-mural university work as well. On top of all this in 1958 I was co-opted to the London County Council Education Committee with which I had two very interesting years, until we left Stepney in 1960.

WH. During that time you were a governor of Risinghill School which one part of the educational establishment regarded as 'the blackboard jungle' and another part as the exemplar of what comprehensive education could attain?

AB. Yes. The Headmaster was Michael Duane. We had a difficult job to get him through the appointment committee. Officers had drawn up a short list. Several of us thought Michael Duane was outstanding, a most remarkable man, but he had said "I don't believe in corporal punishment". Some of the committee were horrified at this - 'how can you run a school like this without corporal punishment?' However, we managed to get the appointment made, and Duane set up the school and ran it without using any corporal punishment - if pupils broke the rules he would give them a good talking to and would think up ingenious punishments. For a year I was in close contact with him. The school worked very well, but in four or five years or so those who had opposed the appointment persuaded the committee that it was no good and they had to get rid of him. There was no way of doing that directly, so the school was closed and Duane was moved sideways to another post. He never got another headship.

WH. *By then you had moved to Bristol?*
AB. Yes, in 1960 I began my association with the College which was to become the University of Bath.

WH. *How did that begin and progress?*
AB. I was appointed to the Bristol College of Science and Technology which in 1960 had just been designated a College of Advanced Technology - a CAT. Our Principal was George Moore, a Bathonian who had put a case very effectively to the committee that was deciding which colleges should be designated CATs, offering the Diploma in Technology. A requirement of the Dip.Tech. was that one tenth of the course should be devoted to non-core subjects, the humanities, languages, economics, history. So a Head of a Department of General Studies was appointed and recruited staff, which included me as Assistant Lecturer in Social and Economic History.

fig 4: The cover of The Industrial Archaeology of Bath, published 1969
Author's Collection

WH. *You also continued with WEA work?*
AB. Yes, at the Bristol Folk House. It was the oldest Further Education establishment in the city and had been set up in 1870 in the docklands to give opportunities to workers in that industry. The Folk House was a real centre of activity and provided facilities for evening classes for the WEA and the University Extra-Mural Department. I taught a WEA class in Social and Economic history, and worked up a syllabus for a course on the history of technology. One of the people who came into the group was Neil Cossons [**fig. 2**], then the new Curator of Technology at Bristol Museum. Over the next four years Neil was very active; among other things he acquired an engine from the Old Mills Colliery in Radstock. It was a big engine, and Neil had to get a crane to take the roof off the engine house. Then it was too big to transport, so Neil took it in parts to an old warehouse in Bristol. It was supposed to go into a new museum building - but that never materialised. Instead an old shed on the dockside was reconditioned and that is now the Industrial Museum, recently re-opened as 'M' Shed.

WH. You and Neil Cossons set up the Bristol Industrial Archaeological Society (BIAS)?

AB. Yes, it grew out of my Folk House class and we had great help from the University Extra-Mural Department who supported us with good speakers. One of the features of Industrial Archaeology (I.A.) is that it is an inter-disciplinary subject and all sorts of people can make contributions. BIAS had a lot of young members, so the families went on site visits - there was quite a holiday atmosphere which was not entirely approved of by the more severe historians. But the Society was very successful, so Neil and I went on to seek wider support for I.A., establishing the national Association for Industrial Archaeology (AIA) in 1973, of which I became the President and, in more recent years, the Honorary President. We went on to develop an international organisation, the International Council for the Conservation of the Industrial Heritage (TICCIH) which still flourishes.

Brenda and I were also linked with 'The New Bristol Group' set up by Tony Benn at a time when he was trying to avoid going to the Lords. We wrote discussion papers on all sorts of policy areas, from the fluoridation of the water supply to education and the libraries.

WH. You published 'The Industrial Archaeology of the Bristol Region'?

AB. Yes, in 1969 [**fig. 3**]. That was a result of linking up with the publisher David St. John Thomas. He was the 'David' of David and Charles and his business partner was Charles Hadfield, the canal historian, and the firm invited Neil and myself to contribute a volume in its series on Industrial Archaeology. I published a pamphlet on The Industrial Archaeology of

fig 5: Professor R. Angus Buchanan at the library at the University of Bath, 23 October 1991
Bath in Time - Bath Central Library Collection

Bath at around the same time [**fig. 4**], and in conjunction with my brother Sandy, a Regional study in the Batsford I.A. series.

WH. The CAT became The University of Bath - what changes did that bring?

AB. We were granted full university status in 1966 and moved to Bath in stages. Our department became the School of Humanities and Social Sciences, and I was responsible for the degree in Social Sciences for thirteen years. Once we got to full University status the relationship with the Council for Scientific and Technological Awards ended, and there was no longer the requirement for the one tenth non-core content in our degrees. The Social Sciences thus became marginalised. The Humanities courses ran down and eventually came to an end, which was a profound disappointment to me. I'm proud of the achievements of the University of Bath and am grateful for its support of my activities, but I greatly regret its failure to develop a strong Humanities Faculty. The Humanities Group had in the 1970s been growing slowly but steadily towards such a Faculty - amongst our staff were two distinguished historians, Sir Christopher Frayling and Professor David Gooding - but the Group wound down after 1986 when the

Degree in Social Sciences, for which it was responsible, was terminated. Since then I've tried to keep History alive in the University through my Centre for the Study of the History of Technology (now re-named The History of Technology Research Unit: HOTRU) and its Seminar and we are grateful for the continuing support of the Dean of the Humanities Faculty and the Head of the Department of Social Policy Studies. **[fig. 5]**

WH. But there were other opportunities?
AB. As historical teaching closed down it gave me the opportunity to do a lot more outside work and a series of Vice Chancellors has been very supportive as they could see it would bring benefit to the University. For example, from 1987 to 1995 I was Director of the National Cataloguing Unit for the Archives of Contemporary Scientists. It came about because Margaret Gowing, who was the Professor of the History of Science and Technology in Oxford, saw that scientists who had been active in wartime and post-war were in need of a service to preserve their records and archives which would otherwise be lost, so she established a unit to catalogue them. When she retired a replacement was needed to take over the work. Our then Vice Chancellor suggested that I should do it, the Royal Society approved and I took over the staff working on the project. We found a room at the University where archives were delivered and stored. The project staff would go through the masses of documents methodically, sort them into groups, weed out some, catalogue the rest,

fig 6: Angus Buchanan, Keith Faulkner and Neil Cossons on the occasion of Keith Faulkner's retirement, 2012
Author's Collection

put them into proper archive boxes, label them and then they would be ready to be dispersed to the relevant bodies. The catalogue records the work of about two hundred and fifty scientists and engineers so far. Now anyone can look up an item of interest in the catalogue, find out where it is, and contact the university or body that holds it for a copy. **[fig. 6]**

WH. You took leading roles in a number of national and international bodies. Can we start with the Newcomen Society, based at the Science Museum, of which you were President 1981-83 and were elected a Fellow in 2010. Why 'Newcomen'?
AB. The Society aims to foster the study of the history of engineering and it is named after Thomas Newcomen, a Devonian, who invented the first viable steam engine in 1712, a beam engine which revolutionised the pumping of water from mines. The Society publishes a journal and organises conferences last year took part in the tercentenary celebrations of his invention.

WH. You were a member of the Properties Committee of the National Trust (NT) for twenty five years, and a Commissioner of the Royal Commission for Historical Monuments in England (RCHME) which is now part of English Heritage and was regarded 'as a symbol of excellence in historic building recording'. Were there particularly memorable properties or sites that you were involved with? And what was the role of a Commissioner in the RCHME?

AB. With the NT I was involved with industrial properties, such as Aberdulais, Dolaucothi, Calke Abbey lime kilns and Lake District Gunpowder industry sites. In the RCHME the Commissioners determined policy and directed the staff. I was particularly involved in industrial sites and supported the publication of books and reports on Textile Mills, Potworks, Docks and Dockyards, Waltham Abbey Royal Gunpowder Mills, canal restoration and so on. It was most interesting work, and at the end of my stint of thirteen years with the RCHME in 1993 I was awarded an OBE 'for services to the history of technology'. About the same time I was elected a Fellow of the Society of Antiquaries of London, and served for a couple of years as Vice-President of this venerable association of scholars.

WH. You have had international recognition in the history of technology as Secretary General and later President of the International Committee for the History of Technology (ICOHTEC), and with the American Society for the History of Technology (SHOT) which awarded you the Da Vinci Medal in

fig 7: A family group of Buchanans at Ticonderoga, New York State in 2008. l-r Tom, Francis, Andy, Alex, Robert, Brenda, Mary, Neil, Julia and Angus
Author's Collection

1989 for promoting the subject. You have also been Visiting Professor or Lecturer in universities in China, at Canberra, Delaware and at Chalmers University (Gothenburg), Sweden, which awarded you an Honorary DSc (Engineering). That suggests a greater academic concentration on the history of technology than is the case in British universities. Why should that be?

AB. Well, that is a complicated question and it requires a careful answer. It certainly seems that there is more sympathy for the history of technology in some other countries than there is in Britain, but that might be a trick of perspective as one tends to see the bright spots in other places rather than everywhere else. In our six-month sabbatical leave in Australia in 1981 for example, when I was at Professor Oliver MacDonagh's Research School in History at the Australian National University (ANU) in Canberra, I was much encouraged by the interest of colleagues and the opportunities to make wide-ranging contacts with engineers concerned about their own historical heritage. Similarly, in Sweden in 1984, when I was invited to serve as Visiting Professor in the History of Technology at Chalmers University for the Autumn Term, there were keen students and staff pursuing courses and research into the subject. The case in China, in 1983, was slightly different, as I had been invited to teach a three-week course in the history of technology at Wuhan on the Yangtse. I found an attentive audience of scholars recruited from all parts of China who were anxious to understand how Britain had come to lead in the process of industrialisation, and my answer was that it resulted from the existence of a relatively 'open' society, encouraging innovation and individual enterprise. I like to think that I contributed a small impetus to the transformation of Chinese industry and society which was then becoming apparent, but it is by no means clear where this process is leading in China.

Meanwhile, Brenda and I have attended an enlightening series of ICOHTEC symposia since I joined at its formation in 1968 at the Paris Congress of the International Council for the History of Science, Technology and Medicine. We have travelled widely over Europe and North America [fig. 7] to attend these and related meetings, and have found ourselves in a large community of like-minded scholars, in contrast with the few committed to this subject in Britain. In the United States, in particular, there is an extensive field of scholarship represented by courses and designated professorial chairs in the history of technology in their universities, with a vigorous society (SHOT) and an excellent journal, 'Technology and Culture'. This can be attributed to the comparative shortness of American historical interest, in which industry figures prominently, but it is also the result of some outstanding scholars adopting the subject and making it a popular area of research for students.

I realise that this is only a partial answer to your question of why the attitude of British universities towards the history of technology has not been as robust as that in some other countries. However, I remain convinced of the importance of the subject, and I hope that British practice in this field will soon be improved.

WH. You and Brenda have been very much involved in local history organisations such as the History of Bath Research Group (HBRG), the Historical Association and in other local activities. How does local history fit into what might be regarded as 'mainstream' history?

AB. Yes, Brenda and I were both founder-members of the HBRG; Brenda served as the first Chairman while I acted as coffee-monitor and washer-up [fig. 8]. I also served a term as Chairman of the Bath Branch of the Historical Association and was a Trustee of the Bath Archaeological Trust (BAT) until this disbanded in 2005. It was BAT that promoted the publication of 'Bath History' of which Brenda became the third Editor - after Sam Hunt and Trevor Fawcett - serving for ten years and producing five volumes. Four of my articles have been published in this journal. I have also been active in

fig 8: Angus on a walk with the History of Bath Research Group, 2011
Photograph by Dan Brown

enterprises to preserve Green Park Station, the Victoria Bridge of James Dredge, and the Kennet and Avon Canal; and, as a biographer of I.K.Brunel [fig. 9], I have taken a special interest in his work in the Bath and Bristol region.

Interest in local history has grown and it is now a reputable and approved subject. The University of Leicester has a Centre for English Local History, the University of the West of England (UWE) has a Regional History Centre and other universities have similar groups. But in many places small disciplines have been swallowed into a single history department.

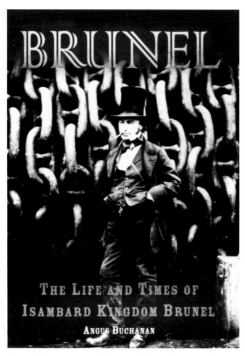

fig 9: The cover of Brunel, The Life and Times
of Isambard Kingdom Brunel, published 2002
Author's Collection

WH. *What are you currently involved with, and
what next?*

AB. HOTRU continues. In 2011 we published
'Landscape with Technology: Essays in Honour
of L.T.C.Rolt' which I edited and to which
Brenda and I both contributed. The volume
reflected Tom Rolt's contribution to engineering
history and industrial conservation. I hope to
prepare a transcript of Brunel's 'Locked Diary'
for publication as a pamphlet in the 'BIAS
Histories' series, to continue local work for
BIAS and Bath societies and involvement with
AIA. ICOTEC will be celebrating its fortieth
symposium in 2013, and we have both been
invited to make contributions. HOTRU will
reach its fiftieth anniversary, all under my
Directorship, in 2014 and we are planning a
publication to mark the event. Meanwhile, I am
preparing some 'Reflections on the History of
Technology', while Brenda is working on a
definitive study of Gunpowder history. We
expect to keep busy!

Principal Publications:

History of Technology:

Technology and Social Progress, (Pergamon 1965)

'Technology, History of" in *Encyclopaedia Britannica* (15th Edition 1974)

The Power of the Machine, (Viking/Penguin 1992)

Industrial Archaeology

Industrial Archaeology in Britain, (Penguin/Pelican 1972, 2nd Edition 1982) (with Neil Cossons)
Industrial Archaeology of the Bristol Region, (David and Charles, Newton Abbot 1969) (with Neil
Cossons) *Industrial History in Pictures: Bristol*, (David and Charles, Newton Abbot, 1979)

Industrial Archaeology of Bristol, (Historical Association, Bristol Branch 1967) (with
C.A.Buchanan) *Industrial Archaeology of Central Southern England*, (Batsford 1980) (with George
Watkins) *Industrial Archaeology of the Stationary Steam Engine*, (Longmans/Allen Lane 1976)

The Engineering Profession

The Engineers: A *History of the Engineering Profession* 1750-1914, (Jessica Kingsley, London 1989)

Nineteenth Century Engineers in the Port of Bristol, (H.A. Bristol Branch 1971)

'Joseph Whitworth' in John Cantrell and Gillian Cookson, *Henry Maudslay & the Pioneers of the Machine Age*, (Tempus, Stroud, 2002)

'Engineers and Government in Nineteenth Century Britain' in Roy MacLeod, *Government and Expertise*, (Cambridge University Press, 1988)

'Providing Infrastructure: Bath and Civil Engineering' in *Innovation and Discovery*, ed. Peter Wallis, (BRLSI, 2008)

I.K.Brunel

Brunel: *The Life and Times of Isambard Kingdom Brunel*, (Hambledon & London 2002) (with Michael Williams) *Brunel's Bristol*, (Redcliffe, Bristol 1982)

'Introduction to L.T.C.Rolt', *Isambard Kingdom Brunel*, (Penguin, 1989)

'I.K. Brunel, Engineer' in Sir Alfred Pugsley, ed. *The Works of Isambard Kingdom Brunel*, (Institution of Civil Engineers & University of Bristol 1976, Cambridge 1980)

Bath History

Industrial Archaeology in Bath, (Bath University Press 1969)

'The Bridges of Bath' in *Bath History III* (Alan Sutton 1990)

'The Floods of Bath' in *Bath History VII*, (Millstream Books, Bath 1998)

'Bath: University City' in *Bath History IX*, (Millstream Books, Bath 2002)

'Brunel in Bath' in *Bath History X*, (Millstream Books, Bath, 2006)

Other Works

History and Industrial Civilisation, (Macmillan, 1979)

Landscape with Technology, Edited and contributed, (Millstream Books, Bath 2011)

'From Trade School to University' in G. Walters (ed.) A *Technological University*: *an experiment in Bath*, (Bath University Press, 1966)

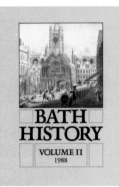
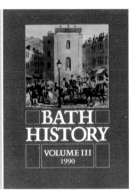
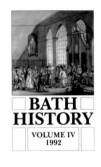

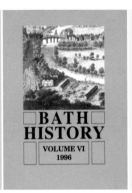

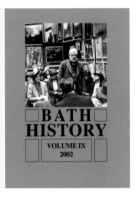

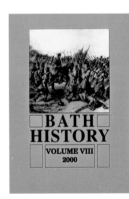
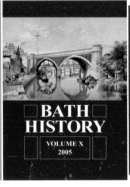

A full index of the first ten volumes of previously published articles is available in Bath History vol. X For further information please visit our website www.bathhistory.org.uk